PERSONAL INJURY & MONEY CLAIMS

LAWPACK

About the author

Felicity Mileham has worked as a barrister since 1997. She is a member of Lincoln's Inn and practised at the Chambers of Brian Higgs, QC.

Thanks and Dedication

Richard Menzies, barrister-at-law, has very kindly allowed me to include the precedent in Appendix 1, Sample 3, Bus Passenger's Claim. A million thanks go to Alexandra Mileham, Helyn Wilson, Pippa Bark (and Matthew), Sally Blanco (and Isabel) for their practical help and willingness to play with my small daughter, without which this book simply would never been written. Finally, and by no means least, I owe the largest debt of gratitude to my husband Richard Wilson, for his willingness to talk about the law at all hours, his legal expertise, his patience and his practical help during the writing of this book. Any mistakes, however, are as ever entirely my own responsibility.

Felicity Mileham

Dedicated to Flora Wilson

Personal Injury & Money Claims
by Felicity Mileham

© 2003 Lawpack Publishing Limited

Lawpack Publishing Limited
76-89 Alscot Road
London SE1 3AW

www.lawpack.co.uk

Printed in Great Britain

ISBN: 1 904053 43 2
All rights reserved.

Crown copyright material is reproduced with the permission of the Controller of HMSO and the Queen's Printer for Scotland.

This Lawpack Guide may not be reproduced in whole or in part in any form without written permission from the publisher.

CONTENTS

APPENDICES

HOW TO USE THIS BOOK

This book is designed for readers without any specialist legal training. It is for those wishing to bring or defend their own claim, for those who want advice on whether or not to use a lawyer (and how to pay for one!), and for those simply wanting to know what to expect before they get involved in a dispute that may lead to litigation.

The book is structured around five basic questions, which take you step by step through analysing your situation, safeguarding your position by gathering the appropriate evidence, and helping you prepare for a satisfactory negotiation or court case. The five questions are as follows:

Do I have a claim or defence?
What sort of compensation or order can the court make?
How do I protect my position from the outset?
How do I bring or defend a claim in court?
How does the court ensure its orders are obeyed?

Do I have a claim or defence?

Chapter 1 will help you to analyse your situation and decide if you have a case in law. It contains a brief overview of the law in many areas, from road traffic accidents, accidents at work, sporting injuries and harassment, to rent claims and nuisance neighbours. General and specific defences are discussed throughout, so that you, by learning about the claim and the possible defences to it, may have the advantage of also analysing the case against you. A strong understanding of the legal basis (and evidential strength) of your opponent's case will help you to be more effective in negotiating and litigating your own.

What sort of compensation or order can the court make?

Chapter 2 deals with damages, other orders to pay money, injunctions and other court orders. The chapter describes how the courts calculate money claims, and discusses the things a litigant can claim for, and those he cannot. There is a description of matters that may reduce an award of damages and, equally important, a discussion on the legal costs of bringing the claim to court.

How do I protect my position from the outset?

Chapter 3 is the chapter which deals with the practicalities of preparing to make your claim or defence. There is an overview of how to gather evidence, and a list of important considerations to make before bringing a claim. Such factors are crucial to a claim; get things wrong and your claim may fail and expensive legal bills may be incurred (which the court may well order you to pay). This chapter also deals with winning without going to court. Insurance-company-run litigation, alternatives to court and out of court settlements are all covered.

How do I bring or defend a claim in court?

Chapter 4 is a practical guide to bringing or defending your own claim in the English and Welsh courts. It will show you how to fill in the appropriate forms and prepare for trial. The courts procedure is outlined so that you can attend the preparatory hearings and the trial with confidence, knowing what to expect, having prepared yourself fully. The chapter also contains a description of how a case may end before the trial occurs; it covers how the courts deal with undefended claims, claims that can be dealt with 'summarily' and claims where there is a 'trial of a preliminary issue'.

How does the court ensure its orders are obeyed?

The final question is actually one of great importance to both a successful claimant and an unsuccessful defendant. Chapter 5 discusses the powers of the court to enforce orders to pay money, orders for possession of land and injunctions. In many situations the successful claimant may have to go back to court in order to obtain satisfaction. The courts have considerable powers including, in some circumstances, the power of imprisonment to ensure that the defendant obeys orders and there is a brief overview of the procedures involved. There is also a discussion on how to enforce an out of court settlement and how to obtain a money payment from the Motor Insurers' Bureau.

If, after thorough examination, you decide that your requirements are not met by this book, or you do not feel confident about writing your own documents or investigating your own claim or defence, consult a solicitor, legal advice centre or Citizens Advice Bureau.

In the Appendices section are example forms and documentation, for reference when preparing your own. When completing a court form, read the notes and instructions carefully. Do not leave any section blank, unless you are told to. If any section is inapplicable, write 'not applicable', 'none' or 'nil' to show that you have not overlooked the section. You should also make copies of the form (the instructions will tell you how many copies the court needs) and do not forget to make at least one copy for your own reference. Always use a pen or type on legal documents, never use pencil and do not cross out or erase anything you have written on your final forms. Always keep legal documents in a safe place and in a location known to your spouse, partner, family or solicitor.

You will find a helpful glossary of terms at the end of this book. Refer to this glossary if you find unfamiliar terms. For your reference, asterisks (*) are used in the text to indicate that a term is included in the glossary, but are only used the first time the term is mentioned in the book.

Note: In the interests of brevity and clarity I have chosen only to refer to 'his' and 'him'. As in Acts of Parliament and other authorities the masculine is deemed to impart the feminine. This is a matter of style only, and is in no way intended to offend.

CHAPTER 1

DO I HAVE A CLAIM OR DEFENCE?

This chapter considers the legal basis of claims for damages* and other compensation or orders*. The legal position is governed by case law*, Acts of Parliament, and/or various Regulations. Knowing the legal strength of your case is invaluable, even if you wish to avoid going to court. By using this chapter you will be able to consider what you and your opponent must prove to the court. This will include:

- assessing what evidence* you need to gather in order to negotiate with your opponent for an early resolution;

- assessing the allegations made by and the evidence produced by your opponent;

- finding out the strengths and weaknesses of your bargaining position.

If the dispute goes so far as to enter the court system, the judge will be considering all the allegations made by the parties in the light of the legal bases set out below.

When a dispute ends up in court, the parties must set out their respective cases in writing. The claimant* submits a document known as a Claim Form* when he initiates the litigation. This contains a section called the 'Particulars of Claim'* where he tells the story of the incident and lists the injuries and losses he has suffered. Sample Particulars of Claim can be found at Appendix 1 and the topic is fully discussed in chapter 4, pages 133-9. You will see from them how detailed the analysis of the accident or complaint must be. The defendant* who intends to contest the claim must be similarly precise in a document he must file at court known as the 'Defence'* (and if he intends to counterclaim*, the Part 20 Claim Form*). Sample Defences can be found at Appendix 2.

INTRODUCTION

In order to claim compensation (or other court orders) the claimant must prove that the defendant acted unlawfully in causing him injury, infringing his rights and/or creating financial loss. This does not mean that the defendant was necessarily committing a crime or acting illegally. Instead, the claimant must prove that the defendant was:

- negligent*;

- in breach of contract*;

- in breach of statutory duty*;

- committing or committed a nuisance* or trespass*; or

- caused injury or loss by assault and battery*, harassment* or false imprisonment*.

Each complaint is known as a 'cause of action'*, and, if proved, will give rise to a court order for damages or any other appropriate remedy. Often the injury or financial loss will have been caused by more than one cause of action, and the claimant may rely on as many or as few as he chooses (and can prove). Also, do note the important duty of the claimant to mitigate (i.e. lessen) his loss* as far as is reasonable (see chapter 2, The duty of the claimant to mitigate his loss).

A defendant will be successful in negotiation or in court if he can show that the claimant has failed to prove his case. He does not have to disprove the claimant as such. However, even if the claimant does succeed in proving the relevant cause of action, the defendant may in turn be able to prove he has a defence*, partial defence or in some circumstances a counterclaim. Thus he may be able to reduce or avoid altogether an award of damages or other order.

Remember that many injuries and financial losses will not give rise to a legal claim. Where an accident occurred through no one's fault, or was caused by the claimant's own carelessness or deliberate action, a claim will not succeed. Some situations which result in loss or injury to a person may simply not fall into any of the categories listed above (an example is the passer-by who fails to come to a person's rescue, leaving him to be injured or worse). In these circumstances, there is no cause of action and the courts are unlikely to order compensation. (If they do, a new law will have been made, and it is possible that the case may be continually appealed until a superior court such as the Court of Appeal* or House of Lords* gives the decisive judgment*.)

ACCIDENTS

Road traffic accidents

It is perhaps not surprising that a large proportion of litigation arises from road traffic accidents. Not only do road traffic accidents cause a great many injuries and damage to property to road users, but also the existence of compulsory insurance against third party injury ensures that there is compensation money available to fight over.

Road traffic accidents are generally based upon the law of negligence*. It is well established that all road users owe a duty to take reasonable care to avoid injuring or causing damage to other road users (including drivers, motorcyclists, cyclists and pedestrians). There are no absolute rules (such as the driver at the rear in a shunt accident being automatically in the wrong); the court will consider each case on its own merits. The judge will ask himself the question, 'did the defendant drive in such a way that he failed to exercise reasonable care to avoid injuring the claimant?' In other words, was the defendant unduly careless in the particular situation that arose?

Was the defendant driver negligent?

Usually accidents are caused by a series of negligent actions or omissions, rather than one single lapse. For example, an accident may seem to be caused simply by the driver driving too fast. However, a careful analysis of the situation will show that the negligent driver also failed to:

- keep a proper look out for other road users;
- use appropriate signals;
- stop in time;
- avoid the other road user's vehicle; and
- observe traffic signals, signs or road markings.

All of these separate acts of carelessness will have contributed to the accident.

Particulars of Claim is a document that enables the judge to see quickly the precise nature of the accident, and helps the parties identify what evidence will be needed to prove the claim or defence. Most importantly, the Particulars of Claim show to the defendant exactly what he is blamed for, so that he can consider his response and marshal his evidence accordingly. It is not enough only to tell the court that the defendant 'failed to drive carefully in all the circumstances'.

The Highway Code* sets out the general standards that drivers (including cyclists, motorcyclists, drivers of long or large vehicles and those towing other vehicles) are expected to use. A breach of a particular paragraph of the Code may not necessarily amount to negligence; however, it is a useful reference for deciding whether or not the defendant was negligent in the particular circumstances. The specific paragraphs breached may be referred to in pre-action letters and in the Particulars of Claim, Defence or Part 20 claim documents, and should be drawn to the judge's attention at trial*.

The body of case law also lays down rules about the standards of care expected of road users. The claimant must show that his case is analogous to a rule stated in a particular reported case decided by a superior court (such as the High Court, Court of Appeal or House of Lords). Conversely, the defendant will succeed if he can distinguish the facts in the reported case from the accident in question, or can argue that the rule should not apply in his case. For hints on how to research case law and other legal rules, see chapter 3, Researching the law further.

Additional rules may apply in accidents involving buses, which is discussed on page 6.

The negligent driver was convicted of a driving offence; can I tell the civil court?

The brief answer is 'yes', as long as the conviction* arose from the same incident which is the subject of your claim for damages. The offences involved could be 'dangerous driving' (Road Traffic Act 1988, section 2) or 'careless or inconsiderate driving' (Road Traffic Act 1988, section 3) or other specific offences. Proof of the conviction will probably, depending on the exact circumstances, amount to evidence of negligent driving. You can obtain, to use in your civil claim, a 'certificate of conviction' from the court where the conviction took place. Practice varies from court to court, so inquire by telephone as to whom the letter should be addressed, and how much the fee for the certificate will be. When you write to the convicting court (a Magistrates or Crown Court) asking for the certificate, ensure you include:

1. the name of the convicted person;

2. the date of the conviction (i.e. the day he pleaded guilty to the offence, or the day he was found guilty at trial);

3. the offence involved.

The defendant may contest the certificate at the civil trial on one of the following grounds, as appropriate:

1. He was not convicted as alleged (i.e. he is not the person named in the certificate, or he was not actually convicted of the offence alleged, etc).

2. He was wrongly convicted (i.e. he did not commit the offence – although even if he is successful and the civil court agrees with him it cannot overturn the conviction or sentence).

3. Although he was convicted as set down in the certificate, the conviction is not relevant to the issues in the civil trial (i.e. the illegal act or omission did not cause the accident).

Can both drivers be considered to have been negligent?

Yes. It is worth remembering that many road accidents happen because both of the drivers involved are careless. Where the judge decides that both parties were negligent he will apportion blame, and either reduce damages on the basis of the claimant's contributory negligence* or, where the defendant has made a successful Part 20 claim (also known as a 'counterclaim'), make 'cross-awards of damages'. Cross-awards of damages occur when the judge decides that both parties have made a good case and awards both parties appropriate damages. Unless the awards are exactly equal, the party awarded the lower amount of damages will end up paying the other party the balance between the two sums. As a result, cross-damages effectively cancel each other out.

Alternatively, the parties, during the negotiation period before litigation begins, may agree that they should share the blame (equally or in different proportions). The settlement* they arrive at can reflect this. For example, the parties may agree to bear each of his own loss and drop any claim for damages against the other driver. Another possible settlement could be where one party offers to pay 75 per cent (or another appropriate percentage) of the claim and all of the costs*.

The accident was caused by mechanical failure, not poor driving; can I claim?

Yes, in some circumstances the driver may be found liable for an accident under the law of negligence, and/or the Occupiers' Liability Act 1957 or the Occupiers' Liability Act 1984 (please see Accidents in or on private property, for further information). If the driver of the faulty vehicle knows that his car has a mechanical fault (or in the circumstances should have known of the fault), he will be liable for the resulting injury and loss. Once the claimant has produced evidence of the fault which caused the accident, the onus shifts to the defendant (i.e. he must produce evidence) to prove that the defect was undetectable despite reasonable vigilance. The court will consider what, if any, inspection, maintenance and repairs ought to have been undertaken. In legal terms, a reasonably undetectable defect is known as a 'latent defect' and is a defence to an action for damages.

The accident victim was not wearing a seatbelt/other appropriate safety equipment; is it relevant?

Yes, the failure to use appropriate safety equipment, such as seatbelts where fitted, may be highly relevant. The failure may amount to contributory negligence and can result in a reduced claim for damages (see page 63, Contributory negligence). The defendant must prove that the claimant's failure to wear the appropriate equipment resulted in some or all of his injury. If he is successful, the judge will reduce the damages by a percentage reflecting the extent to which the claimant failed to take care of his own safety. The case of *Froom v Butcher [1976] QB 286* sets out the guidelines for such reductions. In an accident where, had the claimant been wearing a seatbelt, he would not have suffered any injuries, the damages will be reduced by 25 per cent. If the injuries would have been a 'good deal less severe' if the seatbelt had been worn, a 15 per cent reduction is indicated. The medical expert witness will be able to tell the court the effect of a failure to wear seatbelts or other appropriate equipment on the extent of the injuries (see chapter 3, Gathering evidence).

The failure to ensure that a child* is properly restrained may amount to negligence on the part of the person(s) supervising the child if, as a result, the child is injured in an accident. In the case of *J (a child) v Wilkins (Wynn and another – third parties) [2001] PIQR 179, Times 6 February 2001*, the child's mother and aunt had not ensured that the child was suitably restrained in the car and he was injured in a crash. The defendant admitted he had driven negligently and thus caused the accident, but cited the child's mother and aunt as third parties, claiming that their negligence had contributed to the child being injured. The court agreed and apportioned the liability 75 per cent to the defendant and 25 per cent to the mother and aunt under section 2(1) of the Civil Liability (Contributions) Act 1975.

My accident involved a bus; do any special rules apply?

No, if you are a driver involved in an accident with a bus, coach or similar vehicle. The normal rules of negligence apply (see above) as to whether the defendant driver was negligent. The claimant can sue a negligent driver and the employing bus company – the latter is vicariously liable* for the wrongs committed by its employees in the course of their work.

If, however, you are a passenger who was injured on a bus, you may be able to rely on the bus company's (and its employees') breach of statutory duty as well as its negligence in your claim for compensation. Bus companies must comply with certain duties set out in the Public Service Vehicles (Conduct of Drivers, Inspectors, Conductors and Passengers) Regulations 1990 (as amended). Under these Regulations, drivers and conductors must take all reasonable precautions to ensure the safety of passengers who are entering, leaving or already on the vehicle. A failure to comply with the Regulations amounts to a breach of statutory duty. Drivers and conductors also have a separate common law* duty to take reasonable care for the safety of passengers – a failure to do so will amount to negligence. It may be that the bus company and its employees are both negligent and in breach of statutory duty. However, it is sensible to rely on both causes of action where possible; in rare circumstances you may lose one cause of action but succeed in the other. If you rely on both, you maximise your chances of winning at least one claim and thus obtaining an award of damages.

Accidents in public places

What is a 'public space'?

'Public space' is not a legal term. It is used in this section to describe any land or premises which the public has a right to use or pass over for general or specific purposes. Most premises which seem to be a public space (such as shops, car parks, village greens, etc) will actually be privately owned. Claims against private owners are discussed in Accidents in or on private property, on page 10.

Hazards in public places may be caused by poor maintenance or bad construction. Often uneven paving stones, holes in tarmac, uncovered manholes, potholes, dangerous steps, slippery areas, poor street lighting, and damaged fencing and other street furniture lead to 'tripping and slipping accidents'. Similarly, hazards may have been created as a result of works carried out by various authorities or contractors. These may include objects left in the way of passers-by, inadequate warnings or unguarded works. Other accidents in public spaces may occur when objects fall from buildings or structures on land next to the public area.

The law categorises the various duties to avoid injuring members of the public into negligence, breach of statutory duty and nuisance. Each of these is known as a cause of action. In some circumstances the claimant may be able to prove that more than one of these causes of action applies to the defendant.

Accidents caused by poor maintenance or the condition of the road

Who is the relevant Highway Authority?

Generally, the local council is responsible for a particular road as the Highway Authority under the Highways Act 1980. However, the Crown or other bodies may be designated the authority for a particular road. You will need to use your local facilities, such as the local authority itself, a Citizens Advice Bureau or library to find out the identity of the Highway Authority.

What duty does the Highway Authority owe me?

Under section 41 of the Highways Act 1980, the Highway Authority must maintain (and repair) the roads under its care. The court will look at all of the circumstances to help it decide if the road was unreasonably unsafe. Obviously, the Highway Authority is not obliged to keep the roads and pavements in 'bowling green condition' (in the words of Lord Justice Dillon). Various decided cases have established that the presence of ice or water on the road is not enough on its own to prove the Highway Authority breached its duty. Nor, in tripping or slipping cases, does the mere presence of an uneven surface prove a breach. The claimant must show that in the circumstances the road or pavement was not reasonably safe. The relevant issues may include:

- How did the hazard come about?

- Did the Highway Authority know of the danger?

- What was the Highway Authority's maintenance programme?

- What was the Highway Authority's inspection programme?

- To whom was the danger posed?

- What warnings were given and, if so, were they adequate in all the circumstances?

- How foreseeable was the accident?

Many reported cases have involved situations where the hazard in question was created by the deliberate tampering or the carelessness of individuals (sometimes known as the 'acts of a stranger'). In this sort of case, the court looks particularly at the mischief done, the extent to which the Highway Authority should have foreseen the problem, and whether or not it could and should have taken steps to guard against it arising.

Who is responsible for the condition of the road if the work was done by a contractor?

In most circumstances the Highway Authority will be legally responsible for any breach of the duty to maintain the road, even if he employed a sub-contractor to undertake the work or inspection. This is based on the principle that such duties are 'non-delegable'.

Please see below for the responsibilities imposed on companies digging up the roads for their own purposes (telephone, cable TV, electricity, gas and water companies, etc).

What defences may the Highway Authority seek to rely on?

The Highway Authority may wish to call evidence that it took reasonable care to ensure that the relevant part of the road was not dangerous to persons using it. This is a defence created by section 58 of the Highways Act 1980. If the court is satisfied with the evidence, the claim will fail.

For further discussion of defences, please see Defences, below.

Accidents caused by roadworks, and disrepair caused by utility companies

What duty does the street works contractor owe me?

Persons (whether the Highway Authority itself, or a utility company) digging up the roads have a common law duty to take reasonable care for the safety of road users. The New

Works and Street Works Act 1991 and the Public Utilities Street Works Act 1950 lay down requirements (including safety measures) as to how work and repairs, etc must be undertaken. The court should be told about any failure to fulfil the requirements because it may demonstrate that the company was negligent (a breach of these statutory duties does not give rise to a civil claim for damages, but instead is a criminal offence). An overview of these duties can be found in the following paragraphs. A guide to doing your own legal research can be found at chapter 3.

1. Roadworks

    The company undertaking the works on the street must ensure that the areas of the street that are broken up, or on which equipment or materials are deposited are adequately guarded and lit. Where reasonable, signs giving guidance or direction (i.e. around the dangerous area) should be placed and maintained by the person doing the works. In complying with these requirements, the company must consider the needs of people with a disability, for example, wheelchair users and those with impaired vision.

2. Reinstatement of the road after the works are finished

    The company undertaking the works has a duty to reinstate the road (section 70 of the New Works and Street Works Act 1991). Thus holes must be filled in, street furniture and safety features replaced, equipment and materials removed. The Department for Transport publishes a code of practice relating to street works and street safety (also available on the Internet at www.dft.gov.uk).

Who is to blame if the utility company used a sub-contractor to do the work in question?

In most circumstances the utility company will be legally responsible for any negligence on the principle that, generally, statutory duties are 'non-delegable'.

Accidents caused by the dangerous condition of buildings, structures or trees on land next to a public place, by activities taking place on land next to a public area

A person may be injured by something that originated from land next to the road or other public space. This may be because of activities on private land (such as stray golf balls from a driving range raining down on a public space next to the golf course), or it may be due to the poor condition of the private land or structures on it (such as signposts or masonry falling off buildings, or trees falling down).

Broadly stated, members of the public have the right to enjoy (i.e. 'use' rather than 'obtain pleasure from') public areas for certain purposes, and may expect themselves to be reasonably safe from injury. The causes of action an injured person may rely on are public nuisance and/or negligence. A public nuisance in this context is the interference or disruption of the claimant's right to enjoy the public space. However, some commentators and recent cases suggest that negligence is the more appropriate cause of action (*Clerk & Lindsell on Tort paragraph 19–41 18th edition 2000*). The rest of this section considers negligence claims.

The injured person must first identify who, if anyone, owed him a 'duty of care'. This may be the occupier of the private land from which the hazard originated (i.e. someone with a degree of control over the land in question – usually the tenant or freeholder), or it may be someone undertaking a hazardous activity on the private land. He must also persuade the court that the defendant's acts (or failure to act, depending on the circumstances) posed him a foreseeable risk of injury. Finally, he must bring evidence showing that the hazard resulted in his injury.

Some of the relevant issues for the court to consider in cases like these include:

- the cause of the hazard;
- whether or not the hazard was apparent;
- whether or not there was a duty to inspect the premises for hazards;
- whether there was a duty (and, if so, to what extent) to take preventative steps to avoid the particular hazard, etc.

Accidents occurring to members of the public exercising the 'right to roam'

Please see the following section on Accidents in or on private property, below.

Accidents in or on private property

What is 'private property'?

'Private property' is not a legal term as such. It is used here to describe property belonging to or leased by an individual or company over which the public has no general right of entry. Property in this section includes land, buildings, vehicles, vessels and structures such as scaffolding, ladders, walls and wells. This section concentrates on cases against occupiers of private property for personal injuries caused by the dangerous condition of their property (accidents directly caused by the actions or omission of a person at the property are discussed below). The property may be in a dangerous condition because the occupier created the danger himself, because he has allowed the danger to arise, or because he fails to control the activities of others on his land which then poses a threat to visitors. The difference between dangerous property and dangerous activities on private property is illustrated by the following examples:

Example 1: I am travelling as a passenger in my friend Danny's car. He crashes the car and I am injured. In these circumstances I should bring a claim for damages against Danny. The cause of action will be negligence and the court will consider the manner in which he drove. This is a 'dangerous activity' case – see Road traffic accidents, for further information.

Example 2: I am travelling as a passenger in my friend Danny's car. Whilst we are driving along, the front seat I am sitting in shoots forward without warning and I am injured. I should bring a claim against Danny for damages. In these circumstances my claim will be based on his negligence AND his breach of the Occupiers' Liability Act 1957. The manner in which he drove is irrelevant; the case will instead focus on the dangerous condition of his car and whether or not he knew about the unsafe car seat. This is a 'dangerous property' case – please see below.

Example 3: Lord Fatcat owns two large fields. They are separated by a hedge with a stile built into it. Over the years, the stile has fallen into disrepair and a guest of Lord Fatcat, Mr Smith, is injured when it gives way underneath him. Mr Smith's claim for damages will be based on the dangerous condition of Lord Fatcat's property (breach of the Occupiers' Liability Act 1957 and negligence). This is a 'dangerous property' case – please see below.

Example 4: A fishing competition is organised on Lord Fatcat's estate. One of the participants, Miss Demeanour, is injured by a fellow fisherman's wild efforts at casting a fly. Her claim for damages arises out of the activity she is taking part in and will be against the fisherman (and possibly Lord Fatcat as the organiser of the competition) for negligence. This is a 'dangerous activity' case – see Hobbies, sports and pastimes, for further information.

When a person is injured on someone else's property, his legal case will be affected by the 'standing' he has in relation to the property – was he a lawful visitor, the owner of a private right or a trespasser onto it?

Am I a lawful visitor, trespasser or user of my own right of way?

Lawful visitors

These are members of the public who may be invited or allowed to enter such property for general or specific purposes (such as shoppers entering a shopping mall or shop, or a postman walking up the garden path to deliver a letter). Sometimes a contract* with the landowner gives the visitor a right to enter (such as a car park with a ticketing system).

Owners of private rights

A 'right of way' or other right of access gives its owner the right to enter the land belonging to someone else over which it runs. It is not the same thing as a 'public right of way', a right conferred under the National Parks and Access to the Countryside Act 1949 or a 'right to roam' – see page 16 for further information. When using his private right of way the owner is not a visitor or invitee of the landowner as such, but is lawfully exercising his own right. Such rights are bought and sold in the same way as land and houses; your title deeds or a search of the registers for the property held by HM Land Registry will show you if you own a right of way over someone else's property.

Trespassers

These are people who enter onto someone else's land or buildings without implied or actual permission to do so. An originally lawful visitor becomes a trespasser when he exceeds the owner's permission or the terms of his visit. Once a person is a trespasser, his presence on the land is unlawful (although not necessarily illegal).

What duties does the occupier of the property owe me?

'A common law duty of care' (negligence)

The case law which has built up over the years setting down the duties of property owners to lawful visitors is complex. In order to establish that the defendant has been negligent the claimant must:

1. persuade the court that because of the circumstances the defendant owed him a duty to avoid foreseeable accidents;

2. prove with evidence that the defendant breached that duty (i.e. that the defendant's action or inaction caused the accident); and

3. as a result, prove the claimant's injury and loss occurred.

The court will consider the situation and will try to decide if the defendant should have taken more care of the claimant's safety than he did.

Some legal commentators consider that the common law duty of care has effectively been superseded by the Occupiers' Liability Acts 1957 and 1984 (*Clerk & Lindsell on Torts chapter 10 Sweet & Maxwell 18th edition*). As a result, although claimants often base their claims on both the defendant's negligence and his breach of the duty of care under the Occupiers' Liability Act, in reality the usual focus of the court will be on the latter. The advantage, however, of relying on both causes of action where you can is that it adopts what lawyers call a 'belt and braces approach'. If, for whatever reason, one cause of action fails, the other may survive and succeed. Once the claimant has proved unlawful behaviour by the defendant (whether by negligence or a breach of the Act), he will obtain damages for his loss. It does not matter which cause of action succeeded.

Duties imposed by the Occupiers' Liability Act 1957

The occupier of property (including land, buildings, vehicles, moveable structures such as ships or temporary structures such as scaffolding) must take reasonable care that his visitor is reasonably safe whilst using the premises for the purposes he is allowed to be there. There are no hard and fast rules as to what 'reasonable care' and 'reasonable safety' are; each case must be considered separately. Obviously, the visitor's safety need not be guaranteed by the occupier. The fact that someone has been injured in itself does not automatically mean that the occupier was in breach of his duty. The injured person must persuade the court that the occupier was at fault and that he should have acted differently to how he did.

Don't forget that visitor/occupier relationships can be found in many situations: employer/employee, school/pupil, hospital/patient, retailer/shopper, restaurant owner/diner, etc. The occupier may owe the injured person additional duties as a result of one of these relationships – either because of legislation (such as the Health and Safety at Work Regulations), case law or the contract between them (such as private healthcare and education contracts).

In assessing your case, ask yourself the following questions:

- What was the cause of the accident?

- Did the occupier create the danger?

- Did the occupier know of the dangerous state of his property (or should he have known)?

- What measures should he have taken which would have prevented the accident?

- What are the costs and inconvenience involved in taking such steps?

- What is the age or particular characteristics of the visitor?

- What was the visitor allowed to do on the property?

- What did the visitor do on the property?

- Were there any warning signs or verbal warnings relating to the danger? (For further discussion of warning signs, please see below.)

- Did the occupier's contractors create the hazard? (See below.)

- Did the occupier take steps to ensure that the contractors were reasonably competent, and did he take steps to ensure that the work was properly done? (See a further discussion of the liability of contractors below.)

Duties imposed by the Occupiers' Liability Act 1984

If the occupier knows about a specific danger on his premises (or reasonably believes it exists), knows (or reasonably believes) that a non-visitor is in the vicinity of the danger, AND the risk from the danger is one which he ought reasonably to offer protection against, then he has a duty to take reasonable care that a non-visitor is not injured by it. The wording of the Act is complex, but generally it is thought that the occupier owes a greater duty to his visitors (see above) than to non-visitors and trespassers on his land.

What is meant by an 'occupier'?

An occupier of private property is an individual or company* who has direct and sufficient control or supervision over the property. Therefore, the occupier may be the owner, or the tenant or licensee (including workmen or other contractors). It is possible for more than one person or company to be an 'occupier'.

The claimant must produce evidence that the defendant was the occupier of the property. Matters that may be relevant include:

- On what terms does he use the property (ownership, lease, licences, trespass)?

- What does he use the property for?

- How does he use the property?

- Does he regulate visitors to the property?

- Does he exclude people from the property?

- Does he put up warning notices or 'exclusion clauses' (see below for a description of these)?

- What limitations are there on his usage, etc?

Don't forget that occupier/visitor relationships can be found in many situations, for example, in schools, shops, hospitals or at work. If so, look at other parts of this chapter, as the occupier may have further duties towards a visitor arising from being an employer, hospital or health trust, shop or restaurant owner, or education authority or school.

The effect of warning notices

Evidence of a verbal warning, warning notice or warning in a contract with the visitor may amount to a defence. To decide whether or not the warning was sufficient, the following questions will be relevant:

- How and where was the warning made?

- Was the visitor aware of the warning (or should the visitor have been aware of the warning)?

- Why was the warning given?

- What mischief was the warning seeking to avoid, and was it the mischief that occurred in the accident?

The effect of notices limiting or excluding liability

Private/residential occupiers

Sometimes occupiers put up notices warning visitors of a danger and stating that there will be no liability for injuries or loss even if caused by the occupier's negligence, or limiting liability to a certain sum, etc. Such notices may result in the defendant avoiding paying damages. To decide whether or not such a notice is a sufficient defence, the following questions must be considered:

- How and where was the notice displayed?

- How prominent was it?

- Did the visitor in fact read and understand the notice (or should the visitor have done so)?

- Was the mischief that occurred in the accident the mischief contemplated in the notice, etc?

The clearer the notice or warning and the greater the opportunity it gave the visitor to avoid the risk, the more likely the occupier is to be successful.

Business occupiers

Business occupiers may not disclaim, exclude or limit liability for visitors' personal injuries (or death) where caused by their own negligently looked after property. Any notice purporting to do so cannot amount to a defence and will be ignored by the court. Business occupiers may, however, disclaim, exclude or limit claims for damage to property (although the notice must be 'reasonable' in all the circumstances). These rules are law contained in the Unfair Contract Terms Act 1977 and the reported cases clarifying that Act.

My child was injured; can we sue?

Suing the occupier of dangerous premises

Children can, of course, be compensated for injuries that take place on private property. The duties owed to children, as both visitors and non-visitors under the Occupiers' Liability Acts 1957 and 1984, are exactly the same as those owed to adults. However, occupiers, in looking after their property, must be prepared for children to be less careful than adults. If an occupier wishes to defend the case on the basis that the child failed to take sufficient care for his own safety (the defence of contributory negligence), he will have to prove that the injured child was more careless than a child of his age would usually be. See page 63, for a full explanation of this defence.

Suing those in charge of children

Of course, children should be adequately supervised, although the degree of supervision and discipline required depends on the age and nature of the child. Analysis of the case may show that the child was put at risk of injury because of, or partly because of, inadequate supervision or other carelessness by a parent or someone else 'in loco parentis' (a childminder or school teacher, etc). An injured child may sue that parent or minder for negligence in addition to his claim against the occupier of the premises. Alternatively, the occupier, whose defence is that the child was inadequately supervised, may wish to sue the parent or childminder in order to avoid or reduce damages (this is known as a 'third party action').

Example: Little Tommy (aged 18 months) is playing at the local park which is operated by Somewhereshire County Council when he injures himself on glass found in the sandpit.

He was with his childminder who, at the time of the accident, was chatting to some friends at the other side of the playground. Little Tommy (suing through his litigation friend*) claims damages against the council for failing to keep the sandpit properly clear of hazardous objects. He also can sue his childminder for negligently failing to supervise him adequately. The council can also countersue the childminder for his negligent supervision by way of a Part 20 claim. The judge will decide which, or both, of the council and the childminder should pay the damages and in what proportion.

Please see chapter 3 which will tell you how child claimants (those who have not reached their 18th birthday) can make a claim.

How do I discover who the occupier of the property is?

If you are a visitor, the likelihood is that you will know the occupier. Otherwise, simply banging on the door or writing to the occupier asking for details may well be successful. It may even be worth asking people locally who the occupier is. A simpler way is to search the Land Register (for a small fee) entry for the property. This service is available online to the public at www.landregistry.gov.uk.

I am injured using a public right of way; can I sue?

Please see above.

I am injured using my own private right of way on someone else's land; can I sue?

The occupier of the land over which your right of way passes has a duty under the Occupiers' Liability Act 1984 – please see What duties does the occupier of the property owe me? above.

I am injured whilst exercising the right to roam; can I sue?

The right to roam has not yet been brought into force at the time of this book going to press. When it is, section 2(1) of the Countryside and Rights of Way Act 2000 will allow people to enter and remain on designated access land for the purpose of open air recreation. The Act also provides that people exercising this right to roam are not 'visitors' for the purpose of the 1957 Act. Therefore, if you are injured whilst roaming, you must look to the 1984 Occupiers' Liability Act which has been amended to include the new right. Unfortunately, although written in plain English, the amendment is structured in a very complicated way.

The occupier essentially has the same duty to roamers as he does to trespassers – if he knows about a specific danger on his premises (or reasonably believes it exists), knows (or reasonably believes) that a non-visitor is in the vicinity of the danger, AND the risk from the danger is one which he ought reasonably to offer protection against, then he has a duty to take reasonable care that a non-visitor is not injured by it. Moreover, the occupier must not do anything with the intention of creating a risk for roamers. However, Parliament has ensured that the burden on occupiers is not too onerous. Occupiers are not responsible for the injuries of roamers caused by natural features (including plants, trees and shrubs, or a river, stream, ditch or pond). A roamer passing over, through or under a wall, fence or gate must use the gate or stile properly, and if he does not the occupier is not responsible for injuries caused by the dangerous condition of the wall, fence or gate.

Someone else created the hazard on the occupier's land; whom can I sue?

Often the danger will not have arisen from the occupier's failure to maintain a reasonably safe premises, but from somebody else who has come onto the land and created a hazard.

Independent contractors

Where the occupier's contractor caused the hazard there are two possible defendants. The contractor will be liable for his negligent work – he has simply failed to take reasonable care for the safety of (lawful) visitors to the premises and the visitor suffered a foreseeable injury as a result. The claim against such a contractor will be based on the law of negligence. If the contractor is still on-site and in sufficient control of the premises, he may qualify as an 'occupier' and may be sued under the Occupiers' Liability Act instead or as well. Furthermore, the occupier himself may be liable (in negligence/under the Occupiers' Liability Act) for damages. Was it reasonable for him to hire the contractors; did he take steps to ensure that the contractors were reasonably competent; and did he take steps to ensure that the work was properly done? If the answer is no to any of the above, then the occupier will be liable. For further information about suing more than one defendant, please see chapter 3.

Employees

All employers are liable for the wrongful acts of their employees committed in the course of the employment. All the injured party must do is prove that the employee created the hazard which led to the injury (i.e. he was negligent, etc), and that he did so in the course of his work during his employment by the defendant. Although it is sensible to sue both the employee and the employer, in reality usually the employer's insurers pay any damages that are awarded. To tell the difference between a contractor and an employee, consider whether or not there is a 'contract for services' (contractor), or a 'contract of service' or 'contract of employment' (employee). Often the best indicator is the level of input the contractor or employee has in the way in which the job is carried out – the employer has a greater freedom to direct the way his employees work, and is less able to direct the contractors. Also contractors often have their own employees to do the work, whilst employees usually do not.

Can I sue my landlord for injuries sustained in rented property?

In some circumstances a landlord may be liable for the injuries (including illnesses) of his tenants (and sometimes others lawfully at the property) caused by the dangerous condition of the rented property. The landlord's liability depends on whether the defects arose from the landlord's own action, and whether the defect occurred before the present lease was created or whilst the tenant was in situ.

The property was defective before the current lease was created

Under section 3 of the Defective Premises Act 1972 the tenant may claim damages from his landlord for injuries caused by negligent construction, repair, maintenance or demolition work done by the landlord (or his employers) before the tenancy began. Where a builder was negligent in constructing, repairing, demolishing or other work in relation to the rented premises, the tenant will have a claim against him under the same section.

The defect arose after the tenant had moved in and the landlord has failed to repair it

1. Can the tenant sue?

If the landlord is obliged under the lease or by statute (see below) to carry out repairs to the property or has expressed permission in the lease to enter onto the property and carry out repairs and fails to do so, the tenant may obtain damages for the breach of the tenancy agreement, including any personal injury. Otherwise, when the lease says nothing about repairs, the tenant is responsible for the state of the property and will not be able to claim damages for disrepair. However, if the leased premises is residential and the tenancy agreement is for a period (term) of less than seven years, section 11 of the Landlord and Tenant Act imposes certain repairing obligations on the landlord. (**Note:** This includes statutory tenancies where the original short-term lease has officially expired and the landlord has continued to accept rent on the same terms as before – such leases are often tenancies on a month by month basis.) Section 11 obliges landlords to keep the following in repair and proper working order:

(a) The structure and exterior of the dwelling house, including drains, gutters and external pipes.

(b) Installations in the rented premises that supply water, gas, electricity and sanitation (such as basins, sinks, baths, lavatories, supply pipes, etc), but not the appliances which use the supplies (such as cookers, fridges and washing machines).

(c) Installations in the rented premises that heat water or space, such as the central heating system (including radiators), and hot water cisterns and boilers.

Section 11 only obliges the landlord to repair the installations where their disrepair affects the 'enjoyment' (which means 'use' rather than 'pleasure') of the property. Similarly, the section does not oblige the landlord to install any installations (such as central heating, for example) where they did not exist at the time the lease was agreed. The tenant is also expected to look after the premises in a 'tenant-like manner'. This very circular requirement basically means that the landlord is not liable to repair installations that have been damaged by the tenant's wilful or negligent behaviour.

A landlord who has a duty under the lease or section 11 to repair the defect in question must put matters right within a reasonable time of receiving notification of the defect. If he does not, and the defect causes an injury or property damage, he may be sued.

2. Can someone who is not the tenant sue the landlord for personal injuries?

Any person who may reasonably be expected to be affected by the defects in the premises, but who is not the tenant, can sue the landlord for personal injuries arising from the defect (section 4 of the Defective Premises Act 1972). The claimant must prove that the lease imposed a duty on the landlord to repair or maintain the premises, or gave him the right to enter the premises to carry out maintenance or repairs. People who may sue under this section include spouses, family members and visitors of the tenant, people near the building and even trespassers.

My accident was caused by an activity carried out on the land; can I sue?

As explained above, the law is not entirely clear. The opinion of commentators and the Law Commission suggests that the law of negligence probably applies, and the individual (or his employer where appropriate) responsible for the dangerous activity should be sued in negligence rather than under the Occupiers' Liability Acts.

Injuries in the workplace

Employers have various duties towards the safety of their employees. These duties are laid down by the law of negligence (case law), various Acts of Parliament and their accompanying Regulations covering specific areas of employment safety, as well as the Occupiers' Liabilities Acts of 1957 and 1984. Additionally, government departments, agencies and international bodies (such as the World Health Organisation) publish reports, guidelines and codes of conduct which give advice and guidance on particular safety issues.

This section concentrates on claims based on negligence, and the Health and Safety at Work Act 1974 and related Regulations. It does not cover claims arising in building, mining, quarrying, agricultural, marine, shipbuilding, electricity and oil/gas extraction industries, and others. For a list of some of the legislation in these areas, please see the table of employment safety legislation at Appendix 11. At chapter 3, Researching the law further, you will find further information on how to do your own legal research.

Who is my employer?

Employment contracts impliedly include a form of promise by the employer to ensure that employees will be reasonably safe from injury at work. However, few claims are made on the basis of breach of contract, and the claimant normally relies on negligence and/or breach of statutory duty. Usually there is no dispute over identifying and proving who the employer is. It will probably be a single person or a company. It may be a partnership* (a firm), charity* or unincorporated association* (such as a club). For definitions of these terms, please see the glossary. Guidance in naming the employer correctly in court documents can be found in chapter 4.

What duty does my employer owe me?

There is no magic list of dos and don'ts. The starting point is that the employer has a general duty to avoid exposing his employee to unreasonable foreseeable risks – in other words, 'the ruling principle is that the employer is bound to take reasonable care for the safety of his workman and all other rules or formulas must be taken subject to this principle' (Lord Keith in *Cavanagh v Ulster Weaving [1960] AC 145*). However, as cases get reported over time, a pattern emerged in which the general rule is clarified and summarised. Employers must provide for each employee:

1. reasonably safe premises;

2. reasonably safe machinery and other equipment;

3. competent workers and management; and

4. a reasonably safe 'system of work' (i.e. the rules and procedures governing how the work is done).

Further specific 'statutory duties' are set out in Regulations and Acts. The first step is to ascertain which Regulations, if any, apply to your situation. Most of the duties are not absolute, and are often subject to qualification, such as 'as far as reasonably practicable'. Read the rules carefully – some breaches of Regulations give rise to criminal liability, rather than a claim for damages in the civil courts*. In other cases, the Regulations may not apply to your particular employer, for example, the Crown is not bound automatically by Statutory Regulations (see below). This book refers to some of the rules contained in the following:

*   The Lifting Operations and Lifting Equipment Regulations 1998

*   The Control of Substances Hazardous to Health Regulations 1994

*   Workplace (Health, Safety and Welfare) Regulations 1992

*   Manual Handling Operations Regulations 1992

*   Provision and Use of Work Equipment Regulations 1992

*   Employer's Liability (Defective Equipment) Act 1969

- Health and Safety (Display Screen Equipment) Regulations 1992
- Personal Protective Equipment at Work Regulations 1992
- Occupiers' Liability Act 1957
- Occupiers' Liability Act 1984

The rest of this section looks at the duties (under the law of negligence and the various Regulations) of employers in particular situations. The court will consider all the circumstances of the case. The claimant or defendant should produce evidence at trial of the following matters (the list is not exhaustive), if relevant:

- The use of relevant complaints procedures.
- The reporting of faults procedures.
- The inspection and maintenance programmes.
- The training, practices and standards across the particular industry.
- Any previous accidents.
- The age, experience and skill of relevant employees.
- Any financial and other commercial factors.
- The personnel and discipline records.

The court will also consider the nature of the instructions, training and warnings given to employees and how the company safety rules were enforced. Further guidance for claimants, defendant employers and the court can be found in the published material produced by the government departments, agencies and international bodies mentioned above.

1. My accident was caused by a co-employee

The employer must select, train and instruct properly skilled employees to undertake, manage and superintend the work. In other words, the employer has a duty, broadly, to provide 'safe' co-employees. The employer cannot shift legal responsibility by giving an employee or sub-contractor the task of employing, training or supervising workers. If the employer has not taken reasonable care to provide safe co-employees, he will be liable to be negligent for his own failure.

There is a second way that an employer can be held liable for 'unsafe' colleagues which does not directly involve the employer being in the wrong. In law, employers are vicariously liable* for the negligence (and other torts*) of their employees. The claimant must prove that the co-worker was the employee of the particular employer. Much of the case law in this area comes from accidents where a co-employee was 'horsing around' or deliberately harmed an employee. The courts look at all the circumstances in trying to decide if the wrongful acts complained of occurred 'in the course of the co-employee's employment'. Matters that will be relevant include the following:

- What were the tasks set by the employer?

- In what manner did the employer require the tasks to be done?

- Was the co-employee disobeying orders?

- How experienced were the employees?

- What was known about the employees' personalities?

- Could the employer reasonably foresee the risks of the injury occurring?

This legal rule often results in the injured party suing both the co-employee (for his primary liability in negligence, assault and battery, or other tort) and the employer (for his own negligence and/or breach of statutory duty, and also for the negligence (or other tort) of the co-employee(s)). Once liability is established against either or both, the court will award damages – the claimant does not need to be successful in every cause of action.

2. My accident was caused by the dangerous conditions of the workplace

The employer owes a duty to each employee to provide and maintain a reasonably safe workplace (including access ways). Whether the employer has taken reasonable steps to avoid the dangers and risks is a matter of fact in each case. The court will consider safety precautions; the cause of the hazard; whether the hazard is long-standing, temporary or transitory; the extent to which the employer knew (or should have known) of the hazard; and the particular needs and concerns of the employee. Other factors may also be relevant in a particular situation. It may be that the dangerous condition is caused by an unsafe system of work or an inadequate regime of inspection and maintenance. These must not only exist on paper or in the minds of supervisors, they must also be properly implemented.

The Workplace (Health Safety and Welfare) Regulations 1992, which were brought in under powers conferred by the Health and Safety at Work Act 1974, set standards for ventilation, indoor temperature, lighting, cleanliness, disposal of waste materials, room dimensions and space, workstations and seating, the condition of flooring, the prevention of falling objects, windows, the circulation of pedestrians and vehicles, doors and gates, escalators, sanitary conveniences, washing facilities, drinking water, restrooms and other facilities. Most of the duties are not absolute and are subject to a qualification such as 'as far as reasonably practicable'. The claimant must be prepared to argue that in the particular situation it would have been 'reasonably practicable' to take different action and so avoid the accident. See above for a list of matters that may be relevant.

3. My accident was caused by the nature of the work I was doing

Injuries caused by the way a task is carried out may be the result of the employer's failure to provide a safe system of work, or lack of adequate training and supervision.

If the employer has failed in these duties towards an employee – and the failure has resulted in the injury – then he may well have been negligent.

As for statutory duties, heavy lifting jobs are covered by the Manual Handling Operations Regulations 1992, which were brought in under powers conferred by the Health and Safety at Work Act 1974. Manual handling means 'transporting or supporting a load (including lifting, putting down, pushing, pulling carrying or moving it)'. Under Regulation 4, the employer:

a)   must avoid, as far as reasonably practicable, the need for an employee to undertake a great deal of manual handling which involves the risk of injuring him; or

b)   where it is necessary for the employee to undertake manual handling, the employer must assess the risk of the manual handling task in question and take appropriate steps to reduce the risks to the lowest reasonably practicable level (by introducing a safe system of work), and indicate to the employee at least generally or specifically the weight of each load, and the heaviest side of any load which does not have a centre of gravity.

The Regulations also require the employee to make full and proper use of the system of work instituted by the employer. If evidence shows that the employee failed to follow the orders or protocols which form part of the system of work, he may be unsuccessful in claiming damages for injury. Alternatively, the court may decide that although the employer was negligent/in breach of a statutory duty, in the circumstances the employee was contributorily negligent and may reduce the damages that would otherwise be payable to him (see Contributory negligence on page 63 for further information).

4. My accident was caused by the work equipment

(a) Defective equipment or machinery

Accidents at work involving machinery or other equipment may be caused by various factors. The equipment may be unsuitable for the job it is required to do; it may suffer from a design fault; it may be defective when new, or may become defective after a period of time; or poor maintenance, storage or care may have created a hazard. If the matter goes to trial, an expert witness will probably be required to help the court determine what has gone wrong.

(i)   Section 1(1) of the Employer's Liability (Defective Equipment) Act 1969 makes employers liable to an employee where an injury occurred in the course of his employment, caused by defective equipment provided by the employer for the purposes of the employer's business (i.e. to use at work). Moreover, under the Act, the employer is liable even if the defect is the fault of someone else (a third party) – whether a manufacturer, another employee or an independent contractor.

(ii) Further duties are imposed on employers by the Regulations. The main responsibilities laid down by the Provision and Use of Work Equipment Regulations 1992, which apply to most employers, can be summarised as follows. Employers must:

- ensure that equipment is suitable for the purpose for which it is intended;

- ensure that equipment is maintained in an efficient state, in efficient working order, and in good repair;

- ensure that equipment posing a specific risk to health or safety must only be used by the employee giving the task of using (or modifying, repairing, maintaining or servicing) the equipment, and that adequate training is provided for the employee;

- provide all employees who are using equipment with adequate health and safety information and training and, where appropriate, written instructions relating to the use of the equipment (the written instructions must be readily comprehensible);

- provide fixed guards and/or other protection devices (as appropriate) to prevent access to any dangerous part of the machinery or to stop the movement of any part of the machinery before a person enters the danger zone. The fixed guards or protection devices must be themselves suitable for the purpose, be well-built of sound materials, and must not themselves pose a risk to health and safety, etc.

(b) Other hazards in using equipment

There are various situations in which workers may suffer personal injuries from using equipment that is not in itself defective or obviously hazardous. Some, such as computer screens or headsets, have received recent media interest. Others are generally specific to particular industries. Apart from the common law duty to provide a safe system of work (please see above), various Regulations impose duties on employers in relation to the safe use of equipment. The Health and Safety (Display Screen Equipment) Regulations 1992 are an example. These require employers (amongst other things) to provide breaks or other interruptions for employees working at screens, regular eye and eyesight tests for certain employees (as well as providing them with spectacles or other corrective equipment where appropriate). Employers must also provide certain employees with health and safety training and information about the health and safety aspects of working at workstations.

It is important to look at the actual wording of the relevant Acts and Regulations to determine precisely what the employer's responsibilities are. Further guidance is given in publications by the relevant government departments, the Health and Safety Executive, and other organisations. These are available at TSO bookshops.

5. My injury was caused by the absence/inadequacy of protective gear

The general duty of the employer to take reasonable care for the physical safety of his employees (the law of negligence) may in certain circumstances require him to provide protective equipment such as goggles, gloves or specially designed clothing. A failure to do so may amount to negligence. It is for the claimant to persuade the court that in his situation, considering the job itself, the hazards involved and all other relevant factors, the employer should have provided specific protective equipment.

Furthermore, the Personal Protective Equipment at Work Regulations 1992 may apply to the employer. These stipulate that the employer must 'ensure that suitable personal protective equipment is provided to his employees who may be exposed to a risk to their health and safety while at work except where and to the extent that such a risk has been adequately controlled by other means which are equally or more effective' (Regulation 4(1)). There are further Regulations determining what is meant by 'suitable':

- requiring employers to assess the risks properly;

- maintaining and replacing protective equipment as appropriate;

- providing training and enforcing the use of protective equipment that has been supplied.

6. My accident was caused by a sub-contractor doing work for my employer

A sub-contractor is a term loosely describing a company or person who enters a contract with the employer to do a particular job of work. The contract (a contract for services) is not the same as a contract of employment (a 'contract of service') and the sub-contractor does not become an employee of the employer. In the paragraphs below I have used the term 'employer' to mean the injured claimant's own employer, and 'sub-contractor' to mean the company or individual who has undertaken work for the 'employer' under a separate contract. Of course, in relation to its own employees, the sub-contractor has all the responsibilities of an employer (see above).

If the accident was caused by defective equipment acquired by the employer from a sub-contractor, the employer may be liable under the Employer's Liability (Defective Equipment) Act 1969 (see My accident was caused by the work equipment above, for further information).

Where the sub-contractor's work has caused injury to an employee, even if the employer has used a sub-contractor to undertake supervisory or health and safety work, he still owes his employees a duty to take reasonable care for their safety. It is not enough for him to hire a reputable sub-contractor and try to shift responsibility for his employees' safety on to him. The court will consider all the circumstances of the case to decide whether the employer has failed to provide a reasonable safe place of work, system of work and colleagues (see What duty does my employer owe me? for further information).

7. My accident occurred whilst on someone else's (not my employer's) premises

The employer has a duty to provide a safe place of work and a safe system of work even if he sends an employee to work on property owned by someone else. However, the facts of each case will be examined carefully. Case law suggests that courts will not make employers liable if they have little or no control over the premises. In some circumstances, where reasonable, the employer should foresee particular dangers and devise a protocol for dealing with them.

It may be possible for the injured employee to sue the occupier of the premises where the accident happened under the Occupiers' Liability Act. Please see Accidents in or on private property, for further information. In some circumstances, it may be appropriate to sue both the employer and the occupier of the premises where the accident occurred.

I suffered stress and anxiety at work; can I claim?

Not unless the stress and anxiety manifested itself is a known diagnosed psychiatric illness. There is no duty imposed on employers to prevent the emotions of stress, anxiety, resentment, anger or frustration, etc. Case law shows that this is partly because they are considered as an inevitable part of the job, and do not amount to a personal injury. (Note that unpleasant conditions at work, such as bullying, etc, may form the basis of a claim under employment law. It is an area outside the scope of this book and reference should be made to specialist books on the subject.)

The law counts psychiatric illness as a personal injury and, if the employer is found liable, damages may be awarded. The claimant must prove that some factor at work caused the illness, and that in all the circumstances the employer should have guarded against the situation but failed to do so. The cases about this area of law tend to focus on whether or not the claimant's psychiatric illness was 'foreseeable'. In the legal context, this means the court will consider the likelihood of this employee (or employees like him) suffering psychiatric harm. As a matter of common sense and desirable policy was it so foreseeable that the employer should have anticipated it and taken steps to avoid the injury? It is always for the claimant to prove that his injury was the foreseeable consequence of the employer's wrongdoing.

The Crown is my employer; can I sue?

Yes, the Crown (the institution, not the sovereign herself) can be sued like other employers if it has been negligent or if its employee has been negligent in the course of his employment. Moreover, some Statutory Regulations apply explicitly or by necessary implication to the Crown as well as to other employers, and where this is the case the Crown can be sued for breach. This is the effect of the Crown Proceedings Act 1947. For further discussion of employer's duties and the effect of vicarious liability, please see above.

In litigation, the Crown is sued in the name of the person exercising the Crown's powers and his officers. Thus the Secretary of State for the relevant department is usually the defendant. Note that special procedural rules apply to actions against the Crown (County Court Rules Order 42 and Rules of the Supreme Court Order 77). They can be found in schedule 1 and schedule 2 of the Civil Procedure Rules 1998* respectively (see chapter 3, How to look up legislation, for further information).

The Crown Proceedings Act 1947 only permits actions against the Crown where it is acting as the government of the United Kingdom. It does not authorise litigation against the Crown in its capacity of authority in any other country or territory.

What evidence do I need?

Brief outlines of what the claimant must prove in a claim for damages can be found above. Often 'how did the accident happen?', 'in what way did the defendant act unlawfully?' and 'how did the injury and losses occur?' are questions that can only be answered by experts (safety officers, qualified engineers, doctors or other appropriate professionals). Unlike ordinary witnesses (including the claimant and defendant) who can tell the court only about the facts of the case, expert witnesses are there to give the court their opinions on the facts. They are also able to assist the court by establishing certain facts by using their technical knowledge and skills – examining broken machinery, surveying accident sites and advising what the industry standards and practices are.

Thus these types of claims frequently involve one or both parties calling independent expert evidence* as well as the ordinary witness evidence. Nowadays, such experts are generally jointly instructed by the claimant and defendant; this (usually) minimises the number of experts involved and clarifies the issues considerably. Most significantly, it reduces the litigation costs. Please see chapter 3, Gathering evidence, for further information.

Hobbies, sports and pastimes

Many pastimes and sports carry an inherent risk of injury to those taking part and sometimes to spectators or others nearby. The injured person will have a claim only if he can prove that someone's negligence, breach of contract or other duty (such as breach of statutory duty (including harassment or nuisance)) caused his injury and loss. Carefully analyse what has gone wrong (this may require an expert's report (see chapter 3)) – was it a failure of equipment, inadequate training, carelessness or deliberate harm by a participant, poor spectator management, inadequate security or negligent refereeing/umpiring, etc?

Has someone been negligent?

Damages are recoverable if the defendant is found to have been negligent. Such situations may arise in many different circumstances and may include the following scenarios:

- Accidental injury of the claimant by the defendant during the course of a game, match or other situation (including fellow players and spectators).

- The failure of the referee or umpire to control the game or take other steps to prevent the claimant suffering injury.

- The failure to provide, maintain or check, store or repair equipment properly (liability for defective products is discussed below at Accidents involving defective products).

- The failure to maintain safe premises (see also Accidents in or on private property).

- The failure of a trainer or coach to exercise the proper skill and care expected of him ('professional negligence' – see Negligent professional advice, for further information).

- The failure by organisers of events to control crowds or traffic adequately.

The courts will look at all the circumstances of the accident – did the defendant owe a duty to the claimant to avoid the sort of damage the claimant suffered (i.e. personal injury or damage to property)? Not all accidents will result in a successful claim. For example, some allowance is given for things done in the heat and excitement of a match, and a breach of the rules of the game (such as a foul) does not necessarily amount to negligence. However, if a player made an error of judgment that no reasonable player would have made, and injured the claimant as a result, then he will be held to have been negligent. A referee or umpire has a duty to control the game so as to avoid 'unnecessary risk' to the claimant participant. What constitutes unnecessary risk (and, logically, 'necessary risk') in the particular circumstances will have to be decided in each case according to factors, such as the nature, rules and objects of the sport or activity. The umpire and referee (and by extension all those leading, controlling, organising or training others for an activity) must take into account the age, experience and maturity of the participants and their physical capabilities. For example, people under 18 may have less anticipation of the risk of injury or damage to themselves and others. This affects the way that such people are expected to organise, control or teach an activity.

Has someone committed a battery (assault)?

Battery is the deliberate infliction of unlawful force (i.e. physical touch) on the claimant. The claimant must prove that the defendant intended the physical contact (but not necessarily that he intended to harm the claimant) and that he realised that the touching was unacceptable in the course of everyday life. If the victim of a battery has consented* to the act, he will not have a claim against the defendant. In many sports and activities physical contact with (and even injury inflicted by) other participants is expected and accepted or even necessary, for example, judo, fencing, rugby and even professional ballet. In some sports, such as boxing, (controlled) injury is the aim. Where a claimant has been injured, the real question for the court is 'is the particular physical contact complained of one that the claimant consented to?' and the court will consider the question in the context of the activity undertaken by the claimant. A punch by one participant to another is one thing in boxing, but it would be unacceptable between two rival swimming competitors (see Deliberately caused injuries and violence, below).

Is someone in breach of contract?

Many hobbies and pastimes involve a contract. Examples include membership of a gym; tickets to watch a match, game or event; attendance at a class or training centre; the hiring of a coach or trainer; and participating in an organised event or activity. The contract may be oral or written. Usually the participant will have paid a fee as part of the contract (for a further explanation of the essential features of a contract and how to prove what the terms were, please see Contracts that have gone wrong, below).

The claimant must prove that the defendant breached a term of the contract which resulted in his injury, loss or damage to his property. For example, the trainer, teacher, organiser or event leader acted without reasonable skill and care; or the equipment provided was not the required standard of quality, etc. Compensation for breach of contract is discussed at chapter 2.

Remember that the defendant's behaviour may constitute both a breach of contract and negligence (or conceivably another tort or breach of statutory duty).

My accident was caused because the premises were dangerous; can I sue?

Occupiers of premises, including sports grounds, golf courses, clubs, leisure centres, gyms, studios and buildings where equipment is stored may be liable if, due to the condition of the premises, the claimant injures himself, or his property is damaged. Please see Accidents in or on private property.

My injury was caused by defective equipment

Please see Accidents involving defective products, below.

My injury or loss occurred outside England or Wales

This book does not contain advice on any law other than the English and Welsh law. If the incident complained of occurred elsewhere, England and Wales may not be the correct place to bring a claim. Moreover, incidents happening outside England and Wales will probably be subject to the local law (remember particularly that Scotland and Northern Ireland have their own legal systems).

For an explanation of where claims may be brought, please see chapter 3, Is England & Wales the correct place to bring a claim?

Injuries caused by animals

When an animal injures a person or damages property a claim may be made against the animal's owner. There are two types of claim possible: under the law of negligence and under the Animals Act 1971. As discussed below, if the animal is a 'dangerous one' and the person in charge of it was negligent, a claimant may wish to argue that both causes of action apply (thereby maximising his chance of success).

A dangerous animal caused injury or damage; can I sue?

Under the Animals Act 1971 the keeper of a dangerous animal may be sued for any injury or property damage it causes. A 'keeper' is defined as someone who owns or has the animal in his possession at the time it causes the injury or damage. Where a child under the age of 16 owns the dangerous animal, the keeper for the purposes of litigation is the 'head of that child's household'.

An animal is classed as dangerous if it belongs to a dangerous species (i.e. a species that is not commonly domesticated in the British Isles and when adult has characteristics that makes it likely to cause severe damage if not restrained). Thus bears, lions and elephants have all been held by the courts to be dangerous under the Act.

An animal that does not belong to a dangerous species may also be classed as dangerous if the keeper of the animal knows that his animal has abnormal characteristics (e.g. aggressive tendencies) generally or in particular circumstances, and the type of damage likely to be caused by it was severe. Dogs are not a dangerous species as such. However, a dog may be 'dangerous' within the meaning of the Animals Act if the keeper knows it has dangerous tendencies. In one case, a keeper was found liable when his dog, known to attack people carrying bags, caused damage. An animal which is behaving 'normally' or in an expected way may not give rise to a liability under the Act.

One advantage of claims under the Act is that the claimant need not prove that the keeper did anything wrong or negligent. He will succeed if he can establish that the animal belongs to a dangerous species (or that the keeper knew it had dangerous tendencies), that it was in the keeper's care at the time, and that it caused him injury and/or damage. If, however, the keeper was at fault, the claimant should allege negligence in his Particulars of Claim too. If one cause of action fails (e.g. if the court decides that the animal was not dangerous within the meaning of the Animals Act, or that the keeper was not in fact negligent), the other may go on to win. See below for a discussion of negligence claims relating to animals.

The person in charge of the animal was to blame; can I sue?

A person in charge of any animal may be negligent if he fails to restrain or control it suitably and it causes property damage or injury to the claimant. Cases may include those arising from attacks by animals, or accidents caused by straying or escaping animals. The court will consider whether in all the circumstances (including the species and usual behaviour of the animal in question, the nature of that particular animal in question and the foreseeability of the attack or accident) the defendant had a duty to take care to avoid the danger occurring. The law requires a person to take only reasonable care and not to guard against every eventuality.

My own animal was injured; can I sue?

Animals at law are property ('chattels'), and therefore any damage or injury to an animal is classed as damage to its owner's property. The court will award compensation for monetary losses and costs to the owner arising from the attack or accident. Such compensation may include vet's bills and the cost of special equipment and supplies necessitated by the attack or accident. Where the injured animal was expected to earn profits for its owner (such as a stud or show animal, or one that was to be sold at market), the court may order compensation for any expected losses. In certain circumstances the appropriate compensation may be the cost of replacing the animal. Evidence of all these losses will need to be proved by receipts, estimates and expert reports from appropriate professionals (e.g. a veterinary surgeon, an animal behaviourist, a show judge, a breeder, an agricultural auctioneer, etc).

It is not possible to obtain damages for the claimant's own worry or distress arising from the attack or accident, although if he is injured or suffers 'psychiatric harm', damages may be awarded.

What are the possible defences to animal claims in the civil courts?

The defendant may bring evidence that the claimant brought the attack on himself, for example, by climbing into a lion's cage, or taunting a dog, or intervening in a fight between two animals, or knowingly trespassing into an area patrolled by a guard dog. Moreover, the defendant may be able to prove that the claimant failed to take sufficient care of his own safety and was contributorily negligent.

Will the Dangerous Dogs Act apply to my case?

The Dangerous Dogs Act 1991 – introduced with maximum publicity and often criticised since – regulates the keeping of pit-bull terriers and other proscribed breeds. It creates various criminal offences, but does not directly provide a civil cause of action. Therefore it cannot be used to obtain damages in the civil courts. Most situations will be covered by the Animals Act 1971 and the law of negligence anyway, so damages may be obtained as described above.

However, the victim of an attack by a dog of a proscribed breed may report the matter to the police, and cooperate with any prosecution. If the controller of the dog is convicted of an offence under the Dangerous Dogs Act (or other legislation) for the attack the victim may obtain monetary compensation through the criminal courts*. Either the victim can ask the prosecution to request the court to make a compensation order against the controller, or he can apply to the Criminal Injuries Compensation Board for an award compensating him for his own injuries (see chapter 3).

Where healthcare goes wrong; claims involving a healthcare professional

Claims brought by patients are a specialist area of practice. The law applying to the way professionals carry out their jobs is set out in the law of negligence, the law of assault and battery, and the law of contract. The law relating to the safety of products and equipment is an area of practice know as product liability, and is similarly governed by principles of tort, statute and contract. The area is continually developing and case law is important for setting down the parameters of the duties owed by healthcare professionals and their employers.

What behaviour amounts to negligence?

Each healthcare worker (doctor, anaesthetist, midwife, dentist, pathologist, surgeon, etc) has a duty to exercise reasonable skill and care in the treatment or care of his patient. A hospital has a similar duty in its own right in respect of patients treated in Accident or Emergency, or patients admitted as patients or outpatients. Additionally, NHS healthcare authorities or private healthcare providers are responsible for the negligence of their employees under the principle of 'vicarious liability'.

When assessing whether the professional or hospital was negligent, the court will look carefully at the mistake made. There may have been a misdiagnosis, wrongful or inappropriate treatment, a poorly executed procedure (such as a botched operation), poor nursing standards, cross-contamination or any other failure to look after the defendant's health. The court should ask itself the question 'has the defendant shown the ordinary skill and care expected of a competent professional in the same field (or of a hospital) in the advice given to, or the treatment or care of, the patient?' In other words, the healthcare professional will be judged by the standard of his peers; for example, a defendant hospital doctor will be judged by the standard expected of a doctor in an equivalent post.

The law does not expect healthcare workers to perform miracles, or even to avoid all mistakes. Where a particular procedure, treatment or diagnosis divides medical opinion (e.g. in a developing area of medicine, practice or technology), the law will not find a defendant liable for using a controversial method, as long as that method is recognised by a respectable body of medical opinion.

It is usually essential for a healthcare worker in the same field as the defendant (or the defendant's employee where relevant) to be called as an expert witness to help the court assess whether the defendant's actions were of the expected standard of competence.

What constitutes a 'battery' (unlawful physical contact) by a healthcare worker?

Many medical procedures, from examinations to operations and nursing care, involve the use of physical contact (i.e. a deliberate and perceptible touch) by the healthcare worker and the patient. If done without the consent of the patient, such physical contact would amount to a 'battery' (often described as an assault). In some circumstances it may be appropriate for written consent to be given (by signing a form); in other situations oral consent will suffice. The most important thing is that consent is informed. A patient's consent obtained dishonestly or by other misrepresentation is not a valid consent, and the physical contact will be unlawful (a tort) and illegal (a crime).

Parents may give consent to examinations and procedures on young children (including injections). However, children who have enough understanding and maturity may give consent for themselves. Healthcare workers who touch a patient in a way that is more than what has been consented to, or which is outside the scope of the consent given by the patient, commit a battery, and damages are recoverable for injuries caused by the unauthorised action. However, doctors and other professionals do not need consent from an unconscious patient where a procedure is 'necessary' to preserve life or health.

How do I claim for malfunctioning equipment, or dangerous products such as drugs, vaccines or blood?

Please see Accidents involving defective products, below.

Does the law apply to NHS and private healthcare workers in the same way?

The law of negligence applies to all healthcare workers, whether in public or private employment at the time of the incident in question (please see above). Additionally, the private patient has entered a contract with his healthcare provider for medical and other services. Thus when things go wrong, the patient may have a claim for breach of contract. Aside from other terms that may have been breached, if the defendant has failed to use reasonable skill and care in performing the medical services under the contract, he will be liable. This is a term implied into the contract by the Supply of Goods and Services Act 1982. In many cases, the distinction between a case based on negligence and one based on contract will be academic, but sometimes it will be an advantage to rely on both (if a technicality is fatal to one, the other may nonetheless survive).

What compensation can the court order if the claim succeeds?

By their nature, claims arising from clinical disputes will seek compensation for personal injuries with associated costs. Please see chapter 2 for further information.

Is there an alternative to litigation?

Please see chapter 3, Getting what you want without going to court.

Accidents involving defective products

Where a physical object causes an injury and other loss to a person coming into contact with it, a cause of action may have arisen. The person responsible for the defect may have breached the terms of a contract of sale or supply, may be liable under the Consumer Protection Act 1987 or may have been negligent. Moreover, the facts of the case may amount to more than one of these causes of action. Similarly, the claimant may have claims against more than one defendant (either all under the same cause of action or alternatively under different ones). Unless there is a good reason for not suing a potential defendant, or for not relying on a particular cause of action, it is wise to rely on as many causes of action and defendants as can be proved. That way, the chances of success against at least one are maximised.

Remember also that an employer is vicariously liable for the negligence and other breaches of duty of his employees, but not for sub-contractors. If sub-contractors have been negligent they may be sued directly, and an action will probably lie against them as producers, suppliers, importers or rebranders of defective goods, under the Consumer Protection Act 1987.

What is a 'defective product'?

There is not a single definition of 'product' and lawyers use the term generally to cover various types of items: manufactured goods (machines, vehicles, food, drugs) and other products or physical objects that by virtue of a defect (including design faults, ineffective warnings, misleading labelling or inadequate instructions), may result in the accident. An object is not 'defective' merely because it is dangerous. Many physical objects and substances are by their inherent nature dangerous or pose a threat to health and safety, and those qualities are useful to us. For example, knives are sharp and rat poison is poisonous. The proper use and care of such objects is taken into account when deciding whether they are defective. Note that the Consumer Protection Act 1987 does contain a definition of products that can be the subject of a claim under that particular Act (see below).

How can I claim for a defective product?

Breach of contract

The claimant must prove that there was a contract between himself and the defendant by which he acquired the defective product. Therefore, defective gifts do not come into this category (but there may be a claim in negligence or under the Consumer Protection Act 1987). The contract will probably be a 'contract of sale' (where the claimant brought the product from the defendant), or a 'contract for the supply of goods and services' (where the defendant supplied the product in the course of doing a job of work for the claimant).

The claimant must demonstrate what the terms of the contract stated, such as promises that the product was safe for a particular use, etc (see below). Finally, the claimant must prove that the product was in fact unsafe in the circumstances and that the defect caused the injury. There is no need to prove that the defendant had brought about the defect himself by his action or inaction.

1. What are the terms of the contract?

First, there may be terms that were expressly agreed between the buyer and seller of the product as to its suitability and safety for a particular purpose (orally before the contract was agreed, or in written terms). Second, where the seller, hirer or supplier of goods is acting in the course of his business with a private consumer, various Acts of Parliament insert terms as to the quality of goods supplied under the contract. For example, the item or goods sold, hired or supplied must be of satisfactory quality, they must be fit for the purpose which the consumer told the seller he intended to use them (if he had done so), and they must match the description under which they were sold, hired or supplied. The relevant provisions are found in the Sale of Goods Act 1979 (sections 13 and 14), the Supply of Goods (Implied Terms) Act (1973), and the Supply of Goods and Services Act 1982.

2. What compensation can I obtain if my case is successful?

Damages may be awarded for the following types of loss:

- Pain, suffering and loss of amenity*.

- The value of (or replacement cost of) goods damaged by the defective item.

- Other financial losses arising from the defect.

- The value of the damage to the defective product itself.

Please see the general discussion of damages in contract claims in chapter 2.

Consumer Credit Act 1987

This Act was brought in to comply with a European Directive on consumer protection and other EU countries are similarly obliged to enact the directive. Claims under the Act are for claimants who have suffered injury or property damage caused by a defective product, or by a part contained in a product. In many cases, the defendant may have also been negligent (see below) or in breach of contract (see above). However, there will be many cases in which the Act provides the only cause of action available to the claimant. This may happen where, for example, the claimant did not buy or hire the defective item (i.e. no claim for breach of contract arises), or for some reason the defendant did not owe the claimant a duty of care (and therefore no negligence claim arises).

1. What must the claimant prove?

The claimant must satisfy the court that the thing causing the injury is a product within the meaning of the Act. He must also satisfy the court that the product was defective as defined by the Act. Finally, the claimant must prove that the defendant belongs to one of the four classes of people who are held responsible under the Act.

2. What counts as a product under the Act?

Manufactured goods (including food, drugs, aircrafts, vehicles and vessels), other substances (such as blood and blood products), agricultural produce and fish that have undergone an industrial process (such as canning or cooking), and electricity are all products under the Act. The item may be a raw material or a part used as a component in the finished article. Land (and buildings on land) do not count as products under the Act.

3. What counts as a defect under the Act?

If the condition of an item 'falls below the standard of safety that people are generally entitled to expect', it is termed as defective within the meaning of the Act. This may be because of a malfunction. Inherently dangerous products require proof of malfunction, or evidence that they were supplied with inadequate warnings or instructions appropriate to the circumstances. A product is not defective merely on the basis that current safety standards were higher when it was first made than now, or that newer models have improved safety features.

One of the things the court will take into account when deciding if the product was defective is how long it has been in circulation in the supply chain between creator and the claimant consumer. Most things in life have a shelf life – higher standards of safety are expected of products that are new than those which are not, or those which have suffered a normal level of wear and tear from proper usage.

4. Who can sue under the Act?

The product in question must have been supplied by the defendant in the course of his business. Amateur producers (such as makers of jam at a bring-and-buy sale, or the maker of a home-made car) therefore cannot be sued under the Act (however, they may have been negligent – see below). Most manufactured, extracted and supplied goods pass through many hands before reaching the consumer. The Act defines who may be sued for defects, some of whom may not directly be at fault for the condition of the product but may nonetheless be liable. There are four classes of people or companies who may be sued under the Act. They are producers, rebranders (my term), importers and suppliers.

Producers include the manufacturer, assembler, abstractor or excavator of the product or the industrial processor of the raw material.

Rebranders are people or companies who add their name, trademark or other label to a product manufactured, processed, assembled or abstracted by someone else, so that to the consumer it seems that the rebrander was in fact the producer.

Importers are narrowly defined in the Act as those persons or companies who import the defective product from outside the European Union into any member state (it need not have been the UK).

A supplier is any person who supplies (by selling, hiring, giving, etc) the defective product, in the course of his business, to someone else. The supply in question need not be to the claimant – the definition includes all the people involved in the supply chain. However, a supplier may only be sued if, having been asked by the injured consumer to identify the producers, rebranders or importers within a reasonable time of the injury occurring, he fails to identify those people.

5. What defences are there to this type of claim?

The defendant will succeed if the claimant has not proved each of the elements required (see What must the claimant prove? above). Additionally, the claim will fail if the defendant proves that:

- the defect arose out of his compliance with legal requirements;

- he was not the supplier of the product;

- the defect was not present when it passed through his hands to another person;

- he made only components for the finished article and the components were not faulty; and

- the scientific and technical knowledge at the time the product was in his control was not such that he could have been expected to discover the defect.

6. What compensation is recoverable under the Act?

Damages for personal injury, death and damaged property (worth more that £275) caused by the defective product are recoverable. Any contributory negligence on the part of the claimant will be deducted from any damages awarded. Note that it is not possible under the Act to obtain compensation for the original cost of, or damage to, the defective product itself (although you may in a claim for breach of contract).

Negligence

The claimant must prove that the defendant was the person responsible for the defect itself. Various types of defendant have been held liable (including manufacturers, assemblers and repairers of malfunctioning products, installers, distributors, and even wholesalers and retailers) who have, in the way they have dealt with, handled or stored the item, caused the defect to arise, or who have not provided the necessary safety information. It is vital to a successful claim to prove the defendant's wrongdoing (by action or inaction) and to identify the precise failing of the product.

Example: Where a component of the final product is defective and is incorporated into an otherwise perfectly good product, the maker of the part may be liable to the claimant for his negligent work, and the manufacturer of the finished product may be liable for failing to check the overall safety of the product, or for not using reputable suppliers. Thus there may be more than one defendant, and the court may apportion damages payable by each of them.

How do I prove negligence?

1. The courts will take into account all the surrounding circumstances on the issue of the safety (or otherwise) of a product. This may include any relevant British Standards guidelines (also known as the Kitemark system) or other non-statutory safety standards. Even though such guidelines are not mandatory, they provide a guide to what is considered a safe standard for products.

    As with all negligence claims, normally the claimant must have evidence to prove how the defendant failed to fulfil his duty to take care of the safety of people such as the claimant. Often an expert witness will be necessary. On rare occasions there is no explanation as to what exactly went wrong; merely the simple fact that the product caused the injury or loss. In such circumstances the claimant can ask the court to infer from the evidence of the accident and the injury/loss that the defendant was negligent because the item was in his exclusive control and the defect would not otherwise have occurred. This rule of evidence is known by its Latin tag 'res ipsa loquitur' ('the thing speaks for itself'). Clearly, if there is evidence as to how the defect was caused, there is no need to rely on this principle.

2. If the claimant is successful, he may recover damages to compensate him for any personal injury and damage to property caused by the defective product, including any losses and expenses arising from such injury and damage (see chapter 2, How is compensation for pain, suffering and loss of amenity calculated?). It is not possible to recover compensation for the defective product itself under a negligence claim (unlike a claim for breach of contract).

Example: Narinda is given a new car by her parents for her 18th birthday. When she takes it for a drive the exhaust explodes, injuring her and damaging the car and a laptop computer which was in the boot at the time.

As Narinda did not purchase the car, she cannot bring a claim for breach of contract. Her parents did not supply the car to her in the course of their business, and consequently they cannot be sued under the Consumer Protection Act 1987. However, Narinda can claim against the negligent garage which sold the car to her parents. If successful, she will receive damages for her pain, suffering and loss of amenity – the losses arising from her injuries (such as loss of earnings and the extra cost arising from her injuries, for example, medical bills and the cost of adapting her home). Narinda will also be able to obtain compensation for the damage caused to her property such as the laptop and the clothes she was wearing at the time of the accident. However, under the law of negligence, she will not be compensated for the damage to her car.

Other types of claim

An employer's responsibility for the safety of work equipment is explained in My accident was caused by the work equipment, above. There are other Acts of Parliament dealing with specific areas of product liability, such as the Vaccine Damage Payments Act 1979, but such regimes are outside the scope of this book.

Fatal accidents

Where a person has suffered financial loss and bereavement because a family member has died as a result of someone's wrongful act (e.g. breach of statutory duty, negligence or other tort), he may make a claim under the Fatal Accidents Act 1976. The claim is for damages to compensate him for the monetary losses caused by the deceased's death, and only certain people (see below) may make a claim.

Who conducts the litigation?

The deceased's personal representatives* (executors under a Will or administrators of the estate under the intestacy provisions) bring the claim on behalf of the family members seeking compensation, and are named as claimants. However, if none of the executors or administrators have obtained probate or the letters of administration by six months after the deceased's death, then the family members themselves may bring claims (either separate claims, which should then be joined together to be fought in a single trial; or by naming themselves first, second, third, fourth claimant, etc) against the defendant(s).

Who may be awarded damages under the Fatal Accidents Act 1976?

Only 'dependants' defined by the Act may obtain compensation:

1. The deceased's spouse or former spouse.

2. Any person living with the deceased as the husband or wife of the deceased at the date of death and for at least two years before the date of death.

3. Any parent or other ascendant (e.g. grandparent) of the deceased or any person whom the deceased treated as a parent (including a step-parent).

4. Any child or other descendant (e.g. grandchild) of the deceased.

5. Any child who, although not the deceased's own child, was treated by the deceased as a child of the family (at least during the time the deceased was married).

6. Any brother, sister, aunt or uncle of the deceased, or the child of the deceased's brother, sister, uncle or aunt (including sister, brother, aunt- or uncle-by-marriage).

What does the claimant have to prove?

The claimant must prove that the defendant's behaviour was wrongful (i.e. that he committed a particular tort or other civil wrong), and that it caused the deceased's death. After that, the claimant must call evidence to prove how much money each claiming dependant lost as a result of the death.

What sort of loss can be compensated?

The award(s) will reflect the financial loss of the dependants rather than the injury, loss and damage suffered by the deceased. The deceased's own injury, loss and damage may be the subject of a separate claim for damages which if ordered by the court will ultimately go to the beneficiaries under his Will or the intestacy rules (see chapter 2, Law Reform (Misc. Provisions) Act 1934, for further information). Additionally, under the Fatal Accidents Act 1976, a lump sum will be awarded to the deceased's spouse (or parent(s) if the deceased was under 18).

How does the court calculate damages?

Please see chapter 2, Damages for breach of contract.

CONTRACTS THAT HAVE GONE WRONG

Defective goods

For a discussion of accidents caused by defective goods, please see Accidents involving defective products.

Shoddy workmanship

What claim can I bring for shoddy workmanship?

This section is primarily designed to cover situations where someone who supplies services has failed to do a good enough job. It does not cover defective goods, sale of goods, shipping contracts or building contracts (usually governed by JCT standard contracts) or other such specialist areas.

Generally, the claim will be based on a breach of contract, but the matters complained about may amount to negligence. Sometimes the service provided for by the contract is the giving of professional advice (e.g. by a surveyor or tax advisor). Contracts with professionals frequently require both the giving of advice and the performance of a service (such as a consultant surgeon who diagnoses an illness and then operates on a patient, or a litigation solicitor* who advises on the strength of a case and then conducts the litigation).

This section deals mainly with the performance of tasks. Professional negligence and the related topic of clinical negligence are dealt with separately, although there is a considerable overlap in the areas of law (see Where healthcare goes wrong; claims involving a healthcare professional, above).

Note that there is a professional negligence pre-action protocol* (see chapter 3 for further information).

What is a 'breach of contract'?

When a person has failed to fulfil a promise he made in a contractual agreement with another, he will be in breach of contract. This will give rise to a claim for damages and possibly other types of remedy in the civil court. The claimant must clearly identify the exact promise (known as 'a term of the contract') which has been broken.

Poorly done work

All contracts which involve the defendant performing a service for the claimant contain (by virtue of the Supply of Goods and Services Act 1982, section 13) an implied term that the service is performed with 'reasonable care and skill'. In other words, the defendant must perform the job he is to do with the level of skill and care expected of someone possessing the specialist skill in question. Therefore, the work done by a plumber is compared to the level of competence expected of other plumbers and not by a member of the public. Similarly, car mechanics, kitchen installers, etc are all judged by the standards expected of their peers. Consequently, cases (except perhaps the simplest) require expert evidence to help the court decide exactly how the shoddy work breached the contract.

The supply of defective materials, parts and components in a contract for services

Where the defendant agrees, as part of his contract, to do a particular job in the course of his business and supplies materials, parts or other components, section 4(2) of the Supply of Goods and Services Act 1982 requires them to be of 'satisfactory' quality. If they are not, a breach of contract has occurred.

Can the defendant rely on a disclaimer (exclusion or limitation clause)?

Possibly. One frequently sees a notice in contractual paperwork or notices stating that if anything goes wrong the workman will not be liable at all for loss, injury, etc, or will only be liable for a limited amount or for certain losses. Sometimes the defendant will be able to use such a clause or notice as a defence to a claim for breach of contract. He must prove that the clause was contained in the agreement from the outset (this will be relatively easy if the contract was a written one). Additionally, the defendant must prove that the contractual document containing the exclusion clause was signed, or that the claimant was otherwise given reasonable warning of the clause. The clause must also be worded in a clear way and must cover the situation that has actually occurred. The final hurdle is for the defendant to satisfy the court that section 2 of the Unfair Contract Terms Act 1977 does not render the term invalid. Section 2 says that any clause which attempts to limit or exclude liability for personal injuries or death caused by negligence is void, and clauses seeking to exclude or limit liability for other sorts of loss (e.g. damage to property or financial loss) must have been reasonable at the time the contract was formed, and if not, cannot be relied upon. Whether the term was reasonable is a matter for the judge to decide, taking into account all the circumstances of the case.

I just want the work to be put right, not money compensation

Of course not every shoddy job leads to litigation. Often the person who has done the work will offer to put matters right himself in order to avoid a claim. It is a matter for the potential claimant as to whether he has enough trust left in him to allow this, and it goes without saying that the claimant should not have to pay extra for such work. Where the claimant is not happy for the person who did the poor work (or supplied the poor materials or parts) to put matters right, he is entitled to sue for damages to pay for the work to be remedied or completed (hopefully) properly by someone else. Unfortunately, English law will not generally compel someone to perform the contract properly once something has gone wrong or to repair his own poor work – the usual remedy is damages, which exposes the claimant to the danger that the workman may not be worth the money.

The shoddy work was done by a sub-contractor

The only person who can sue for breaches of contract are the parties to that contract. In the case of sub-contracts (and sub-sub-contracts, etc) the claimant only has a contract with the contractor, who in turn has a contract with the sub-contractor. There are two options: sue the contractor for his own breach of contract, or sue the sub-contractor in the tort of negligence where applicable. The contractor may be in breach of section 13 of the Supply of Goods and Services Act 1982; not only has he to carry out his own job with reasonable skill and care, but he must also take steps to ensure that the subcontractor will act with reasonable skill and care (*Metaalhandel JA Magnus BV v Ardfields Transport Ltd and Eastfell Ltd (trading as Jones Transport) [1988] 1 Lloyds Rep 197*). The sub-contractor may have been negligent if it can be established in all the circumstances that he owes a 'duty of care' to the claimant, and that the damage that arose from his negligence was foreseeable. Under the Contracts (Rights of Third Parties) Act 1999, a person who is not party to the contract (known as the 'third party') may nonetheless sue for a breach of contract in certain circumstances – where the contract expressly allows him to do so; or where the breached term confers on him a benefit, and the contract does not appear to exclude the enforcement of the term by third parties. The term 'benefit' means that if the third party has benefited from the contract (e.g. the work fixed by the contract has been completed for him), he may sue for breach of contract under the Act.

Can I withhold further payment of money where the work is shoddy?

If the shoddy work is a breach of contract (see above) and amounts to a 'fundamental' breach of contract (i.e. the quality of the particular piece of work is of major importance to the contract), the complainant may end the contractual relationship with the person undertaking the work. This has the effect of neither party being obliged to perform further actions under the contract (such as to finish the work or to pay further instalments). The complainant must make clear that he wishes to terminate the contract, and that no more payments will be made. A claim may then be brought for damages (see chapter 2 for how such damages are calculated).

Negligent professional advice

A professional in this context is a person who undertakes a particular activity and holds himself out to have a skill and experience of that area. The term is not confined to members of a professional body, such as the Law Society (solicitors) or the General Council of the Bar (barristers*), for example. For a discussion on poorly carried out work by a professional, see above. This section will contain a brief overview of what happens when a professional gives negligent advice. As mentioned already, some professional work will involve both giving advice and then undertaking some further work, such as a surgeon making a diagnosis and then performing the operation. Accordingly, this section should be read in conjunction with Contracts that have gone wrong. Note that there is a professional negligence pre-action protocol (see chapter 3 for further information).

What is 'negligent advice'?

The duty of a professional to give advice usually originates in a contract. Implied into that contract is the stipulation that he shall give that advice with 'reasonable skill and care' (section 13 of the Supply of Goods and Services Act 1982). In other words, the advice must not be incompetent or careless. Additionally, in certain circumstances, 'negligent advice' may amount to a tort of negligence. For this, the claimant must prove that the professional, in acting as he did, failed to show the degree of skill and care expected of a reasonably competent person of his position. Where the advice was not given to the claimant directly, but came to him second-hand, the claimant will also have to prove that the professional knew that the claimant would be given the advice, that the advice related to a particular matter relevant to the claimant, and that it was reasonable for the claimant to have relied upon the advice (*Caparo Industries plc v Dickman [1990] AC 605 HL*).

Thus there is often a liability in tort and contract at the same time. If you can, it is wise to allege both causes of action in the claim; if one fails for some reason, the other may survive. As long as one cause of action wins, the claimant will be awarded damages.

Holidays

Can we sue if our holiday goes wrong?

It depends on the situation. Obviously, if bad weather or an earthquake ruined your cycling holiday in the Alps, there is unlikely to be any redress in law. On the other hand, if someone is at fault resulting in your holiday being spoilt, the chances are that you can obtain compensation. Cases fall into three categories:

- Holidays in England and Wales that have gone wrong.

- Holidays where an English or Welsh based travel agent or tour operator is at fault.

- Other holidays abroad that have gone wrong.

For a discussion on how compensation is calculated in holiday cases, please see chapter 2.

My holiday was in England or Wales; how do I sue?

A holiday may go wrong for many reasons: the accommodation or facilities may be sub-standard or even dangerous, the staff may not provide a competent service, or the promised entertainments and excursions may not live up to the advertisement in the brochure. Many of these disappointments will amount to a breach of contract, a breach of the Occupiers' Liability Acts or negligence. A claim can be brought in the English/Welsh courts. The Occupiers' Liability Acts are dealt with at Accidents in or on private property. The other two causes of action are discussed below.

Breach of contract

The agreement between the parties may be oral or written (or both). However, usually contracts will be on the holiday company or hotel's standard form. The claimant must analyse the contract carefully – did the defendant fail to provide exactly what he had promised? Additionally, every contract in which a person provides a service to a consumer is subject to the (implied) term that the service provider will act with 'reasonable skill and care' (Supply of Goods and Services Act 1982, section 13). A breach of any of these terms (of course, there may have been multiple breaches) will give rise to a claim for damages in court.

Negligence

In order to establish that the defendant has been negligent, the claimant must:

1. persuade the judge that, because of the circumstances, the defendant had a duty to ensure that no foreseeable injury, loss or damage happened to the claimant;

2. prove, with evidence, that the defendant breached that duty (i.e. that his actions or inaction caused the injury, loss or damage); and

3.   bring evidence of his injury, loss or damage.

My holiday abroad was organised by an English or Welsh travel agent; can I sue?

If the travel agent has not provided a reasonably safe service, or the accommodation, facilities and amenities do not live up to what was promised, there will be a claim. Note that ABTA (the Association of British Travel Agents) runs an arbitration scheme for complaints against its members – this is a way of obtaining compensation without going to court. Note that a strict time limit of nine months applies – see www.abta.com for further information.

The holiday did not measure up to the description in the brochure

No matter where in the world the holiday took place, if the holiday was provided by an English or Welsh travel agent or tour operator a claim may be brought if the agent is at fault. The holidaymaker must prove that the holiday provider was in breach of an express or implied term of the contract.

1. A breach of an express term of the contract

It may be that the holiday company has failed to provide the facilities it promised to, or that the facilities, amenities or activities are not of the promised quality. If so, there will be a straightforward claim for breach of contract.

It is important, however, to check the terms of the contract first. The small print usually provides for the holiday company to substitute a particular hotel or other amenity with another, without being in breach of the contract. Such terms will be regulated by the Unfair Terms in Consumer Contracts Regulations 1999 (which applies to consumer contracts subject to the company's standard terms). An 'unfair term' will be invalid, and the holiday company will not be able to rely on it. Under the Regulations, an unfair term is one that 'causes a significant imbalance in the parties' rights and obligations arising under the contract to the detriment of the consumer' (Regulation 5(1)). It is not possible to argue that the price is unfair per se.

2. A breach of an implied term

Inserted into such contracts is the requirement that the holiday company must provide its service (i.e. arrange the holiday in question) with 'reasonable skill and care' (section 13 of the Supply of Goods and Services Act 1982).

3. An accident caused by unsafe premises

The claimant has two options: to sue (if possible) under the law of the country where the accident happened (for which the advice of a local lawyer will be necessary), or, where appropriate, to sue the travel agent under English law. For further information on claiming abroad or suing foreign defendants in England/Wales, please see chapter 3.

When claiming against an English or Welsh holiday provider for an accident that occurred abroad, the claimant must satisfy the judge that there was a breach of contract or other negligence, or a breach of the duty under the Occupiers' Liability Acts (if the agent is an occupier of the premises).

The Occupiers' Liability Acts are discussed above. As for breach of contract, section 13 of the Supply of Goods and Services Act 1982 inserts into every contract a duty for the travel agent to take 'reasonable skill and care' in providing services. The court in the case of *Wilson v Best Travel Ltd [1993] 1 All ER* decided that travel agents must not include hotels in their brochures that are not reasonably safe. One of the ways they can avoid liability is to ensure that the local Safety Regulations have been complied with (even if those safety laws are not as rigorous as their British equivalent). Where there are no local Safety Regulations that apply, the travel agent should perhaps check whether it was so unsafe that a guest would refuse (reasonably) to stay there if he knew about its unsafe condition.

4. An accident caused by unsafe equipment or goods (including food)

Again, the claimant has two options: to sue (if possible) under the law of the country where the accident happened (for which the advice of a local lawyer will be necessary), or, where appropriate, to sue the travel agent under English law. For further information about claiming abroad or suing foreign defendants in England/Wales, please see chapter 3.

When claiming against an English or Welsh holiday provider for an incident that occurred abroad, the claimant must satisfy the judge that there was a breach of contract or other negligence. It may be even possible to bring a claim under the Consumer Protection Act (see above). A claim for a breach of contract is just that – the claimant must prove that the defendant has broken a particular term of the contract and, as a result, personal injury, loss or damage has occurred. A claim in negligence must persuade the court that in the circumstances the defendant holiday provider owed a duty to take care of the safety of the claimant, and failed to do so, resulting in injury, loss or damage to him.

DELIBERATELY CAUSED INJURIES AND VIOLENCE

Clinical negligence (incidents involving the healthcare professions)

Medical procedures often involve a healthcare worker (doctor, nurse, dentist, etc) touching the body of a patient. Where the physical contact is not consented to, or exceeds the consent given, by the patient, a 'battery' is committed. Please see Where healthcare goes wrong; claims involving a healthcare professional.

Can I obtain damages if I am the victim of a crime?

Generally, yes. Harassment and false imprisonment are crimes that also may form the basis of a civil claim for damages. Drivers convicted of careless or dangerous driving will probably also have been negligent in civil law terms and thereby liable for damages (see

Road traffic accidents for a discussion of negligent driving cases and how to rely on relevant driving convictions in court). A person who deliberately or recklessly causes an injury to another may have committed a crime. The criminal law calls such actions grievous bodily harm (GBH), actual bodily harm (ABH), common assault, putting a person in fear of violence, indecent assault and rape, etc. In the civil law, these offences are all classed as 'battery'. 'Assault' is a separate tort where the defendant does something to make the victim think that the defendant is about to inflict unlawful physical contact on him.

Both assault and battery are torts and give the victim the right to claim damages in the civil courts. There is one exception to this general rule. The defendant will not have to pay damages (Offences Against the Person Act 1861, sections 44 and 45) if he is:

1. convicted and imprisoned for a minor offence of criminal assault or battery, or has paid the money the court sentenced him to pay; or

2. acquitted* and given a certificate of judgment by the magistrate.

Note that if the defendant acted in the course of his employment, his employer will still be vicariously liable and can be named as the defendant in a civil claim. Only the defendant himself can rely on the defence in section 45 of the Offences Against the Person Act 1861 (*Dyer v Munday [1895] 1QB 742*).

Should I pursue compensation in the criminal or civil courts?

It is not possible to recover damages or compensation twice. Usually the criminal case will be heard first. The court may, in straightforward cases, include a compensation order to compensate the victim for injury, loss or damage. This type of order was designed to provide a quick and easy method of awarding compensation to victims of crime. It was not supposed to replace the civil claims for damages.

The disadvantages of compensation in the criminal courts include the fact that the judge or magistrates must take the defendant's financial position into account (unlike the civil courts), and that magistrates are limited (amongst other things) to awards of £2,000. Moreover, it is more difficult to prove a case against a defendant in the criminal courts, in that the magistrates or jury can only convict if they are satisfied 'beyond reasonable doubt' that the defendant committed the crime. In the civil courts the judge only needs to be convinced that the defendant 'probably' committed the act complained of, in order to judge the case in favour of the claimant. However, the advantages of compensation orders include less delay, no legal costs, and compensation can include an element representing fear and anxiety (which is not available in the civil courts except for the Harassment Act 1997 claims or where psychiatric illness has resulted).

Do not forget that the victims of violent crime can seek a compensation award from the Criminal Injuries Compensation Board. This is suitable for more serious cases where the defendant cannot afford the appropriate level of damages. The scheme is funded by the state. See chapter 3 for further information.

Note that bringing a civil claim is not the same thing as a private prosecution. A private prosecution is where a private individual rather than the Crown prosecutes the defendant. The defendant, if found guilty, will be sentenced in the normal way. Private prosecutions are part of the criminal law and are not within the scope of this book.

Suing in the civil courts

Assault and battery

An assault, technically, does not involve physical contact. An assault is committed when the defendant, acting deliberately (or possibly negligently, the law is not clear) causes the claimant to fear that he (the defendant) is about to inflict physical contact on him. Thus the tort is concerned with the threat of violence, rather than actual bodily violence. Therefore, shaking a fist at someone may, in some circumstances, amount to an assault. Pointing a gun at someone almost certainly would.

The tort of battery is where the defendant deliberately inflicts unlawful force on the claimant's body without his consent. Obviously, violence will be unlawful. However, the physical contact need not be violent as such – a mere touch may constitute a battery. Of course, the courts recognise that a certain amount of physical contact is all part of everyday life and not every touch will be unlawful. The court will look carefully at the context of the physical contact between the parties.

In practical terms, any physical contact that results in an injury can be the subject of a civil claim for damages. In the split second before the attack (or for even longer than that), the claimant may have been aware of the impending battery and therefore may have suffered an assault as well. Usually the two are termed together 'assault and battery' (sometimes also known as 'trespass to the person') and where injury has resulted, the court is not likely to split hairs over the precise difference.

Defences to assault and battery

The defences of 'consent' and 'justification' may be raised by the defendant in civil claims for assault and battery, where appropriate. Where the claimant has consented, actually or impliedly, to the type and degree of physical contact, then the claim for battery will not succeed. However, if the physical contact exceeds the degree, or is of a different type from that consented to, then the defence will not succeed. Additionally, consent that has been obtained through fraud, or some form of coercion, is not true consent and the defence will not be successful.

Justification is where the defendant can prove to the court's satisfaction that the circumstances of the case make the battery lawful. Self-defence, reasonable force to prevent a crime or a breach of the peace, assisting officers of the law, and the claimant being a danger to himself and others are all examples of justification. Another well-known example is the reasonable chastisement of a child by a parent or certain persons in authority over a child. What the courts will tolerate as reasonable is of course affected by modern day sensibilities, and this defence is the subject of political debate and government review. In the future, it could well be banned.

The deliberate infliction of psychiatric injury

By case law, following the decision of *Wilkinson v Downton [1897] 2 QB 57*, a claimant can recover personal injury damages for a psychiatric condition brought on by the deliberate actions of the defendant. This covers those cases where the defendant had deliberately set out to harm the claimant, but where no physical contact had occurred or been threatened. Nowadays, most situations are probably covered by the new statutory tort of harassment (see below).

Harassment

In June 1997 the Protection from Harassment Act came into force. It had been brought in as a result of a growing perception that there was no effective law against 'stalking', although it is generally thought to apply to non-stalking situations as well. The Act created a new civil tort of harassment (section 3) as well as the criminal offences of harassment and 'putting a person in fear of violence'. The Act does not define harassment, except to stipulate that it is behaviour that occurs on more than one occasion. In other words, harassment is a 'course of conduct'. Over the next few years cases will come before the civil and criminal courts which will enable the courts to define harassing behaviour. Nuisance telephone calls, malicious letters, threatening behaviour, intimidation, pestering and other forms of anti-social behaviour directed against one or more persons will probably all amount to harassment.

A successful claimant can recover damages not only for damage to property and injury resulting from the harassment, but also for anxiety. This is exceptional, as the judge cannot normally take into account anxiety or distress falling short of psychiatric injury when awarding damages. It remains to be seen how the courts quantify damages for anxiety and distress in harassment cases.

False imprisonment

False imprisonment is a crime as well as a civil wrong (tort). It is the deliberate or reckless restraint of the victim's freedom of movement from a particular place. The restraint may be achieved by physical means or by intimidation. The victim need not have been 'taken prisoner' as such. Merely blocking the victim's means of exit or escape will be sufficient. The victim does not have to realise that he is being restrained. However, lawful restraint (such as lawful arrest) cannot amount to false imprisonment and the defendant is entitled, where appropriate, to claim lawful restraint as a defence.

PROBLEMS RELATING TO THE OWNERSHIP OF A HOUSE, BUILDING OR OTHER LAND

Evictions and obtaining rent from tenants

This section cannot pretend to explain the complex landlord and tenant law in any depth. Often the validity of landlords' attempts to evict their tenants will turn on questions of whether or not a tenancy or licence was created, whether or not a notice served by the landlord to the tenant contained the precise and necessary information in the prescribed form, and whether or not the dates given in the form were calculated correctly. These questions are highly technical, depending upon a mix of statutory requirements and common law rules. Accordingly, this section is designed to give a brief overview of possession actions (cases where the landlord wishes to evict tenants) in straightforward cases of residential, private and individual tenants of 'dwelling houses'. Agricultural and business tenancies are not discussed; nor are tenancies that began before 15 January 1989 (these latter tenancies are governed by the Rent Act 1977 and are known as 'regulated tenancies'); neither are lodging arrangements where a person lodges with a landlord or employer.

(Further recommended reading: *Defending Possession Proceedings* by Jan Luba QC, Nic Madge and Derek McConnell, 5th edition, Legal Action Group 2002.)

Can the landlord just evict tenants or licensees?

Tenancy still continuing

Unless allowed to by court order or the provisions of the lease, a landlord may not evict a tenant whilst the tenancy is still continuing. To do so is breach of the tenancy agreement and unlawful eviction. The tenant may take his landlord to court in order to obtain an injunction (letting him back in the house) and damages.

Where the tenancy has come to an end

Even if a residential tenancy has come to an end, and the tenants remain in the property without permission, the landlord may not evict them himself and must obtain a court order for possession. The law is set out in the various Acts relating to rented property including the Rent Act 1977, The Housing Act 1988, the Housing Act 1985 and for otherwise unprotected tenancies, the Protection From Eviction Act 1977. Note that in such a situation, where the tenants are 'holding over', the landlord must be very careful not to grant a new tenancy by accepting rent, etc.

How may the landlord lawfully obtain possession of the rented premises?

You must decide the characteristics of your tenancy in the following areas:

1. The length of the tenancy period (and therefore the type of tenancy).

2. How and when the tenancy may be brought to an end.

3. Whether the tenancy is protected by a statutory regime (sometimes, and misleadingly, known as 'security of tenure').

These factors together will determine how much notice the landlord must give before bringing proceedings, and also which grounds the landlord may use to obtain a possession order and other orders against the tenant.

1. How to work out the length and type of the tenancy

First consider what the original agreement between the landlord and tenant was. Most tenancies nowadays are written leases in a standard form where the landlord has just filled in the blank spaces for the amount of rent and when it is payable, and so on. A tenancy granted orally is perfectly valid, although it is perhaps more difficult to prove exactly what the agreement was.

Tenancies for a fixed term

The tenancy may have been expressly granted for a particular length of time (such as a year) in which case it is known as a tenancy 'for a term of years'.

Periodic tenancies

Alternatively, the tenancy may be an ongoing one with no such agreement for an end date. The legal basis for such a tenancy is that it is actually being granted afresh over and over again, such as from week to week, month to month, or quarterly (every three months) each time the rent is received. Such tenancies are called periodic tenancies. The length of a periodic tenancy is generally the period the rent is calculated by – thus where rent is expressed to be '£X per week' the tenancy will be a weekly periodic; if rent is expressed as '£Y per month' the tenancy will be a monthly periodic; if rent is calculated as '£Z per quarter' the tenancy lasts for a quarter of a year, and so on. Although the rent is calculated for one period of time, such as a week, sometimes it is payable less or more frequently; this makes no difference to the rule I have just set out. Therefore if a rent is expressed as '£X per week' but is payable at the end of each month the tenancy will be a weekly periodic tenancy, not a monthly one. The important thing is not when the rent is payable, but how it is calculated.

2. Bringing a tenancy to an end

(a) Tenants

A tenant is bound to continue paying rent and observing any other promises made in the tenancy (such as to keep the property in good order, do repairs, etc) until the end of a tenancy. If he wishes to leave early and end his obligation to pay rent, etc he must either:

(i)   'surrender' the tenancy by agreement with the landlord (by a formal document known as a 'deed', or by vacating the property and leaving the keys with the landlord who then accepts the property back or relets it);

(ii) wait until the tenancy has expired (tenancies for a 'term of years'); or

(iii) serve a valid Notice to Quit on the landlord (periodic tenancies).

(b) How to work out the Notice to Quit period

Without going into detail about the requirements of a valid Notice to Quit (they are hardly used nowadays), it is relevant to mention that the length of notice given in a Notice to Quit depends on the length of the periodic tenancy. The notice period contained in a Notice to Quit should end on the last day of the next whole period of the tenancy. Thus where a tenant or landlord of a periodic tenancy decides, in the middle of a period of the tenancy, that he wishes the tenancy to come to an end, he should serve his Notice to Quit before the beginning of the next tenancy period stating that it will expire on the date at the end of that period. The rule is slightly modified in the case of weekly periodic tenancies, where instead of the notice period lasting only one week, the notice period mentioned in the Notice to Quit must be four weeks.

3. What statutory regime applies

If the landlord is a local authority or other public sector landlord, the Housing Act 1985 may apply ('secure tenancies'). Private sector tenancies created before 15 January 1989 may be protected by the Rent Act 1977 ('regulated tenancies'), and those created on or after 15 January 1989 may be protected by the Housing Act 1988 ('assured' and 'assured shorthold' tenancies). Readers should refer to the relevant Act to see if the tenancy in question qualifies for protection.

Secure tenancies (public sector tenancies)

A secure tenancy is a residential tenancy where the landlord is a public body such as a local authority or housing action trust. The full definition is set out in the Housing Act 1985.

The landlord must send the tenant a Notice Seeking Possession (NSP) before bringing a claim for possession in court. The NSP must set out the ground(s) on which possession is sought, and specify the date after which the landlord may take proceedings in court. The specified date should be the earliest date at which the landlord could bring the tenancy to an end at common law (see above). In the case of a weekly periodic tenancy the date is at least four weeks after the beginning of the next rent period (please see above). The NSP will remain valid for a year after the specified date, and court proceedings must be brought within that time (or the tenant will be able to defend the case on the basis that the NSP has lapsed).

At the hearing of the landlord's claim for possession he must bring evidence that he served a valid NSP and prove that one or more of the grounds for possession exist. The most common ground for possession is that the tenant has fallen into arrears with his rent payments; other grounds include that the tenant has breached other terms of the tenancy agreement, caused a nuisance or annoyance, or that the remaining occupier of the property caused his partner to leave the property through the threat or occurrence of domestic violence, etc. Some grounds require the landlord to prove that he has offered the tenant suitable alternative accommodation.

Assured tenancies (private sector tenancies)

Unless the tenant 'surrenders' an assured tenancy (and this is accepted by the landlord), or moves out when the original rental period ends, the tenancy will only come to an end if the court orders possession. When a fixed term tenancy comes to the end of his term, and there is no new lease signed, but the tenant continues to live at the property and the landlord continues to demand and accept rent from him, the tenancy becomes a 'statutory periodic tenancy'. When a fixed term tenancy has not expired or become a statutory periodic tenancy the landlord may only obtain possession for limited reasons – including the mortgage lender wishing to sell the property, rent arrears (see below), persistent delays in paying rent, breach of any tenant's obligation in the lease, causing nuisance or annoyance, domestic violence towards an occupier who has now left the premises, etc. Periodic tenancies, including statutory periodic tenancies, may be repossessed on one or more of a wider selection of grounds. The 17 grounds are set out in schedule 2 of the Housing Act 1988.

The first step for the landlord is to serve the tenant with a Notice complying with section 8 of the Housing Act 1988 (a 'Section 8 Notice'). The Section 8 Notice must:

- be in the official prescribed form;
- tell the tenant that the landlord intends to begin proceedings for possession;
- state which ground(s) are relied upon, together with full particulars;
- state that the proceedings will not be commenced before a particular date; and
- state that the proceedings will be brought within 12 months of that date.

The particular date given must be calculated according to the rules set out in the Housing Act 1988. The calculation depends on the ground relied on. Where ground 14 (nuisance, annoyance or criminal conviction) is mentioned, the date must be no earlier than the date the Section 8 Notice is served on the tenant. Where grounds 1, 2, 5, 6, 7, 9 and 16 are relied upon (alone or with other grounds), the date is either at least two months from the date of service, or if the tenancy is a periodic tenancy the date that would be stated in a valid

Notice to Quit served on the date of service, if that is later. For information on how Notice to Quit periods are calculated, please see How to work out the Notice to Quit period, above. For Section 8 Notices relying on any of the other remaining grounds (for example, the various rent arrears grounds), the particular date must not be earlier than two weeks from the date of service of the notice. Except in cases where ground 8 is relied upon, the court can dispense with the requirement to serve a Section 8 Notice if it is 'just' and equitable' in the circumstances to do so.

The most common reason for repossession by a landlord is for the tenant's rent arrears. If some rent is due (ground 10 of schedule 2 to the Housing Act 1988) or the tenant has persistently failed to pay rent on time (ground 11), the landlord must further satisfy the court that it is 'reasonable' in all the circumstances to make an order for possession. Where the landlord relies instead on ground 8, he must prove that a particular amount of rent is due and in arrears (both at the time of the Section 8 Notice and at the hearing) – eight weeks' rent in the case of weekly tenancies, two months' rent in the case of monthly tenancies and three months' rent in the case of quarterly tenancies, etc. The judge must make the possession order in those circumstances. The judge will also order the tenant to pay the arrears. Obviously, if the arrears have been paid off by the time of the hearing no order will be made (unless another ground is relied upon and satisfied), although the tenant will probably be ordered to pay the landlord's legal costs. Once the possession order is made there can be no further chance for the tenant; the tenancy is at an end.

Assured shorthold tenancies (private sector tenancies)

Assured shortholds are, as the name suggests, a type of assured tenancy under the Housing Act 1988. Since 28 February 1997 most newly created residential tenancies are assured shorthold tenancies. The main difference between assured tenancies and assured shorthold tenancies is that once a periodic tenancy exists, in addition to the landlord's ability to repossess under the Section 8 Notice procedure set out above, he may evict the tenant under the section 21 procedure. A periodic tenancy exists if it was either granted by the landlord at the outset, or the tenant remains in the property and continues to pay rent after the expiry of the original fixed term, in which case, a 'statutory periodic tenancy' arises.

The section 21 procedure is set out at section 21 of the Housing Act 1988. It allows landlords to have their property back without having to bring evidence that the tenant is at fault, or using any of the other grounds set out in schedule 2. All the landlord must do is prove in court that:

- at the date of the hearing the tenancy is a periodic one (whether it was from the outset or has arisen subsequently as a statutory periodic tenancy); and

- he gave the tenant at least two months' notice (in writing) prior to him informing the tenant that he required possession of the property (and that where the tenancy was a periodic tenancy when he served the notice that the two-month period expired on the last day of the period of the tenancy).

If these criteria are satisfied the court must grant the possession order and the tenancy is at an end.

Ejecting trespassers (including squatters)

What is a 'trespass'?

A trespass occurs when someone who either entered the claimant's land (including buildings) without permission or having originally had permission has exceeded the terms of the permission. A person is also a trespasser if he directly causes an object to intrude over, rest on or become embedded in the claimant's land – the object involved could be a nail, ladder or even a building. The trespass may be a one-off event or a continuing state of affairs. It is a common law of tort in English law (although there is also a criminal offence of 'aggravated trespass', which is outside the scope of this book).

A trespass may occur in many situations, for example:

- A person may stray onto land.

- Squatters may take up residence.

- A next-door neighbour may begin to use land without permission in order to park vehicles, use access ways, erect a fence or build onto it.

- A person may allow his animals to run onto land or use it to store equipment or dump rubbish on it.

- A former tenant can commit a trespass by remaining in the property after the lease has come to an end, and without a new lease being agreed. Note, however, this statute provides that most residential tenancies only come to an end with a court order, and under both statute and common law if a tenant remains in the property after the term of his tenancy has expired, and pays rent to the landlord who continues to accept it, then a new tenancy has almost certainly arisen. In such circumstances, the tenant is not committing a trespass by remaining in the property.

The principal remedies available for trespass are an order for possession (recovery of land), damages (compensating the claimant for the loss of enjoying or using his land, but probably not for personal injuries, which are confined to negligence claims) and injunctions.

Who has the right to take action against trespassers?

Trespass is a tort historically designed to protect the rights of landowners. The person who possesses the land (including buildings) may bring the action against a trespasser. Possession in this sense means the owner, the tenant of the land, the beneficiary of the land under a trust or any other person who has 'exclusive possession' (i.e. a person who is entitled to exclude other people from the property (including part of a building) in question). The claimant does not need to prove that he is the owner of the land in question as such, but he must bring evidence to show that he has a better claim to possession than the defendant.

Can I just eject the trespasser myself?

Yes. Under common law a person is allowed to use reasonable force to remove a trespasser. What is 'reasonable' depends on the circumstances, and the court is unlikely to condone any physical manhandling of the trespasser except in the most extreme and urgent of situations. The alternative is to take the trespasser to court to obtain a possession order (also known as a 'recovery of land order'), and/or an injunction, and damages.

How do I recover my land or eject the trespasser by court order?

The claimant must prove the following elements:

- that he possesses the land or building in question;

- that the defendant has deliberately entered the land himself, or has caused an object physically to intrude, embed or rest on the land.

If he wishes to receive compensation, rather than just nominal damages, the claimant must also prove his loss (see chapter 2, Damages for trespass to land for further information). The procedure for starting possession claims against trespassers is set out in chapter 5. There is a special procedure under the Civil Procedure Rules, Part 55 for claims that include a request that the court grant a possession order. Other claims may be made under the Part 7 procedure described in the same chapter.

What happens if I do not know the name(s) of the trespasser?

A claim may be brought against 'persons unknown' – please see chapter 4 for further information.

Are there any specific defences to the tort of trespass to land?

There are many instances of either common law or statutory provisions allowing persons to enter the property of another, from the powers of the police and other law enforcement agencies to enter property to the establishment of a right to roam under the Countryside and Rights of Way Act 2000 (not yet brought in). Such rights can be raised in defence and are often described as a 'defence of justification'. Please also see below for a general discussion of defences.

Nuisance (interference with a person's enjoyment or use of his own land)

What is a 'nuisance'?

Whilst a direct and deliberate encroachment onto the claimant's land is a trespass (please see Ejecting trespassers, above), a nuisance is committed by someone acting in a way that interferes with the claimant's use and enjoyment of his own land (including rented land or buildings). 'Enjoyment' in this sense does not mean pleasure as such, but is the landowner's right to use his land as an amenity. Moreover, the act complained of must be 'substantial' (i.e. not trivial) and 'unreasonable' (i.e. more than just an unpleasantness of everyday life which the law expects the landowner to put up with). The courts will take into account whether or not the claimant (or the claimant's business) is abnormally sensitive to loss or damage from the activity complained of and will also consider the character of the neighbourhood. The courts have to balance the rights of landowners to do what they want with their own land (including their right to run a business on it) with the responsibility they have for damage to another landowner's health, land or business; to abnormally sensitive claimants; or to a location where such inconveniences are more common than elsewhere.

There is a special category of nuisance where one possessor of land does something on his land or uses his land in a particular way which causes an escape route onto the land of the claimant, resulting in damages. This is known colloquially as a 'Rylands and Fletcher' claim and is based on the judge-made law in the case of *Rylands v Fletcher [1886] LR 3 HL 330*. Examples include a reservoir flooding adjoining land, cattle escaping and grazing another's land, deliberately planted plants which invade land nearby, and fire or explosions, gases or noxious fumes which cause damage. Unlike nuisance (or even negligence) proper there is no need to prove that the defendant was in any way to blame for the escape. The simple fact that it happened is enough to establish liability. This is a principle known as 'strict liability' and is an unusual feature in the law of tort.

What must the claimant prove?

As well as bringing evidence that the defendant caused the nuisance, knowingly risking foreseeable damage to the claimant's use or enjoyment of his property (or doing so maliciously), the claimant must also produce evidence of his loss, damage or injury which constitutes the interference with his use or enjoyment of his land.

The defendant may be the creator of the nuisance, or he may simply be an occupier of the premises where the nuisance emanates from (sued on the basis that he failed to take reasonable steps to repair or otherwise remedy the danger on his land). Note also the legal principles set out previously with regard to the occupier's liability in negligence and for breach of statutory duty. The claimant may be able to prove that more than one cause of action apply to the facts of his case.

What about relying on other torts as well?

There are many overlaps between nuisance, Rylands and Fletcher and other torts. One act complained of may amount not only to nuisance, and/or Rylands and Fletcher, but also to trespass, negligence or occupier's liability (see the rest of this chapter generally). Where possible, it is of course sensible to rely on as many torts as can be established by evidence – this maximises the chances of success on at least one of them, and then the court will grant the claimant his remedy as appropriate.

Are there any alternatives to bringing a claim?

Instead of going to court it may be possible to report a nuisance to the local environmental health department. They are able to take action against those who perpetrate statutory nuisances (such as noise, smells, etc) under the Environmental Protection Act 1990 and other legislation. Such procedures are out of the scope of this book – please refer to your local authority for details on how to make a complaint.

Are there any special defences to nuisance claims?

Please see below for a general discussion of defences. Many activities that would otherwise constitute nuisance are permitted by a specific Act of Parliament – although careful attention must be paid to the type and level of nuisance permitted by the statute; where the permission is exceeded there will be no defence to that extent.

If a nuisance has gone on for a long time without being successfully challenged in court and stopped by a court order, the defendant may be able to establish that he has a common law right to continue with the activity. This is known as the doctrine of 'prescription', by which a person can gain a prescriptive right to do something. The defendant must prove that the activity was carried out without secrecy, permission or the use of force; that the level of inconvenience was continual; and that this went on for a period of at least 20 years affecting the claimant and the people who owned the property before him.

Interference with rights of way or other accesses; blocking of light, etc

There are many types of property which are at risk from damage or interference by others. A window may be overshadowed by a fast growing hedge, a private right of way (or right of drainage, etc) over someone else's property may be blocked, or a party wall which depends on a 'right of support' over a neighbour's property may be threatened by building works, or undermining or encroaching vegetation. Such occurrences may form the basis of a claim in trespass to land or nuisance. Statutory procedures set out in the Access to Neighbouring Land Act 1992 and the Part Wall Act 1996 may be relevant. The area is a complex and technical one and is outside the remit of this book.

DEFENCES

What is a 'defence'?

A 'defence' is a term for the facts and legal arguments relied upon by the defendant to avoid an order for damages, injunction, possession or other court order. Defences fall broadly into four categories:

1. Denying the factual basis of the claim.

2. Raising a technical legal defence.

3. Contributory negligence by the claimant (this may be a partial or complete defence).

4. Challenging the amount of damages claimed (or challenging the basis of another type of court order).

Filling in the Defence Form

Whichever defence is relied upon, it is important to remember that the Defence Form must be verified by a statement of truth* – the defendant must confirm that the facts contained in the defence document are true. A defendant who has signed the statement not believing the truth of the facts in the defence is in contempt of court. The court may bring proceedings against him for the contempt. Contempt of court is punishable by up to two years in prison and/or a fine.

The Defence Form is a document that the defendant uses to tell the court and the claimant of his defence. It should carefully set out his response to each of the allegations made by the claimant. Each statement made by the claimant in the Particulars of Claim must either be:

1. 'admitted' – in which case the issue is no longer 'live' and the court accepts the fact without hearing any evidence from either party; or

2. 'not admitted' – where the defendant has no knowledge or evidence of whether the allegation is true or not, and therefore simply requires the claimant to call evidence to prove the fact; or

3. 'denied' – where the defendant disagrees with the fact or entitlement alleged and puts forward his own version. The court will hear evidence (or legal argument if appropriate) from both sides and make findings as to which version it prefers.

Please see chapter 4, Part 7 claims and Appendix 2 for further information.

Denying liability

Denying legal entitlement

The claimant must satisfy the court that the defendant is legally liable to compensate him for each item of injury and loss. His claim is founded upon a cause of action (e.g. negligence, breach of statutory duty, battery, harassment, trespass, nuisance, statutory possession or breach of contract, etc). A close analysis of the Particulars of Claim may reveal that a crucial element in the cause of action is not present. The basic and necessary elements of the various causes of action are set out in the rest of this chapter. For example, a particular Act of Parliament or set of Regulations cited in the Particulars of Claim may not apply to the defendant (or to the claimant or to the situation generally, as the case may be). Similarly, the claimant may not have alleged a fact crucial to the cause of action. There is no need to argue complex points of law in the defence, but it should clearly allege that the claim fails to amount to negligence/battery/breach of Statutory Regulation, etc. See sample paragraphs 1 and 5 in Appendix 2 on page 190.

Challenging the facts

Many cases will come down to a straightforward fight on the facts. The essence of this type of defence is that the defendant:

1. challenges the claimant's evidence; and

2. brings his own evidence in order to persuade the court that no negligence, battery, breach of statutory duty, etc, took place.

See sample paragraphs 2–5 and 7–9 set out in Appendix 2 on pages 190-91.

Denying causation

The claimant must prove that the defendant's behaviour or omission caused his loss and injury. Where there is no evidence to prove this, or the claimant's evidence has been successfully discredited by the defendant at trial, a crucial element of his cause of action, namely 'causation', has not been proved. He should state clearly in the defence that he denies that any behaviour on his part (whether admitted or not) caused the claimant's loss and injury.

Challenging the claimant's evidence of causation may be a matter of common sense. In some situations, however, the judge may need the assistance of specialist help (e.g. if a particular chemical caused a disease, a mechanical failure caused a crash, a surgical treatment caused an injury, or a claimant's pre-existing medical condition was made worse by an injury). It may therefore be necessary to call expert evidence to prove or challenge causation, as well as to give opinion on other matters. Expert evidence is dealt with under Expert witnesses, on page 83.

The injury, loss or damage was caused by something beyond the defendant's control

When the defendant has committed a wrongful act towards the claimant, but another factor that is beyond the defendant's control then contributes to the claimant's injury, loss or damage, the court must decide if the defendant is responsible to the claimant. This principle was known as 'novus actus interveniens'; in other words, the 'intervening act' has broken the series of events between the defendant's wrong and the claimant's loss, injury or damage.

The court will look carefully at the chain of events leading up to the injury to see if the factor (whether an act of nature, the act of a third party or the act of the claimant) introduced a new, possibly unforeseen, element into what has happened.

Legal defences

Consent (permission or licence)

If the defendant proves that the claimant consented to the specific behaviour complained of, he will have a defence. The consent may have been given expressly (in words) by the claimant, or else inferred from his conduct. Obviously, where the claimant has only consented to the defendant's behaviour under coercion or fraud, the defence will fail.

The claimant knows about and accepts the risk of the defendant's behaviour

This defence is related to the defence of consent (see above). If successful, it has the effect of ruling that, even though the defendant's actions caused the injury and loss, the claimant is to blame for his own injury. The defendant must prove that the claimant, by his words or actions at the time of the accident, has voluntarily waived his right to claim against the defendant for the risk posed by the defendant's behaviour.

The defence will not succeed where the claimant merely knew about the risk. It is unlikely to apply in accident at work claims.

Self-defence, defence of another person or property, or the prevention of a crime

These are defences to battery and are self-explanatory. The court will take into account all the surrounding circumstances to decide if it was reasonable for the defendant to commit what would otherwise be a battery on the claimant, and also to decide if the amount of force used was reasonable and proportionate to the perceived danger.

Limitation

The Limitation Act 1980 places a time limit on the period in which the claimant may bring a claim against the defendant; once the relevant time limit has expired, the defendant may assert that the claim is 'statute-barred'. Even the strongest claim cannot proceed once a successful limitation* defence has been proved. However, the defendant must be careful to raise the issue himself; the claimant will not mention it. The only way for the court to hear argument that the claim is statute-barred by the Limitation Act (or other provision) is for the defendant to include the appropriate paragraph in the Defence Form. Of course, he does not need to rely on it if he does not want to and he may also formally waive the right to rely on the Act.

The Act sets out various limitation periods*. Most claims based on personal injuries will have a limitation period of three years, which can be extended in certain circumstances. A six-year rule applies to most other torts, breaches of contracts and causes of action. There are special rules dealing with child claimants and patients* under the Mental Health Act. To find out what limitation period applies to the claim and for a discussion on how to calculate the period, see chapter 3.

The claimant was himself acting wrongfully

The fact that the claimant was acting wrongfully or even illegally is not usually relevant to a claim for personal injury and will not amount to a defence. Only in certain exceptional cases will the court decide that a claimant was acting so wrongfully or illegally at the time the defendant was negligent, or in breach of statutory duty, etc, that he should not benefit from the legal process. The case law in this area is somewhat complex and possibly contradictory, and a discussion of this area (known in Latin as 'ex turpi causa non oritur actio') is outside the scope of this book.

Reasonableness

There are two ways in which the defendant's reasonableness is a defence:

1. In certain situations, Acts of Parliament or Regulations provide that if the defendant can prove he was in fact acting reasonably in the circumstances, he will not be liable. An example of this is the Protection against Harassment Act 1997. This defence may therefore amount to a justification of the defendant's otherwise wrongful actions.

2. Other legislation and rules of law provide that the defendant has only to act reasonably or take reasonable steps in the circumstances to ensure the claimant's safety, etc. Thus the defendant, in proving he has taken those reasonable steps or acted reasonably, disproves the claimant's claim that he has breached a duty towards him. An example of where this might be an issue is the (defendant) driver's duty to take reasonable care for the safety of other road users.

Either way, if the defendant is successful, the claimant will not be able to succeed on his claim. Defendants should look carefully at the legislation that the claimant is relying upon to see if this defence is available. A sample paragraph for inclusion in the defence is shown at paragraph 6 in Appendix 2 on page 190.

Contributory negligence

The defendant may allege that the claimant's actions or omissions were the only cause of the loss or injury complained of, rather than anything the defendant has done or failed to do. In that case, he is asserting that the claimant has failed to make out the cause of action (see above). However, where the defendant believes that the claimant by his action or inaction was partly to blame for the loss and injury suffered, he can rely on section 1 of the Law Reform (Contributory Negligence) Act 1945. If the court finds that the accident is partly the fault of the claimant, the claimant's damages will be reduced proportionately to the extent to which he was to blame. Thus the claimant who is found to have been 50 per cent to blame for the accident or injury will have his damages reduced by 50 per cent. An example of this defence can be found at paragraph 11 in Appendix 2 on page 191.

A claimant who contributed to his own injury by reacting in the 'agony of the moment' will not be held to be contributorily negligent.

Challenging the amount of damages claimed

Types of damage that may not be recoverable

It is worth checking that each item of damage claimed is something that the court will order compensation for. A discussion on what types of loss, injury and damage the claimant can recover damages for is found at How is compensation for pain, suffering and loss of amenity calculated? on page 67. If an item is not recoverable, the defendant should state in the defence that the entitlement to it (or the type of loss or damage) is disputed.

Failure to mitigate loss

The claimant has a general duty to mitigate his loss. This means that he must take reasonable steps to minimise his expenses and losses (including future losses) caused by the defendant's action. Everything will depend on the circumstances of the case and the options open to the claimant, as his loss and expenses become clear after the incident. For example, the court may decide that it would have been reasonable for the claimant to have undertaken recommended medical treatment, or retrained so as to obtain future employment, or to have used a contractor who provided the lowest estimate. If the claimant has incurred extra expense or increased his damage or injury by not taking these reasonable steps, that extra expense or increased expense will not be awarded in damages. Accordingly, where this defence succeeds, it takes the form of:

1. a reduction of the amount claimed with respect to a particular item of loss or injury; or

2. no award of damages with respect to a particular item of loss or injury.

CHAPTER 2

WHAT SORT OF COMPENSATION OR ORDER CAN THE COURT MAKE?

This chapter is divided into sections covering damages and other orders to pay money, injunctions and orders for possession. The two methods of calculating damages are those used in:

1. claims based on one or more of the various torts; and

2. breach of contract cases.

These are described below, but the starting point is damages in personal injury cases (including clinical negligence), which is really a branch of tortious damage. There are also sections on damages claims arising after the death of a person (brought under the Fatal Accidents Act 1976 or the Law Reform (Miscellaneous Provisions) Act 1934).

DAMAGES

The law in England and Wales generally attempts to compensate an injured person for the loss he has suffered, rather than punish the person responsible for the injuries. Once liability has been decided (or for some causes of action, such as negligence, liability has been proven), the court turns to the claimant to prove his loss. Loss may be an actual or direct loss (such as injury, damage to vehicles, clothes, etc) or a consequential loss arising from the direct loss (such as lost earnings, medical and care expenses, etc). The principles underlying the calculation of loss in tort cases differ from those in cases of breach of contract. It would seem, however, that the courts treat personal injury damages in the same way, whatever cause of action has been established.

Damages for personal injury

The claimant's claim for damages will comprise:

- Special damages*: these represent the actual and consequential expenses and other losses, quantifiable in monetary terms, incurred between the accident and trial (such as damaged clothing, vehicle repairs or loss of earnings). Special damages must be set out in the schedule attached to the Particulars of Claim (see chapter 4).

- General damages: damages for pain and suffering (past and future) arising from the injury, and anticipated future costs and losses, such as future medical expenses or equipment, future loss of earnings or the 'handicap on the labour market' (i.e. where the claimant cannot expect to earn as much because of the accident).

The courts will generally only consider the case once. The award of damages must encompass any future losses, pain and suffering or loss of amenity. In certain circumstances the court will consider making an award for the time being and revisiting the claim at a later date – see Provisional damages, below.

Special damages are generally mere exercises in proof and calculation. General damages are not so obviously quantifiable. The courts have had to devise a system which translates pain and suffering from an injury into a sum of damages. Similarly, the court has devised methods of calculating future losses to take account of the advantages of being awarded a lump sum in advance of the likely time of loss (this is sometimes called the 'benefit of accelerated receipt').

How is compensation for pain, suffering and loss of amenity calculated?

As the phrase suggests, this element of the award compensates for the pain and other suffering occasioned by an injury. The area is governed by case law and other guidelines, such as the Judicial Studies Board Guidelines*. These have resulted in a loose 'tariff' system, so that both claimants and defendants (and the insurance industry) can calculate the likely amount of an award from the outset. In other words, every injury has its 'value' in terms of damages. The law will take into account the following elements:

- The pain suffered.

- The recovery rate and prognosis.

- Whether the symptoms are permanent.

- The extent of the treatment required (past and future).

- Whether the symptoms have accelerated the onset of any other condition.

- Whether the injuries have reduced life expectancy.

- The effect of the injury on the practicalities and enjoyment of everyday life, including damage to relationships, loss of job satisfaction, as well as the ability to work and to look after oneself, to resume normal duties and responsibilities, and to pursue hobbies and interests.

- The degree of shock, embarrassment, anxiety and any other emotional effects of the injury (although no claim can be made for this element alone).

- The age of the claimant.

The starting place is the Judicial Studies Board Guidelines. These class symptoms into general categories covering psychiatric conditions, paralysis, orthopaedic injuries, injuries to internal organs, injuries affecting the senses, scarring, facial injuries and brain damage. Within these categories, broad bands of likely awards reflect the severity or otherwise of the symptoms. The Judicial Studies Board Guidelines are reproduced in the various textbooks used by lawyers. These resources also contain hundreds of case reports and the damages awarded (usually called the 'quantum of general damages for personal injury'). You may find one of these textbooks in a library: *Kemp and Kemp: the Quantum of Damages*, *Current Law* and *Butterworths Personal Injury Litigation Service*.

Lawyers calculate general damages awards by taking the following steps. It is not a precise art, but the more research one does and the more comparable cases one finds, the easier it is to pinpoint the appropriate award. They:

- identify the guideline range from the Judicial Studies Board Guidelines;

- research case law to ascertain how the courts deal with cases of the same nature to yours, trying to identify a reported case that is as near as possible on the facts;

- account for inflation (see below).

Because inflation renders the damages awarded and the Judicial Studies Board Guidelines are out of date within a short period of time, lawyers update the likely award by using the following formula:

$$\frac{\text{Today's RPI} \times £[\text{expected award}]}{\text{RPI at the time of the award}}$$

The monthly Retail Price Index (RPI)* is reported in *Current Law*, and in tables set out in *Kemp & Kemp* and *Butterworths Personal Injury Litigation Service*. A Citizens Advice Bureau or library may be able to help you obtain any of these publications or the RPI.

Example: An award of £5,000 was made in March 1993 when the RPI was 139.30. The value of the award in December 2000 when the RPI was 171.7 is calculated as follows:

$$(171.7 \times £5,000) \div 139.3 = £6,162.95$$

Thus, at the date of calculation, December 2000, the award would be the equivalent of £6,162 and the court would take that into account when deciding the actual amount.

Where a person suffers more than one injury, the court is anxious to avoid 'double recovery'. This is where the compensation for different elements is not merely added up, but there is some overlapping of compensation. Thus, in crude terms, the court will not add up, say, £1,000 for a whiplash injury, £450 for a hand injury and £300 for a head injury, and award £1,750. It will take into account that the pain and suffering come largely from multiple injuries and, where appropriate, will consider the pain, suffering and loss of amenity together. In this example, therefore, and all other things being equal, the court would award a sum less than £1,750.

Case study: Joan Brown's stationary motorbike was hit from behind by a car. She was knocked to the ground and an ambulance was called. At Accident and Emergency she was found to have sustained a 3cm cut to her face, a soft tissue injury to her neck, and bruising to both knees and her upper legs. Her wound was cleaned and 'glued', she was given analgesics and a surgical collar, and was discharged.

Joan, who is 34 years old, stayed in bed for one week and could not go to work. Her birthday party had to be cancelled and she was unable to resume her hobby of windsurfing for six months. When the specialist examined her, he agreed with the diagnosis and noted that her facial cut had healed after five weeks with a faint but permanent scar and the bruising on her legs had settled after two weeks. Her neck was very stiff and painful for two weeks after the accident and thereafter began to improve. Joan still suffered some residual symptoms when examined by the specialist six months after the accident. The specialist believed that the symptoms would settle completely in a further three months (nine months after the accident).

The award will take into account the following:

- Joan has suffered multiple minor injuries and the court will not look at each injury separately, but rather consider them together.

- Joan suffered pain and discomfort for the first two weeks from her neck injury, the bruising and the cut; she was in bed for one week.

- After two weeks, her symptoms began to settle, with her bruising improving first, then the cut healed and finally her neck symptoms resolved. This occurred within nine months after the accident.

- She missed one week of work, could not windsurf for six months and was disappointed to miss her birthday party.

- Joan's everyday life and her ability to care for herself were not affected beyond the first two weeks, when her mother came to look after her.

- She is a young woman, and in the specialist's view the injuries she sustained will have no long-term implications for her.

What happens if there was a previous injury or a further accident before trial?

A defendant is only liable for the damage and injury he has caused. Where a claimant had a pre-existing condition, the court will only grant compensation to the extent to which the claimant was further injured, suffered loss, etc. Similarly, where before the trial or settlement the claimant suffers a separate incident, accident or disease, the court must avoid making the defendant compensate for the aggravation or exacerbation of any symptoms, or the increase of any loss caused by the second event. This is a matter in which medical evidence is particularly helpful.

How are expenses and financial loss arising to the date of trial or settlement calculated?

This element of a damages claim is known as 'special damages', and is made up of direct types of damage and consequential losses. Special damages are calculated arithmetically. The claimant must prove his loss by satisfying the court that he has incurred each expense or suffered each item of loss as a result of the accident. He must also quantify each item claimed by providing receipts and estimates. The court expects him also to mitigate his loss (see The duty of the claimant to mitigate his loss, below). A failure to mitigate a particular loss may result in only partial recovery of the amount claimed.

English and Welsh law requires the claimant to set out everything he is claiming at the outset. A 'schedule of special damages' is a pre-action stage required by the personal injury pre-action protocol (see chapter 3). This sets out each item of loss or expense and the amount claimed. Of course, as the matter progresses it will be necessary to update the schedule from time to time.

The items that can be claimed include:

- the cost of repairing property damaged in the accident (e.g. clothing, spectacles, car, motorcycle or bicycle) or, if uneconomic, the value of the item prior to the accident;

- the cost of treatment (including private healthcare, prescription charges and travel expenses to hospital);

- the costs of disability (including nursing charges and other reasonable paid help, the cost of necessary equipment such as crutches or a specially adapted car, and the increased costs of normal expenditure attributable to the injuries such as transport, home heating, etc);

- the value of the unpaid care provided by a member of the family or friend to the claimant and the costs incurred by such carers visiting hospital, or taking unpaid time off work;

- the loss of earnings (net of contractual sick pay) or loss of earnings disregarding statutory sick pay (the value of the latter will be deducted by the defendant and paid to the government under the Recovery of Benefits scheme (see below), as well as the value of other employment benefits).

For a sample schedule of special damages, see chapter 4.

Are DSS benefits considered when calculating damages?

Under the Social Security (Recovery of Benefits) Act 1997, a defendant is obliged to repay the government for any social security benefits paid to the claimant as a result of the injury or disease for up to five years from the accident or, in the case of disease, from the date of the first benefit claim in respect of it. The defendant must apply to the DSS for a certificate of recoverable benefits (known as a CRU Certificate), and this will tell him how much benefit must be repaid to the government.

The classes of recoverable benefits are listed at Appendix 11. They fall broadly into three categories:

1. Loss of earnings

2. Costs of care

3. Loss of mobility

Where the claimant is claiming for a type of loss, such as loss of earnings, the defendant will deduct the amount of any recoverable benefits paid during that time relating to his loss of earnings. The deduction can only be made from that particular element of his claim. It cannot be deducted from another area of damage, such as the element for pain and suffering. Nor can the deduction create a payment to the claimant of less than nil; the claimant cannot end up owing the defendant for deductions made by the defendant.

How is compensation for future losses and expenses calculated?

These are often known as 'general damages for future loss'. The calculations are made from the date of trial or settlement. The aim is to compensate the claimant for any future losses arising from the accident (although not for future pain and discomfort of any disability which is contemplated in the general damages for pain and suffering component – see above). There is no magic formula that will apply to all cases – the court will need to take into account various contingencies and tailor the different arithmetical or statistical tools to provide the most accurate level of compensation. For example, the chances of future promotion, early retirement or the statistical probability of a woman taking time out of employment to have children will all be relevant and will reflect not only the amount of damages, but also the way they are calculated.

Some types of damage will be a single item of expenditure; others will be a repeated loss or expense. In some cases, the claimant may only have needs for a few years; in others, the disability or condition may be permanent, in which case life expectancy or retirement age may be part of the calculation.

The list below is not exhaustive but damages may include, where appropriate:

- the future loss of earnings and/or loss of earning capacity (also known as the 'handicap on the labour market');

- the future costs of nursing care or other professional help (housekeeping, maintenance of the home, etc);

- the future costs of medication, treatment or equipment;

- the cost of adapting a home/car to meet the claimant's particular needs;

- the higher costs of living occasioned by the claimant's continuing condition;

- the loss of future pension rights because of his inability to maintain the pre-accident expected contributions.

The claimant must prove the likelihood of him suffering continuing or future losses and the reasonableness of the sums involved. He will need to produce estimates and other documentary proof of future costs. Medical evidence of a relevant specialist will be needed to prove evidence of the claimant's future care and treatment needs and also evidence of his future ability to work. Similarly, where the claimant claims a future loss of earnings (because he cannot work at all, or his working life has been curtailed by the injuries) or a handicap on the labour market, a forensic employment specialist will need to give evidence on his behalf.

Once a figure is obtained for each type of loss, the parties will need to establish if this is a 'once-only' expense, or if it is regularly recurring. An example of a once-only expense may be the increased cost of purchasing and adapting a bungalow – a figure that is easily obtainable.

Those items (such as specially adapted vehicles or equipment) which will only be incurred from time to time are, similarly, easy to calculate. An example may be the purchase of a wheelchair at £1,000 and its replacement every five years. Where the claimant can be expected to need a wheelchair for the rest of his life (he is 46 and has a life expectancy of 75, say) the future costs of wheelchairs for him will be: £1,000 × 5 (the number of times he will have to replace the wheelchair in his lifetime). Generally, the payment of a lump sum for such expenses will not take into account inflation and other future price rises.

Other ongoing losses can be calculated on an annual basis (except for the loss of earning capacity – see below). This is a complex area and it is recommended that readers who are claiming or defending a case with significant periods of lost future earnings or reduced life expectancy take legal advice. This guide can only give an indication of the court's approach.

Once an annual figure of loss and expense is calculated, it must be multiplied by a suitable amount known as the 'multiplicand', to reflect the future period of continuing loss. The starting point is to consider the actual number of years the claimant is expecting to suffer this loss – is it for a short period or is it permanent? Lawyers use a series of actuarial tables called the Ogden Tables* (now in their fourth edition), to find the appropriate multiplicand.

What is 'loss of earning capacity' and how is it calculated?

This phrase covers various types of damage to the future prospects of earning an income. It includes situations where the injuries have handicapped the claimant on the labour market, damaged his prospects of promotion, or increased the likelihood of the claimant having to retire early or obtain lower paid work. Quantifying such losses is not easy and often the starting point is one or two years' net pay.

Damages in Fatal Accident Act 1976 claims

A claim under the Fatal Accidents Act 1976 is brought on behalf of the deceased's dependants (generally members of his family) for their own losses (see chapter 1, Fatal accidents, for further information). They must prove that the defendant's wrongful act (negligence, breach of statutory duty, etc) caused the death of the deceased, and they must also prove their own dependence upon him and corresponding loss.

The award of damages will reflect the financial losses of the dependants, rather than the injury, loss or damage suffered by the deceased. The court can only award the following:

1.   £7,500 damages for bereavement – only to the spouse of the deceased, or if the deceased was a child and unmarried at the time of his death, to his parents (if he was legitimate) or to his mother only (where he was illegitimate).

2.   The amount the deceased would have given to his dependant.

3. Any extra expenses the dependant has incurred as a result of the deceased's death.

4. Any particular financial loss the dependant has suffered as a result of the deceased's death.

Although it may not be possible to be exact about the figures, the court will strive to make its estimation of the losses suffered by the dependants as a result of the accident and death. Various methods are used by the courts to establish what each dependant should be awarded. Where the deceased was working, it may be a matter of simply working out what percentage of his earnings would be available for the dependants.

Once the value of the dependency is ascertained the court will take into account:

1. any contributory negligence on the part of the deceased (see chapter 1);

2. the interest on the damages;

3. any benefits or savings made as a result of the accident by the deceased, including contractual sick pay, social security benefits, some pension payments, some redundancy payouts, and savings on living expenses caused by a stay in hospital or a similar provider;

4. the proportion each dependant should receive of the calculated amount;

5. any award of damages for bereavement.

Damages awarded in tort cases (other than for personal injury)

What is compensation for?

The aim of the damages is to place the successful claimant in the position as if the tort had never happened.

What types of loss and damage may be compensated?

The types of loss and damage which may be subject to a claim for damages are known as 'heads' of damage. The following is a list (not-exhaustive) of the heads of damage which are relevant to the torts covered by this book.

• Physical injuries (see Damages for personal injury, above) and consequential losses.

• Damaged or destroyed chattels (physical objects).

• Damage to land (including buildings).

• Loss of financial benefit (but only where the essence of the tort complained of is the defendant's responsibility for protecting the claimant's economic interest (*Street on Torts*, John Murphy Lexis Nexis 2003 at page 240)).

How does the court work out damages?

Physical and other personal injuries

The method of working out physical injuries damages is described separately at Damages for personal injury, above. For awards under the Criminal Injuries Compensation Scheme (an alternative to bringing a claim in the civil courts), please see chapter 3.

Damages for harassment

Where the harassment has caused personal injury (including psychiatric injury), or damage to chattels or land, the damages will be calculated on the usual bases – see the rest of this section. Under the Harassment Act 1997, however, it is possible to recover additional damages for distress and anxiety. The court will hear the claimant's evidence on the effects of the harassment and the distress and anxiety suffered, and will award a sum of general damages in compensation (see above). Until a body of legal precedent begins to indicate the level of awards for this type of claim, the measurement is somewhat arbitrary. It may be useful to draw the court's attention to the relevant tariff set out for mental anxiety, etc in the Criminal Injuries Compensation Scheme (see chapter 3 for further information and www.cica.org.uk).

Damaged and destroyed chattels

Other damages are usually worked out on the basis of the 'diminution of value' in the damaged or destroyed item. Depending on the circumstances, this will be represented by the cost of putting the damage right, or where this is impossible (or uneconomic – such as in the case of a written-off car), the market value of the object before the tort was committed. The court will take into account the extent to which repairs will improve the object and will reduce the amount of damages accordingly – the defendant should only have to pay for the damage he is legally responsible for. Thus the claimant will not always be awarded the full replacement value for destroyed objects.

Damages for trespass to land

In cases of trespass to land it is not necessary to prove loss or damage in order to establish the defendant's liability (unlike negligence or breach of statutory duty where the fact of injury, loss or damage is an essential element of the wrongdoing). Thus where the claimant is successful in a claim, but suffered no actual damage to his land, he may be awarded nominal damages.

Where the claimant has proved that the land was unlawfully occupied (e.g. by squatters, or some types of statutorily unprotected tenants 'holding over' the property after the expiry of a lease), the court will order the defendant to pay mesne profits (pronounced 'mean') rather than damages. Mesne profits are roughly the equivalent to a reasonable market rent for the property occupied for the duration of the occupancy. Where the land occupied was the claimant's home, the court may order an additional sum to reflect the insult of the trespass – a type of somewhat arbitrarily measured general damages. Unlawfully evicted claimants may obtain exemplary damages* from their landlord where the landlord made a profit by the unlawful eviction.

In other trespass cases, where damage has occurred to the claimant's land (including buildings), the damages will be measured by the extent to which the market sale value of the land is diminished. Where, in the circumstances, it is impossible to ascertain the market value of the land, or the cost of repairing the damage exceeds the diminution in value, or it is reasonable to carry out the repairs, the court will order the defendant to pay the cost of repair instead.

Damages for breach of contract (including failure to pay rent)

General principles

The court tries to put the claimant in the position he would have been in if the contract had been properly performed. Occasionally this is not possible, and the court will then try to put the parties in the position they were in before the contract was performed (i.e. award the claimant expenses which he incurred after the formation of the contract in the hope that the contract would be properly performed, including, where appropriate, money paid to the defendant as to the contract price).

The court may rule that some types of damage arising from the breach of contract are too 'remote' to make the defendant compensate the claimant; thus some elements of the claimant's claim may be disallowed. The case that set down the test for ascertaining unacceptably remote damage was *Hadley v Baxendale [1854] 9 Exch 341*, and it was later refined by *Victoria Laundry (Windsor) Ltd v Newman Industries Ltd [1949] 2 KB 528* and *The Heron II [1969] 1 AC 350*. First, damage which arises 'in the normal course' of things can be compensated. More unusual or remote damage can only be compensated if both parties had enough knowledge of the circumstances at the outset to have foreseen that there was a risk of the unusual, or more remote, damage arising. Often loss of profits or a business opportunity come into this latter category. Remoteness of damage is sometimes raised in the Defence by the defendant to deny all or some of the amount claimed by the claimant.

The defendant failed to pay money owed under the contract

Where one party has defaulted payments under the contract (which includes a failure to pay rent to a landlord), the court will order the defendant to pay the debt as damages.

The defendant failed to do the work properly or at all

Where one party has failed to do work under the contract, or failed to do it properly, then the damages will be the reasonable costs of doing the work or putting it right, or the reasonable out of pocket expenses of obtaining the service from another provider. Remember that where the contract was for a service that was to give a particular enjoyment to, or have a special similar significance for, the claimant (such as contracts involving weddings or holidays), the claimant will additionally be able to recover a sum for disappointment, distress, etc (general damages). Note, however, that the law does not allow the claimant to get the work done for free, and therefore the original contract price will be taken into account. Where, however, there has been a total failure to do any work, it may be more appropriate for the claimant to seek damages for the contract price (or instalments paid) and any out of pocket expenses incurred as a result of entering the contract.

Damages awarded under the Law Reform (Miscellaneous Provisions) Act 1934

Under this Act, the deceased's personal representatives (i.e. his executors or person administering his estate under the intestacy rules) may take over any litigation the deceased was involved in at the time of his death, or may start any litigation which he would have been entitled to begin at the time of death. The damages represent the deceased's losses up to the time of his death. Any money awarded will be paid into his estate and distributed according to his Will or the intestacy rules.

The damages will comprise all those types of injury, loss and damage which the claimant could have claimed against the defendant, whatever the cause of action (for which, please see the rest of this chapter). Certain types of damage, therefore, may not be recovered on behalf of the deceased, many of which will be self-evident:

- Damages for bereavement.

- Any loss of income after the date of death.

- Losses to the estate as a result of the death (except for funerary expenses), which are losses that will be suffered by the dependants or legatees rather than the deceased himself.

- Exemplary damages. These are an additional type of damages designed to compensate the successful claimant over and above his actual measurable losses and injuries. They mark the outrage of the court at the defendant's behaviour, are fairly rare in practice and are the subject of much academic debate and some controversy. In any event, Parliament has banned the award of exemplary damages in this type of claim.

Where the death was caused by someone, a Fatal Accidents Act 1976 claim on behalf of the deceased's dependants may be appropriate. Under that Act, the first three types of loss listed above are recoverable (please see page 72 for further information).

Other factors that the court will take into account when calculating damages

The duty of the claimant to mitigate his loss

The claimant has a positive duty to take reasonable steps to minimise the damage he has suffered. The court will take account of the claimant's circumstances in deciding what is reasonable. A failure to take the reasonable steps may result in a proportion of the damages suffered not being recovered.

Insurance payouts and other sums of money

Insurance payouts are ignored by the court – a defendant cannot take advantage of the fact that he has injured and caused loss to a claimant who has received or who will receive a sum of money from his insurers. The court simply looks at the liability between the claimant and defendant. But the claimant who receives damages will, in due course, under his contract of insurance, have to repay his insurer for any payouts made.

Similarly, pension payments and charitable donations, gifts or grants that are received by the claimant are ignored in the calculation of damages awards. However, where an employer is liable for an employee's injury, any redundancy payment (or part of that redundancy payment) may be deducted.

Tax

When courts are assessing financial loss which would normally attract tax, such as earnings or profits, they must take into account that the claimant, had he not made the loss owing to the tort or breach of contract, would have only had the benefit of a net figure. The court will, therefore, be careful not to award sums gross of tax. Accordingly, the claimant should bring evidence of his figures net of tax.

Contributory negligence

This is a defence, or partial defence, available to claims based on tort, and occasionally on claims for breach of contract (but only when the defendant's liability to the claimant is identical in both contract and tort). Where the judge finds that the claimant has been contributorily negligent he will determine to what extent that was the case, and reduce the final calculation of damages accordingly. Please see chapter 1 for further information.

Other matters relating to damages

Provisional damages

The courts have power in certain cases to consider and award damages in two tranches. This will be where there is a 'measurable' chance that the claimant will in the future, as a result of the accident or injury, develop a serious disease or that his condition will seriously deteriorate. Such a future development must be over and above the normal development of the disease, so as to justify the court looking twice at the issue of damages. In practical terms the first (or 'provisional') award will therefore not be a 'once and for all' award. This power allows the court to be more accurate in difficult cases where the injuries have an uncertain outcome.

Interim payments

A claimant may apply to the court for an order that the defendant pay him a proportion of the likely final award before the trial has taken place. The application* is made by an Application Notice* (see chapter 4, Applications in the period before trial), and copies must be served on the defendant at least 14 days before the hearing date of the application. Both the claimant and defendant may rely on witness statements* at the hearing and the judge will consider the evidence contained in statements of case, the Application Notice and witness statements, together with any documentation relied upon.

The claimant must satisfy that:

- the period for filing the Acknowledgement of Service* has expired; and

- the defendant is insured for the claim, or the defendant's liability is to be met by an insurer or the Motor Insurers' Bureau*, or the defendant is a public body; or

- the defendant has admitted liability to pay damages to him, or the court has made a judgment against the defendant with damages to be assessed; or

- the court is satisfied that if the claim went to trial, the claimant would obtain judgment for a substantial amount of damages against the defendant.

The court will consider any claim by the defendant that the claimant was contributorily negligent (see Contributory negligence) and also any counterclaim brought.

Interest on damages

The court has the power to award interest on damages claims. This is a notional compensation for the claimant for the lapse of time between the accident or injury and the award of compensation by the court (or time of settlement). Special damages and general damages are treated differently in that they have different periods and rates of interest. Of course, only past losses are considered for interest; future losses will not attract interest.

Special damages

Period: from the date of the accident to trial (or date of settlement).

Rate: half the High Court Special Investment Account rate (currently seven per cent).

General damages

Period: from the date of issue of the claim*.

Rate: currently three per cent.

INJUNCTIONS

An injunction is a type of court order ordering a person to refrain from an activity, or to do a particular thing, in order to stop a civil wrong taking place, now or in the future. Injunctions may be appropriate in both tort and breach of contract claims. In contract cases, the injunction may prohibit the defendant from doing something he promised in the contract not to do or, as one commentator puts it, 'to take steps to undo what he has already done in breach of contract'(*Cheshire, Fifoot and Furmston's Law of Contract,* 14th edition, Butterworths 2001, page 701).

An injunction obtained before the trial of the dispute is known as an 'interim' injunction. An injunction can be limited in time or permanent, as appropriate. Injunctions will only be made against the defendant (or proposed defendant). This remedy is available only at the discretion of the court, unlike damages or possession orders.

Injunctions may be granted in harassment cases to restrain the defendant's harassing behaviour. Under section 3 of the Protection from Harassment Act 1997, if the defendant has breached the injunction and continued with the harassment, the claimant can ask the court to issue a warrant for the defendant's arrest, so that he may be brought to (civil) court by the police and dealt with for that breach.

SPECIFIC PERFORMANCE

This is a remedy available only for breach of contract in limited circumstances. The court orders the defendant to do what he promised to do under the contract. It tends to operate in cases where the defendant was to provide a service or take some action, rather than agreed to pay money, or is obliged to give up possession of land. Like injunctions, specific performance is a discretionary remedy. It will not be granted if damages are an adequate remedy, or if the claimant is also in breach of contract. There is no point to specific performance if the parties are reluctant to continue to work together.

POSSESSION ORDERS

An order for possession is a common law remedy which orders the defendant to give up his possession of land (including buildings). Where the claimant has successfully established that the defendant no longer has a right to remain (and under some statutes, it is reasonable to grant possession), the court must order possession. The court can, of course, make other orders as appropriate, such as damages, mesne profits or injunctions (for which, see above).

How long will the court give the defendant to leave the premises?

This depends on the category of the defendant:

- Trespassers, generally, must leave the premises immediately.

- Secure and assured (including assured shorthold) tenants who have lost a case based upon mandatory grounds for possession in the Housing Act 1985, or the amended Housing Act 1988, will be given up to 14 days, except where the court accepts that the tenant would suffer exceptional hardship if not allowed to stay for longer – here the court may grant up to 42 days before the tenant must leave the premises. Mandatory grounds are those grounds set out in the Acts where the claimant does not have to prove that it is reasonable to grant possession.

- Secure and assured (including assured shorthold) tenants who have lost a case based upon discretionary grounds for possession in the Housing Act 1985 or Housing Act 1988 (as amended) may have their possession delayed by the possession order being granted and then stayed* or suspended, or a further direction that the execution of the order is to be delayed. The court may impose conditions such as continuing the payment of rent, and paying the arrears in instalments. This is, of course, a double-edged sword – the tenant effectively gets a second chance and remains in the property, but he has the possession order 'hanging over him' ready to be activated if he fails to keep to the conditions, etc, and of course, the tenancy itself is brought to an end. A discretionary ground under the Acts is one where the claimant must prove that in the circumstances it is reasonable to grant the possession order. The court must specify the period of the delay, stay or suspension, although it can be for as long as it thinks fit in the circumstances.

OTHER REMEDIES

Other remedies available for the claimant to seek include a 'declaration' (in which the judge, having heard the evidence, formally declares a particular fact to exist). This is often used to confirm the ownership of an item or land where there has been a dispute. Judicial Review remedies (quashing, or resubmitting judicial or quasi-judicial decisions for further consideration, etc) are not within the scope of this book; neither are remedies for 'unjust enrichment', breach of trust, declarations of incompatibility under the Human Rights Act 1998 (not nearly so exciting as it sounds!) or any international law remedies.

CHAPTER 3

HOW DO I PROTECT MY POSITION FROM THE OUTSET?

GATHERING EVIDENCE

What is 'evidence'?

'Evidence' is material that proves what events have taken place and what is happening at the moment. It comes in many forms, including the memories of people who were involved, the paperwork generated at the time and the physical state of objects (e.g. a dented car or an injury). For a more detailed discussion of the categories of evidence, please see below. The judge arrives at his judgment by considering the tested evidence of the parties. It is very important, therefore, for both parties to think very carefully about what evidence they need to obtain to prove each element of the claim or defence.

How is evidence dealt with at trial?

The claimant must prove his claim with evidence. This means that he must formally submit evidence to the judge at trial to prove each element of his case. The evidence must establish all the facts, which will enable the judge to make an order against the defendant. Thus, in a negligence case, the evidence should show how the defendant owed the claimant a legal duty to take care to avoid causing injury and loss to the claimant, and that he breached that duty. In contract claims the evidence must show that the defendant was in breach of the contract. In every type of case the claimant's evidence must show the amount and extent of his loss and injury so that the court can precisely work out the correct amount of compensation or the right type of order.

Once the claimant has put his evidence before the judge, the defendant may test it by completing cross-examinations* of the witnesses and by pointing out weaknesses and gaps in the other evidence. If the defendant wishes to put forward an alternative case in his defence, he then does so by putting his own evidence before the judge. Finally, the claimant has his own opportunity to challenge the defendant's evidence by cross-examination.

What are the types of evidence?

1. Oral evidence

Oral evidence is the evidence given by witnesses in court from the witness box, usually under oath. The parties are required to submit a written witness statement by each witness to the court and to each other prior to trial (please see chapter 4). This enables everyone to assess the strength of the evidence and allows proper preparation for trial. Witness statements also reduce the time a witness is in the witness box, as usually the witness swears an oath, adopts the contents of his statement as true and moves straight on to cross-examination without having to repeat his statement. Witnesses fall into two categories – witnesses of fact and expert witnesses.

The responsibility for paying the expenses of a witness to come to court, lost earnings and the professional fees of any expert witnesses fall on the party calling him. However, such costs may be recouped wholly, or in part, if the court orders the other side to pay an order for costs.

Witnesses of fact

Witnesses of fact are called by a party to tell the court what they have seen or heard. The parties themselves (the claimant and defendant(s)) may of course give evidence in support of their cases. There may be other people who saw something relating to the accident or incident in question. Others may be able to give evidence of relevant background circumstances. Unfavourable witnesses do not have to be called, or their written statements disclosed to the other side. However, the other side may wish to call them, and they are free to do so.

Expert witnesses

A party should call an expert witness if evidence of a technical subject is necessary. It is very important that the right expert is instructed – his main role is to explain to the judge the technical details of the matter in dispute. Having looked at the facts of the case (by making his own examinations, measurements, calculations and researches), he can give his professional opinion on what has happened. Of course, the judge makes the final decision, but expert evidence is vital to help him do so.

The expert must be independent (i.e. not involved personally in the case) so the claimant or defendant may not give expert evidence even if they have the relevant professional expertise. Often an expert is jointly instructed by both claimant and defendant. The aim of jointly instructing experts is to ensure absolute impartiality, minimise costs and avoid litigation where possible. Pre-action protocols formally require parties to attempt joint instruction of experts and, in any case, it is considered best practice to do so. To see if a pre-action protocol applies to your case, please see below.

The permission of the judge is required before you can rely on the report and oral evidence of an expert. The judge will consider whether to grant permission at the directions hearing* (see chapter 4 for further information).

2. Documentary or paper evidence

There are many different types of document that may be relevant to the case that can be included in the evidence put forward ('adduced') by a party. All documents that are relevant but not 'privileged' must be disclosed to the other side at a certain stage before trial. Once disclosed, the documents can be used as evidence at the trial. Disclosure* is discussed further in chapter 4.

It is important, where possible, to keep the originals of all documents that belong to you, and to obtain photocopies of ones that do not. During preparations for the trial, photocopies of all the documentary evidence will be placed in a file (the trial bundle), and copies made for the claimant, defendant(s), judge and one to go in the witness box for witnesses to refer to when they give evidence. For a further explanation of what other material goes into the trial bundle, please see chapter 4. For an explanation of what a privileged document* is, please see below.

A document, once disclosed, may be used by any party to support his case. A party who discloses a document because he must do so (see chapter 4), does not have to use it as evidence when he puts his case before the judge. However, it is perfectly proper for the other party to cross-examine him about it, or otherwise bring it to the judge's attention and rely on it in support of his own case.

3. Physical evidence, photographs and video evidence

There are many occasions where a case can be better presented by the production of physical evidence. This may take the form of photographs or video evidence (including surveillance or CCTV, etc) being shown to the judge, or it may entail a physical object being brought to court. Photographs (or video footage) of the site of an accident are usually very useful, for example, in road traffic accidents, or tripping and slipping type accidents caused by uneven surfaces. Photographs can also be useful where the condition of land or buildings forms the heart of the case, for example, a boundary dispute, a claim for shoddy workmanship or a disrepair in rented premises. Photographs (and to some extent video footage) are a graphic way of showing the judge the extent of the injuries and other physical damage (such as cars) involved. Where equipment has been defective or inadequate, the object itself may be exhibited (unless, of course, photographs are more appropriate).

The photographs, video or object are exhibited in the witness statement of the witness who made or obtained it. An example in chapter 4 shows how this is done. Once the witness has confirmed his witness statement and identified the photograph, video or object, it can be shown to the judge. Expert witnesses may have produced their own photographs and video evidence and, where relevant, will have to examine and consider the photographs, videos and objects produced by other witnesses.

With this type of evidence it is very important to note how and when it was obtained, and who did so. The witness statement of the person who will be producing it at the trial should therefore identify who took photographs or video footage or obtained an object. Do note precisely what time and date it was taken and how it was processed, treated and stored after that. Remember, also, that when the disclosure stage has been reached the original photographs, videos and objects will have to be viewed by the other side, and then copies taken. Moreover, when trial bundles are prepared, they will have to contain copies of any photographs that are to be used. It is worth, therefore, retaining the negatives and ordering sufficient reprints at the outset. Each photograph should be numbered for easy identification and copies should be numbered to match the originals.

4. Site visits

On rare occasions, the judge may consider (or be persuaded) that a site view is necessary. This involves all the parties and their lawyers meeting with the judge at the site so that the judge has the opportunity of seeing it for himself. He then may have certain informal questions for the parties in order to clarify in his mind exactly what is in dispute relating to the site. Site visits are probably most often used in boundary and other land disputes between neighbours, but may, for example, be useful in road traffic claims where the lie of the land or respective sight lines of drivers is significant.

How to collect evidence

The responsibility for collecting evidence falls to the party who intends to rely on it. A party cannot succeed without calling evidence to prove his claim or defence. Most of the evidence will be gathered at the stage when a party is assessing whether or not he has a case or defence, and some evidence will be obtained in order to comply with the pre-action protocol that applies to the case. Occasionally further evidence is gathered or turns up in the period of preparation before or even during the trial.

1. How do I make my own witness statement?

Guidance on the format and content of witness statements is given at page 148.

2. How do I obtain witness statements from other people?

The first stage is to obtain the names and addresses of those who may be able to help you. Friends, acquaintances and passers-by may all have witnessed one or more aspect of the case, such as the accident, the aftermath of the accident and the extent of the injury or damage, the defendant's unlawful behaviour, or the effect of the incident on you and your health, etc. If the police attended the incident in question (such as an accident or crime), you should write to the relevant police station asking for the official police report and details of any willing witnesses (a small fee will be charged, which counts as a legal cost).

The second stage is to find out if potential witnesses have:

(a) any useful evidence to give; and

(b) whether they are willing to give evidence by giving a witness statement and attending court on your behalf.

A sample letter is given on the following page.

The third stage is to put the evidence in the form it needs to be for the court. It may be that the witness has already made a statement in the appropriate form, complying with the standard format (described on page 148). If not, you should type (or write out legibly) the statement in the witness' own words adding the necessary formalities, such as the opening sentence 'I [*name*] of [*address*] will say as follows...' and the statement of truth (see chapter 4). Leave a space blank for him to sign and date the statement and send it back to him (retaining a copy for yourself). If the witness is exhibiting any documents, photographs, videos or other evidence, remember to identify it. An example of how to exhibit evidence in a witness statement is shown on page 149. Make it clear to the witness that if he has any

Example request for a witness statement

[*Address*]

[*Date*]

Dear Mr Snooks

Potential court case arising from [*describe the nature of your claim, e.g. road traffic accident*].

[I am writing to you regarding the above incident, having obtained your name and address from [*explain how*]. You are a potential witness and I wondered if you would be willing to give evidence on my behalf.] [You may remember our conversation of [*date*] when you agreed to give evidence on my behalf.]

Being a witness entails preparing a witness statement and, if necessary, going to court and giving oral evidence at a trial. I would, of course, be prepared to type up your witness statement from notes or dictation provided by you, in order for you to verify and sign it. You will be fully consulted on your availability to attend court (if this turns out to be necessary) and any other requirements you may have. Furthermore, I will pay you reasonable travel expenses and your loss of earnings incurred in this matter.

If you are willing to give evidence on my behalf, please could you let me know by [*telephone, fax, letter, email, etc*] on [*number or address*]. If you are able, your evidence should cover the following matters:

- Who you are.
- How you came to witness [*the incident*].
- What you saw and heard.
- What was said and by whom.
- Include any maps or diagrams where appropriate.

I suggest that you send me a letter which I can then type up and put into the official witness statement format for you to check over, correct, verify and sign. If you would prefer, I am happy to speak with you and take notes which I can then turn into a witness statement for you to check, correct, verify and sign. Alternatively, you may wish to produce a witness statement without my help and I can lend you [*title of the book*] which will show you how to do so.

I look forward to hearing from you.

Yours sincerely

Mr Smith

changes to make to the statement he should do so and initial the amendments (as one might correct a cheque, for instance).

Once your witness has returned, signed and dated the statement, you are ready to send it to the other side. The judge will order the parties to exchange* witness statements when he gives directions*. This means that the parties must send each other copies of the witness statements they are going to use at the trial, which is explained further on page 148. If you decide that you do not wish to rely on a particular witness, you do not have to. If the date for exchange of witness statements has not yet passed, you do not need to send the other side his statement. However, if the witness statements have already been exchanged, the other side may want to call the witness to give oral evidence anyway, and may obtain a witness summons* to compel him to attend the trial.

3. What can be done about reluctant witnesses?

If a witness is reluctant to attend court to give oral evidence or to produce documents, the court can order him to attend (and produce the relevant documents). Such an order is called a 'witness summons' (formerly known as a 'subpoena'*). The party wishing to call the witness must ask the court to issue the summons (the procedure is governed by Part 34 of the Civil Procedure Rules 1998). If there are less than seven days to go before the beginning of the trial, or the witness is required to attend at court on a date other than the formal trial, a judge at the court must give permission for the summons to be issued. Otherwise, no such permission is needed. To obtain permission an application under Part 23 of the Civil Procedure Rules 1998 should be made. For guidance as to how to apply under Part 23, please see Applications in the period before trial, on page 152.

If the witness fails to comply with a summons issued by the High Court, he is in contempt of court (punishable by a fine or up to two years' imprisonment). Disobedience of a witness to a County court* witness summons is punishable by a fine of up to £1,000. The disobedient witness may also be ordered to pay any legal costs which have arisen and have been wasted as a result of his non-compliance.

4. How do I obtain an expert's report?

In deciding whom to instruct you should ensure that the expert is qualified to deal with the area required (obviously, it is pointless asking, for example, an orthopaedic surgeon to comment on psychiatric illness and depression) and, if possible, that he has court experience as an expert witness. Experts with forensic experience (i.e. experience of giving evidence in court) are preferable, as they will be familiar with the way in which courts analyse matters such as causation and prognosis.

Once identified, the expert must be formally instructed to produce a report. The letter of instruction must be neutral. This means that it should not try to influence the expert's judgment or conceal facts. Where the expert is to be instructed jointly by both parties, this must be made clear in the letter, and both parties must agree the wording of the letter. A sample letter of instruction for personal injury cases is contained in Appendix 3, whilst a sample letter for use in cases where a specific pre-action protocol does not apply can be found at Appendix 7.

5. Hints on collecting documentary evidence

Once you have worked out what the elements of your case or defence are, you will have an idea of the type of documentary evidence that will prove them. For further guidance, Appendices 3 and 4 contain lists of the types of document owned by the defendant that may be relevant in personal injury and clinical negligence cases (the other pre-action protocols are not so helpful in this respect). The table below suggests some of the types of documentary evidence that may be needed to prove certain facts:

Event or appointment	Financial costs ('loss')	Wages/ work record	Injury or state of health	Relevant correspondence
Journal of witness and attendance notes of meetings	Estimate	Employer's records and correspondence	Medical records	Letters (including faxes)
Appointments diary	Receipt	Pay slips	Doctor's letter or certificate	Emails
Employer's accident log book	Bank statement or building society book	Bank statement or building society book		Telephone attendance notes
Policeman's notebook/report	Travel tickets	Benefit book		
Contract, lease or agreement (including any standard terms or other conditions referred to)	Prescription slips			

Witnesses of fact and experts may have documentary evidence of their own to put to the court. Such documents should be exhibited in the witness statement or report (see the example in chapter 4). Where relevant documents are owned by others, you will have to request copies from them by telephone or letter yourself. It is possible to obtain a court order for a witness to produce documents at the trial by way of a witness summons (please see further at What can be done about reluctant witnesses? above). Prospective parties may obtain a court order to oblige another prospective party to disclose a particular document (or class of documents) under Part 31.16 of the Civil Procedure Rules 1998 before a claim is even issued. It is also possible to obtain a court order that someone who is not a claimant or defendant in the case must disclose a particular document or class of document (Civil Procedure Rules 1998, Part 31.17). Moreover, the Data Protection Act 1998 allows the inspection of certain documents held by various organisations and individuals about oneself.

6. Collecting physical and photographic evidence

It is perfectly acceptable for witnesses (particularly the claimant and defendant) to take photographs, film a video film or preserve relevant objects. Usually the circumstances of the case will not call for specialist equipment or technical expertise. Occasionally it is wise to instruct a professional to do so (e.g. a personal detective to undertake surveillance). In such circumstances they will be 'witnesses of fact'; able to give the court evidence of what they have recorded.

RESEARCHING THE LAW FURTHER

Do I need to do any legal research?

Of course not. You are entitled to put the facts before the court and let the judge decide. However, it will save a great deal of time and money, and will avoid your need to appeal, if you are sure of the case before you begin, can present legal arguments to the judge, and can assist him in making the correct decision. Principles set down in Acts of Parliament or case law determine if someone's behaviour is unlawful. A proper understanding of the law will enable you to:

- work out the strength of the claim;

- work out the strength of the defence or counterclaim;

- work out what damages or other compensation may be ordered by the judge;

- comply with pre-action protocols and other requirements;

- negotiate effectively with the other party;

- avoid unnecessary litigation and minimise costs;

- present your case clearly in court.

England and Wales does not have a single book or code containing all the laws ever made. This is because, historically, it has a common law tradition and the law comes from many different sources. The most common of these are Acts of Parliament, Statutory Regulations and case law. Therefore researching the law can become a bit of a paper trail.

How do I decide what I need to research?

Substantive law

The 'substantive' (civil) law is a term used by lawyers to describe the rights and remedies that citizens have against individuals, companies and the State who act unlawfully. It is a collective term for the body of law that includes tort, contract, equity, land, etc. This book can be used as the starting place for legal research. Use chapter 1 of this book to work out if you have a claim or defence. It contains a brief overview of the substantive law in many dispute situations. Chapter 2 describes the law of 'remedies'. A more detailed discussion of the substantive law can be found in textbooks, articles and on the Internet.

Procedural law

Chapters 3, 4 and 5 mainly describe the 'procedural law' of England and Wales. These are the rules (found mainly in the Statutory Regulations, Acts of Parliament and some case law) that govern how cases are brought to court. The answers to questions such as 'which court do I sue in?', 'which form must I use?', 'what are the time limits?', 'what happens next?', 'what can the judge order?' and 'how can I appeal or enforce the order?' are to be found in procedural law.

How to use textbooks or other commentaries

Textbooks and articles are a very good starting-off point. They tend to fall into one of three categories, so choose one with the level of detail you are comfortable with. These are:

1.   books for the layman (with no legal experience at all);

2.   student textbooks; and

3.   practitioners' textbooks (reference works for barristers and solicitors).

Obviously, the books for the layman will be the most simplistic, and practitioners' textbooks the most detailed. Although some specialist practitioners' books can be very expensive, general works published in paperback are often very affordable and up to date. They do not necessarily assume a high level of knowledge, and many have user-friendly tables, flowcharts and diagrams to help the reader.

When you have discovered a textbook that covers the area you want to research, check that it has a comprehensive index, a table of case law (an index listing all the reported cases mentioned in the book – useful for finding out whether a book refers to a particular case and providing you with the official citation), and tables of legislation and Statutory Instruments. These will help you find the original source of the law, whether it is a judgment by the Court of Appeal or House of Lords, a Regulation or a section in an Act of Parliament.

Textbooks and articles are generally not quoted to the judge at trial. They should be used to look up and explain relevant legal principles and concepts, and also to allow you to look up references to reported cases, Regulations or Acts of Parliament.

How to look up legislation (Acts of Parliament and Statutory Instruments)

At the time of writing, the Lord Chancellor's Department is preparing the Statute Law Database. The intention is to make all statutes (Acts of the UK Parliament) available on the Internet. It is for practical use (rather than academic historical research), as all statutes that were on the statute book since 1 February 1991 and all new legislation made since then will be included.

Until the Statute Law Database is up and running, some legislation is available online. The HMSO website publishes all the Acts of Parliament enacted since the beginning of 1988 (www.legislation.hmso.gov.uk). It is also possible to buy copies of new legislation at The Stationery Office Ltd (they also have an online bookshop at www.tso.co.uk). Local libraries may have copies of statutes or commentaries, such as *Halsbury's Statutes* or *Halsbury's Laws of England*. Law libraries at universities and other educational institutions or courts (such as the Supreme Court Library at the Royal Courts of Justice) may allow you to look up a specific piece of legislation.

Remember to establish if the Act or Regulations are up to date, and whether that particular section is in force. General Acts of Parliament are passed by the UK Parliament at Westminster and are given the Royal Assent. Usually the government minister responsible sets a date for each section to come into force, and sometimes parts of the Act will begin to operate before others. For example, at the date of writing this book the Countryside and Rights of Way Act 2000 has been enacted (i.e. passed by the Westminster Parliament), but the much vaunted right to roam clauses have not come into force.

How case law works

Case law is the body of rules made by judges over time. Case law may either clarify the meaning or application of a section or clause in legislation; or else set down a new principle of law (or extend an existing one) to cover the particular circumstances of the case. Case law is made by the senior courts (known as the 'courts of record'). All courts must follow the rulings (where they are relevant to the case) of the courts above them, although not of the courts of their own level (except the Court of Appeal). Therefore, the County courts must follow the principles laid down in the High Court, the Court of Appeal and the House of Lords; the High Court must follow those laid down in the Court of Appeal and House of Lords, and so on.

When researching case law it is essential to:

- try to obtain the official report of the judgment;

- try to work out how your case is similar to and different from the reported case;

- read the judgment very carefully;

- work out the actual passage where the judge formulates the principle of law and applies it to the facts of the reported case;

- decide if the principle should be applied to your case or not.

Presenting a legal argument in court

Prepare for yourself a note of the points of law you wish to refer the judge to (known as a 'skeleton of argument' or 'skeleton argument'). If you wish to, you can make a copy for the other side and the judge, which may be handed out at the beginning of the trial. It is possible that the judge will have directed that the parties exchange any skeleton arguments (and send the court copies) on a certain date before trial, in which case, of course, you should comply.

Be clear about which sections of the Act, Regulation or reported case applies to your case, and where possible make clean photocopies of the relevant section, rule or case for the judge and your opponent.

IMPORTANT CONSIDERATIONS BEFORE MAKING A CLAIM

Must I have a solicitor?

No. Generally, every person has the right to conduct their own case in court. Alternatively, parties may instruct a solicitor to represent them at any stage. If higher court advocacy is involved, a barrister may be instructed by the solicitor on your behalf to speak for you at hearings and to conduct the trial. Trade unions and other interest groups often provide legal services to their members, as do insurers. Recent changes to the civil court rules (known as the 'Woolf reforms') have recognised that litigants-in-person* are appearing more frequently in the courts. The reforms aim to modernise the rules that govern procedure. Plainer English has been used and (generally) one set of rules applies to both the County and the High Court. Court forms are now accompanied by comprehensive notes and leaflets available at the courts and online, explaining some of the more common questions that arise from members of the public. Finally, judges are usually aware of the needs of the litigant who is not represented by a lawyer.

The question of whether you would be disadvantaged by not having a solicitor is more difficult to answer. The advantage of having a lawyer conduct your case is that the day-to-day handling of the case and preparation for trial are out of your hands. A lawyer can advise you on the strength of your case, deal with technicalities which arise and conduct negotiations on your behalf. Furthermore, barristers and solicitor-advocates* are used to presenting cases in court, not only making legal arguments but also examining and cross-examining witnesses.

Your final decision on whether to instruct a solicitor should take into account three factors:

1. Your personality and personal circumstances.

2. The complexity of the case.

3. Your financial position.

Chapter 1 will help you to assess the complexity of the case. How do I fund my claim?, below, discusses alternative ways of paying for legal representation. Below are some issues that should be taken into account when considering your personality and personal circumstances: the need to be articulate and the emotional pressures of litigation.

1. The need to be articulate

Conducting a court case involves filling in forms, putting a case or evidence in writing, giving evidence by speaking aloud in court, being cross-examined and cross-examining the other party's witnesses (including experts). All these activities will be very closely scrutinised by the other party's lawyers and the judge. Furthermore, there will be evidence to gather, witnesses to liaise with, negotiations to be conducted and decisions taken about the conduct of the case. Obviously, a person who is confident and articulate in relation to his case will be in a much stronger position than one who is not.

2. The emotional pressures of litigation

The other factor that should not be underestimated is the emotional cost of litigation. A person involved in a court case usually starts off feeling aggrieved (due to suffering injury or loss, or because he feels wrongly accused) and subsequently suffers the stress of having to deal with the bureaucratic and tactical side of litigation (the attendant paperwork, costs and deadlines), as well as the pressures of simply being at court (finding the court, the inevitable delays, attending hearings, seeing the other side in court, dealing with the other side's lawyers, etc). The stress of being involved in a court case as a party or witness is significant enough; without the support and expertise of a lawyer, it may be all the greater.

How do I fund my claim?

There are three different types of expense that arise from litigation:

1. Court fees.

2. Lawyers' fees and other disbursements, such as witness expenses, etc.

3. An award of damages and interest.

An award of damages (and interest) will form the subject matter of the dispute, and is explained further in chapter 2. Court fees and lawyers' fees are known as 'costs'. Inevitably, both parties will run up costs, even if the case never gets as far as trial. If the case settles before trial, the parties may agree which of them (if either) recovers his costs from the other. Otherwise, the parties can ask the judge to decide if either of them may recoup his costs (or part of them) from the other. The court has absolute discretion (except in small claims track* cases which are subject to special rules) and will take into account various matters, including who has 'won', compliance with any pre-action protocol which applies to the case, and the general conduct of the litigation by the parties. Frequently the parties decide, or the judge rules, that neither party may recoup his legal costs from the other. Therefore it is vital to think about the potential costs of litigation before you begin; you may never get your money back, even if you win your claim or defence.

1. Do I qualify for Community Legal Services Funding (formerly known as Legal Aid)?

On 1 April 2000, the old Legal Aid* system was officially replaced by Community Legal Services Funding*, under the Access to Justice Act 1999. It is a means-tested scheme where qualifying litigants' legal costs are paid by the State. There are three hurdles to overcome to qualify for funding:

1. Your claim must be one for which legal services funding is available.

2. You must be in financial need (as defined by the Regulations).

3. Your case must 'merit' funding (which usually means that it must be likely to win, or that it is in the public interest to bring the case to court).

Community Legal Services Funding is not available for claims for injury, death or damage to property based on negligence. Thus most personal injury claims (such as those arising from road traffic accidents or 'tripping and slipping' cases) will not qualify for State funding. Funding is available for clinical negligence claims (see chapter 1, Where healthcare goes wrong) and for claims involving deliberately caused injuries, such as assaults (batteries), intentional causation of harm* and harassment (see chapter 1, Deliberately caused injuries and violence). The other types of claim (or defence) that do not qualify for legal services funding include boundary disputes, matters of company law or partnership law, or matters arising out of the carrying on of a business.

Community Legal Services Funding is administered by franchised solicitors who will be able to tell you whether you qualify for funding, help you fill in the (inevitable!) forms and explain more about how the scheme works.

2. Will my insurers pay my legal expenses?

Many insurance policies (such as car, health, professional or home) will give you cover for legal expenses. This means that the insurance provider will either pay the legal fees of a solicitor of your choosing, or (more usually) provide their own in-house legal services, or instruct a solicitor on your behalf. Look closely at the terms of your policy and discuss cover with your insurance company to find out what cover you have, and whether there are any limitations on it. If, at the end of the case, you are awarded your legal costs by the judge (or the other side agrees to pay), they will be assessed in the normal way and paid to the insurer. For an explanation of how legal costs may be awarded, please see chapter 4.

3. How do 'no win, no fee' (conditional fee) agreements work?

Any glimpse at advertising hoardings or daytime television will show that there has been a development in this area of financing claims. It is central to government policy and goes hand in hand with the curtailing of public funding for certain types of claim (particularly personal injury claims).

A conditional fee agreement* (a CFA) is an agreement between a solicitor and his client in which the solicitor agrees to provide advocacy or litigation services on a no win, no fee* basis. Where the client is successful in obtaining a payment of damages from the other side (whether in court or in an out of court settlement) he will have to pay the legal fees of his solicitor plus a success fee. The success fee is agreed between the solicitor and client at the outset, and is measured as a percentage of the legal fees. Statute sets a limit of 100 per cent, but the Law Society recommends a success fee of 25 per cent. The legal costs and the success fee may be recoverable from the other side upon settlement (see chapter 2) or at the end of the hearing or trial (see chapter 4). Note also that a barrister (who has to be instructed by a solicitor) can also undertake conditional fee work. Speak to your solicitor to see if this will be possible.

4. Getting free advice and representation

There are various organisations that provide free advice to litigants. Often this will take the form of initial advice on the merits of a claim and help with filling in forms. Citizens Advice Bureaux are staffed by lawyers and other volunteers. They can be found in town centres and at help desks at court. Legal advice centres serve a similar function and are staffed by qualified and trainee solicitors and barristers. In special cases, solicitors' firms or barristers (instructed through solicitors) will agree to represent a litigant 'pro bono'*, in other words, for free. It may be worth checking to see if the students at the law faculty of a local university or law college run a student advice centre. For victims of clinical negligence (medical accidents), the charity Action for Victims of Medical Accidents (AVMA) provides advice and support (see their website at www.avma.org.uk).

5. Can someone who is not a lawyer represent me in court?

A litigant may, with the permission of the judge, have a non-lawyer beside him in open court hearings for moral and practical assistance with his case. Such a person is known as a 'Mckenzie friend'*. Permission will be granted if the judge agrees that in the interests of justice, or for reasons of fairness, the litigant requires a Mckenzie friend.

In small claims track hearings a 'lay advisor' may present the case for the litigant, as long as the litigant is also present. In fast track* and multi-track* hearings, however, the litigant has to speak for himself.

6. What happens if I decide to pay the solicitor myself?

When you instruct a solicitor you enter a contract with the firm. One of the first things that will be dealt with, before he agrees to act for you, is the terms and conditions of the contract. You may be given details of the hourly rates charged by the various levels of fee earners and an estimate of the likely cost of funding your claim or defence. If you are unsure about the financial implications of instructing a solicitor, ask for clarification. The cost of court fees and experts' professional fees will be included in the solicitor's charges, as will the fees (brief fees) of any barrister instructed on your behalf. Many solicitors will ask you to make a payment on account so that he can begin working on your behalf.

The legal fees you have incurred may be recoverable from the other side upon settlement of your claim or at the end of the trial or hearing (please see chapter 4 for further information).

7. What costs may I incur even if I do not use a solicitor?

There will be court fees to pay at each stage of litigation, and the costs of you and your witnesses to attend court (travel expenses and loss of earnings for you and your witnesses, plus the professional fees of expert witnesses). There are also more hidden costs of litigation, such as telephone calls, Internet charges and faxes, photocopying expenses, postal charges and the cost of books. Remember, too, that you will have to spend time dealing with the case and attending court. The rules by which the court will order one party to pay a sum to the other to compensate him for his time spent taking the case to court are set out in chapter 4.

Do I have to bring the claim, or can someone else obtain damages for me?

If you are the person who has suffered the injury, loss or damage, or if you are being sued by someone, you will be named as claimant or defendant and will generally be expected to bring your own case (with the help of lawyers if you wish). However, certain people cannot conduct their own litigation – there are special rules for child claimants, the mentally ill and the deceased.

1. Children who have not reached their 18th birthday

Unless the court orders otherwise, a child cannot conduct litigation. Although the child is named as a party (i.e. a claimant or defendant) in the normal way, a litigation friend is appointed to act in his interests and make all the necessary decisions connected with the litigation (e.g. filling in forms, instructing a lawyer, obtaining evidence and conducting negotiations). The appointment of a litigation friend automatically ceases on the child's 18th birthday, and (unless he is also mentally disordered – see below) he must take over the conduct of the case himself. On reaching 18 the litigant must let all the other parties know the situation and indicate if he wishes to continue with the case.

In some circumstances, depending on the age of the child and the nature of the claim, the judge may order that a litigation friend is not needed. A child may make a formal application to the court for such an order.

Damages awarded to a child claimant will usually be 'paid into court' and invested by the court on the child's behalf until he reaches the age of 18. However, the court may make different arrangements if appropriate (such as allowing out a payment before his 18th birthday for a good reason). Additionally, out of court settlements involving a child party must be approved by a judge. The judge will look at the terms of the agreement to see that the child's interests have been protected (even if the child has been represented throughout by a litigation friend and lawyers).

2. Mentally disordered litigants

A person suffering from a mental disorder that renders him incapable of managing his own affairs can be a party in litigation (i.e. can be a claimant or defendant). Such a person is known as a 'patient'. However, the case must be conducted on the patient's behalf by a litigation friend. If a person is capable of managing his affairs at the beginning of his case, but becomes mentally ill to the extent that he can no longer do so, a litigation friend should be appointed to continue the conduct of the case. Conversely, if a person who has a litigation friend becomes well enough to manage his own affairs, the judge will make an order terminating the appointment of the litigation friend.

3. How do I become a litigation friend?

Part 21 of the Civil Procedure Rules 1998 governs how a person becomes a litigation friend. There are useful leaflets available at court (or online at www.courtservice.gov.uk) that explain how this can be done. Unless there is a previous court order appointing a litigation friend or there is a person authorised by the Mental Health Act 1983 entitled to act as litigation friend in the case, no permission of the court is needed. The litigation friend is self-appointed.

A prospective litigation friend must file either a certificate of his authorisation under the Mental Health Act 1983 or a certificate of suitability at court (Form N235). The certificate of suitability certifies that he:

(a) is able to conduct the proceedings fairly and competently;

(b) has no conflict of interest with the child or patient; and

(c) solemnly promises to pay any costs which the child or patient is ordered to pay during or at the end of the case (known as an 'undertaking').

The certificate must be filed at the same time as the claim is issued (where the child or patient is the claimant), or at the first occasion the litigation friend takes a formal step in the case (where the child or patient is the defendant).

A 'conflict of interest' is where two people have different and conflicting aims in the way a case is managed or in the outcome of a claim.

Example: Tommy (aged 4) is injured when his mother drives her car negligently into a tree. He needs compensation and a family friend suggests that his mother should be his litigation friend.

His mother cannot be Tommy's litigation friend. There is a conflict of interest between them as Tommy is the prospective claimant and his mother is the prospective defendant. She may wish to deny the claim, or minimise the damages she pays out. As Tommy's interest is to prove that his mother drove negligently and obtain the maximum in damages from her insurers, his interest is directly opposed to hers. Tommy will have to be represented by another litigation friend.

4. The claimant (or potential claimant) has died; who can sue on his behalf?

With the exception of defamation cases, all the claims or potential claims a person has at the time of his death continue afterwards. The Law Reform (Miscellaneous Provisions) Act 1934 enables personal representatives to step into the deceased's shoes, so to speak, to begin or continue any litigation. The law imposes a special time limit on when claims may be started (see below). The deceased's personal representative is either an executor named in a valid Will or, where the deceased had no valid Will (known as being 'intestate'), a person appointed by the court to act as an administrator of his estate.

In such a case the personal representatives will become the claimants. They must conduct the litigation as any claimant would. However, it is well to bear in mind the possible practical difficulties of bringing a case without the chief witness. Any damages that are awarded will become part of the deceased's estate; the personal representatives must then distribute the estate according to the deceased's Will (or the intestacy rules if they apply).

See also chapter 1, Fatal accidents.

5. Many of us have a claim against one defendant; can we sue together?

In theory, there is no limit to the number of claimants that can bring an action against a defendant or defendants in a single claim. The Claim Form may get a bit complicated by including the various claims between the first, second and third claimants (etc) and the first, second and third defendants (etc). For ease of administration and in the interests of fairness it may be appropriate for the judge to order separate trials of the claims, or make representative or group litigation orders*.

Representative orders

Representative orders* are used to limit the complexity and length of litigation and therefore reduce the costs involved. It is appropriate where a group of potential claimants have a common grievance against the same defendant(s), especially where factual issues such as 'causation' (see page 60 for further information) or particular legal questions are common to each case, and other areas of fact are not in dispute.

Group litigation orders

Sometimes a group of potential claimants will have cases that raise common or related issues of fact or law. Where individuals begin separate cases (sometimes in different courts and against different defendants) the court can make a group litigation order, which provides for all the cases to be managed together.

Is it too late to sue?

The claimant only has a certain amount of time (known as the 'limitation period') in which to issue his claim against each defendant. Any claim that is brought after the time limit has expired is 'statute-barred'. The Limitation Act 1980 lays down various limitation periods according to each cause of action, or type of claim.

What happens if I am too late?

Your claim will not succeed. Where the claim is statute-barred, the defendant can rely on a defence of limitation. This means that if he can satisfy the judge that the relevant time limit or limitation period has finished, he will win. The defence is a legal one and, no matter how strong the claim was or weak the defendant's evidence is, is absolute.

Where the injury, damage or loss is occurring every day (known as 'continuing' damage), or where there is a series of incidents causing fresh injury, loss or damage each time, the claimant may only claim compensation for those which fall within the relevant limitation period. This is discussed further below in Where injuries are caused by repeated acts.

Can I extend the limitation period?

It is possible to obtain the court's permission to extend the limitation period, or rather to disapply the limitation period, in personal injury cases. The court will only do so if it thinks that the balance of fairness requires it. In other words, it must weigh up the unfairness ('prejudice') to the claimant (him not being able to bring his claim due to the expiry of the limitation period) with the unfairness to the defendant (in having a personal injury action being brought against him after the three years allowed by law).

Such applications usually arise once the defendant has pleaded a defence of limitation in his defence papers (see Limitation on page 62 and the sample Defences at Appendix 2 for further information). The claimant should apply to the court using a Part 23 Application Notice. The court will consider all the circumstances leading up to the issue of the claim including:

- the length of time that has elapsed;

- the reasons for the claimant's delay;

- the conduct of the defendant in responding to requests for relevant information;

- whether or not the quality of the evidence will be affected by the delay; and

- the steps taken by the claimant to obtain legal or expert advice relating to the claim.

How do I calculate whether I am in time?

When calculating the date the limitation expires, it is important to remember that the limitation period begins on 'the day after the relevant day' (usually the day on which the injury, loss or damage happened, or the 'date of knowledge'). The limitation period then ends on the last day of the time allowed by the Act.

1. Personal injuries arising from a breach of duty (including negligence, breach of contract or nuisance)

The limitation for claiming damages for personal injury is generally three years from the date when the injury occurred. However, there are special provisions for dealing with cases where there is a series of wrongful incidents (causing 'continuing damage') and where the injury is not apparent at the time of the wrongful incident which caused it.

(a) One-off accidents

Most personal injuries are caused by accidents. A single mishap causes the initial injury there and then. In such situations the claimant has three years from the date of the accident to issue a claim in court (section 11 of the Limitation Act 1980). Such accidents may arise in all sorts of situations: at work, on the roads, in public places or on someone else's land.

(b) Where the injury does not arise immediately

In some situations an injury develops or becomes apparent some time after the negligent act, breach of contract or act of nuisance complained of. The claimant may only suffer symptoms years after the event. The situation is governed by section 14 of the Law Reform (Miscellaneous Provisions) Act 1934 and related case law. The law allows him time to:

(i)   realise that the injury is significant enough to make a claim for damages;

(ii) investigate whether the injury is attributable to the behaviour of the potential defendant; and

(iii) discover the identity of the person or company who is to become the defendant.

Once the injured person has obtained these answers (known as the 'date of knowledge' in the Act), the three-year time limit begins to run.

Example 1: Mrs Brown is told by a consultant on 5 December 2003 that the pains she is suffering are caused by a medical instrument negligently left inside her after an operation four years before. She remembers that the operation was performed by Professor McKay at Anytown District Hospital.

Mrs Brown has three years from 5 December 2003 to issue a claim against Anytown District Hospital and Professor McKay. The limitation period will begin on 6 December 2003 and the last day for issuing her claim will be on 5 December 2006.

Example 2: Bhupinder Talal is told by her specialist on 14 July 2003 that she has developed a rare eye condition which threatens her sight. On 8 August 2003 she is reminded by a friend of an incident of chemical contamination of the local water supply by a water company that occurred in March 1998. She consults an expert on water contamination and on 20 November 2003 receives his report which confirms that there is a high probability that the contamination caused her eye condition.

Miss Talal has three years from 20 November 2003 to issue a claim against the water company. The limitation period runs from 21 November 2003 to 20 November 2006 inclusive.

When considering a defence of limitation in such cases, the judge may make a decision that the claimant should reasonably have known the relevant facts at a certain date. This may result in the three-year time limit running earlier than the claimant expected. For example, a claimant may have ignored obvious symptoms until after the date on which it would have been reasonable to obtain expert advice. Alternatively, he may not have bothered to find out the identity of the defendant when he should have done. The court will identify the date of knowledge, having considered all the circumstances. If the claim was issued later than three years from that date, then the claim will fail. It may be possible to persuade the court to disapply the limitation period – please see above at Can I extend the limitation period?

(c) Where injuries are caused by repeated acts

Where an injury or disease is caused by repeated wrongful acts, such as an industrial disease caused by a long-term exposure to dangerous chemicals, the claimant can recover damages sustained within the limitation period. This means that he can recover compensation for the three years immediately prior to the issue of his claim.

Example: Brian has worked in a very noisy factory since 1990. In 1994 he noticed that he was having hearing problems. On 1 October 1995 his specialist confirmed that the noise in the factory had caused his problems and the condition would get steadily worse if he continued to work in the factory. Brian continues in his job and there is no change to the sound levels he is exposed to. On 1 May 1999 Brian issues a claim for damages against his employer in his local County court.

Because Brian's employer's negligence and breach of statutory duty is 'continuing' (i.e. occurring afresh each day Brian goes into work), a new limitation period arises each day he suffers damage. The first cause of action probably arose in 1990 when the first injury to his hearing started, but because his date of knowledge under the Act is not until he is aware of the significance of his injury, and the fact that it was caused by employers (1 October 1995), the limitation period begins on 2 October 1995 and runs to 1 October 1998. Each limitation period more than three years old has expired. Therefore, as Brian only issued his claim for personal injury damages on 1 May 1999, every incident of negligence/breach of statutory duty before 2 May 1996 is statute-barred. Thus he will only be able to claim damages for the incidents of excessive noise that occurred on or after 2 May 1996.

2. Claims for personal injury damages arising from assault (battery) and intentional causation of harm

The claimant has six years from the date the injury was suffered to bring a claim for damages (Limitation Act 1980, section 2).

3. Claims under the Protection from Harassment Act 1997

The Protection from Harassment Act 1997 came into force on 16 June 1997, and thus any acts of harassment on or after that date may be the subject of a claim (but not acts taking place before that date). Harassment is behaviour which is a 'course of conduct, occurring on more than one occasion'. The first incident alone does not amount to harassment under the Act. A right to bring a claim under the Act (cause of action) arises only when the defendant's course of conduct amounts to harassment. The incidents may only amount to harassment on the second, third, twentieth or fiftieth occasion, depending on the nature of the behaviour complained of. Once the defendant's behaviour amounts to harassment the claimant has six years in which to issue the claim (Limitation Act 1980, section 2).

4. Consumer Protection Act Claims

Where a claim for personal injury damages is made under Part 1 of the Consumer Protection Act 1987 (see chapter 1, Defective goods) the limitation period is usually three years from the date when the injury or damage was sustained, or the claimant's date of knowledge, whichever is the later. For an explanation of the date of knowledge, please see above.

5. Other claims for compensation (which do not include a request for damages for personal injuries)

The general rule is that the claimant, for claims based on tort and simple contract, has six years to issue his claim at court. The starting date for the six-year period depends on the type of claim.

If the claim arises out of someone's negligence, then the period begins to run on the day after the loss or damage was suffered. If the damage was not discoverable at the time it was suffered, then the claimant has only three years from the date on which the damage could have been discovered to bring a claim. (This was brought in to deal with cases where damage or injury is undetectable by current technology at the time it occurs.) However, no claim based on negligence may be brought more than 15 years after the negligent act which caused the damage.

If the claim is based only on a breach of contract (including the breach of a contractual duty to take reasonable care), the six-year period begins to run on the day after the breach, whether or not the damage was discoverable within the limitation period.

6. Cases relating to land disputes (where damages are not sought for personal injury)

The limitation period for the recovery of rent from a tenant is six years from when the rent became due (Limitation Act 1980, section 19). To recover land from the defendant the landowner has 12 years from the day the trespass began (or 30 years if the potential claimant is a child or patient), after which his ownership comes to an end and the squatter acquires ownership (Limitation Act 1980, sections 15 and 17). Claims based upon the tort of nuisance must be brought within six years of the damage occurring.

7. Where the claimant (or potential claimant) has died

Where the potential claimant has died, there are two possible types of claim that may be made:

(a) Under section 1 of the Law Reform (Miscellaneous Provisions) Act 1934 the deceased's personal representatives (executors or administrators) may issue a claim for compensation for wrongs suffered by the deceased before his death. This applies to all types of claim (including negligence, breach of contract, nuisance, harassment, trespass, etc), except defamation. The personal representatives may also take over litigation already started by the deceased at the time of his death. The personal representatives have three years from the date of the deceased's death, or three years from the personal representative's date of knowledge of the cause of action arising (or the later of the two dates) to begin a claim or to take over the litigation. For a discussion of how to work out the date of knowledge in personal injury cases, please see Where the injury does not arise immediately, above. Any damages awarded are paid into the deceased's estate to be distributed according to his Will or, where there was no valid Will, under the intestacy rules.

(b) A claim by the deceased's dependants for compensation for their own losses caused by the death of the deceased in a fatal accident caused by the defendant. Such a claim is governed by the Fatal Accidents Act 1976, and a more detailed explanation can be found in chapter 2. The personal representatives are named as claimants, except where they have failed to bring a claim within six months of the death, when the dependants themselves are allowed to bring the claim. In such circumstances, the Limitation Act 1980 provides that a Fatal Accidents Act claim should be brought within three years of whichever is the later; the date of the relevant death, or the date of knowledge of the person for whose benefit the action is brought. An explanation of the date of knowledge can be found above at Where the injury does not arise immediately. Note that an application to disapply the time limits may be made (see Can I extend the limitation period? for further information).

8. Where the claimant is a child (i.e. has not yet reached his 18th birthday)

Generally, the relevant limitation period (usually six or three years – see above) begins on his 18th birthday (Limitation Act 1980, sections 28(1) and 28A).

9. Where the claimant is suffering from a mental disorder

Generally, the relevant limitation period (usually three or six years) begins to run when he ceases to suffer from the mental disorder (Limitation Act 1980, sections 28 and 28A).

Suing the correct defendant

In order to gain compensation or another order for a legal wrong, you must identify who is responsible for it in law. The second stage is correctly to identify them in the Claim Form. This section deals with these issues and explains how the different types of defendant are sued.

1. Who is responsible?

You will have to analyse your case and think 'who owed me a statutory duty?', 'whose negligence caused the accident?', 'who breached the contract?' Detailed explanations of the various types of claim (or causes of action) are set out in chapter 1. Most of the time, the question of legal liability will be easily answered. In some situations there may be more than one defendant (either because the loss was caused jointly by more than one person, or because loss, injury or damage was caused separately by more than one defendant) and it is convenient to have all the evidence heard together in one trial. Do not forget, however, that you only have a limited time to find out who is liable, and to bring your claim, see above. If there is more than one defendant, the court may not allow you to bring a second claim against a different person if the first claim fails. Suing everyone at the same time in one claim also keeps down the costs.

Example 1: I am injured in a car accident which was caused by the negligent driving of two separate drivers.

It is sensible (although I am not obliged to do so) to claim against them both, naming the drivers as first and second defendant respectively. If I am successful against them both, the judge will decide how the damages are to be apportioned between them. If I lose against one, but win against the other, the judge will work out what damages the unsuccessful defendant must pay me.

Example 2: I have a biopsy performed and the pathology laboratory run by the local health trust negligently fails to notice an abnormality. I then move to a different health authority's area where my new GP negligently fails to pick up further warning symptoms of my condition. As a result, I suffer unnecessary pain and discomfort and my condition is undetected for some time.

I should sue both the pathologist and GP involved as they both have been negligent. Furthermore, their respective employers are vicariously liable for their negligence, so I should also sue the two health authorities.

2. How do I name the defendant correctly in the Claim Form?

It depends on the type of person the defendant is (his legal 'capacity'). Note that with hit-and-run accidents there is no one to sue, and claims should be made to the Motor Insurers' Bureau under their compensation scheme for victims of untraced drivers (see below).

(a) Suing an individual

Where the wrongdoer is an individual person, he should be sued in his own name. Often a person may be 'trading as', under a different name. If the case relates to the individual in his work capacity, the 'trading as' name should also be included in the Claim Form.

Example 1: I am injured by Sam Browne in a car accident. He was driving to work at the time of the accident. He is a greengrocer, trading under the name of 'Sam's Greens'.

In this instance, the fact that he is a greengrocer is irrelevant to his negligent driving – I should sue him in the name of 'Sam Browne'.

Example 2: I am injured at Sam Browne's shop when I slip on a banana skin negligently left by him on the floor. The shop is called 'Sam's Greens' and is owned by Sam Browne (not a limited company).

Here, Sam Browne's job and trading name are relevant to the case. I can name him as 'Sam Browne, trading as Sam's Greens'.

(b) Suing an individual's employer (vicarious liability)

Where an individual's act commits a tort in the course of his employment, the law also holds his employer liable (responsible) for the consequences of that tort. This is known as 'vicarious liability', and both the wrongdoer and the employer may be sued. Thus where an employee, employed by an individual, company, firm or Limited Liability Partnership, is negligent whilst at work, both he and his employer (individual, company, firm or LLP, etc) can be named as first and second defendants. The advantage of this rule is that often an employee will not be able to pay any damages or costs awarded if the claimant is successful, whereas the employer is more likely to be able to do so (and will probably be insured against such a claim). Because vicarious liability is parallel to actual liability and depends on the employee acting in the course of his employment, it is wise to sue both the employee and the employer. It is possible to sue an employer for vicarious liability of an employee where the identity of the particular employee cannot be established. The body of law on what the phrase 'in the course of employment' is, is complex and seemingly contradictory, especially in cases where the defendant employee was disobeying orders or acting deliberately. A detailed explanation is not within the scope of this book. However, the following simple examples illustrate the basic principle:

Example 1: I am shopping in 'Sam's Greens' which is a greengrocer's shop owned and run by Sam Browne. Theresa Wilson, the shop assistant, negligently hits me with a crate of lettuces she is lifting.

Theresa Wilson is primarily liable. Sam Browne, her employer, is vicariously liable as she has been negligent while in the course of her employment. I should name 'Theresa Wilson' as the first defendant, and 'Sam Browne trading as Sam's Greens' as the second defendant.

Example 2: Theresa Wilson, driving on her way to work at 'Sam's Greens', negligently drives her car into me causing me injury.

In this example, Theresa Wilson was merely getting to work, not 'acting in the course of her employment' when she commits the negligent act, and therefore Sam Browne is not vicariously liable. I should sue Theresa Wilson.

Example 3: Sam Browne employs Tina Smith as a driver to make deliveries of vegetables around the local area in a van. Whilst on her delivery round, Tina causes a road accident in which I am injured.

Here, Tina was acting in the course of her employment when she commits the negligent act – driving is part of her job. I should sue Tina Smith (first defendant) and 'Sam Browne, trading as Sam's Greens' (second defendant).

(c) Suing a company

In law, companies are legal entities. As soon as a company is 'incorporated' (i.e. is formed into a corporation), it becomes a creature distinct from the people who run it or own it. In other words a company is a legal person (as opposed to an actual person) under the law. Thus a company can own a duty of care and enter contracts (through its officers and employees) like any ordinary person. When things go wrong, therefore, a company may be held liable to those who suffer. Moreover, the company can be held vicariously liable for the torts committed by its employees (see above).

You will be able to tell if you are dealing with a company because the letters 'plc'* or 'Ltd'* usually appear as part of the name. The letterheading used by the company will reveal the company's official address (the 'registered address') where correspondence may be sent. If in doubt, it is possible to find out if a company is in fact incorporated, by doing a search of the register at Companies House (for a small fee).

Example: Sam Browne has decided to form a limited company to carry on his expanding greengrocer's business. On 4 July 2000 'Sam's Greens Limited' is incorporated. On 6 September 2000, I slip on a wet floor in his shop and injure myself. My claim should be against 'Sam's Greens Ltd'.

(d) Suing a firm or partnership

A firm or partnership, unlike a company, is not a legal entity separate from its members. Each partner will therefore be personally liable:

(i)   for his own wrongful acts;

(ii) for the wrongful acts of his fellow partners committed in the normal course of the firm's business; and

(iii) for the wrongful acts of the employees of the partnership committed whilst acting in the course of their employment (vicarious liability).

Where the partners are defendants under (ii) or (iii) above, they are sued in the name of the firm, 'Thompson, Thompson and Smythe, a firm'. Only those partners at the time of the act complained of will be held liable.

Example 1: Gary is a partner in a firm of solicitors. Driving on his way to work one morning he negligently causes a collision that creates damage to someone else's car.

Gary is personally liable for his own negligence. When he was driving to work he was not acting in the course of the firm's business, so his co-partners will not be liable for damages.

Example 2: A client visits Gary's firm's offices for an appointment. Unfortunately, she trips on a rickety stair and injures herself.

In this instance the partners in the firm will be held liable (jointly and separately) for their unsafe premises. This is because the firm is the occupier of the premises, and the premises is where they carry on their business.

Example 3: Mary Matthews consults Gary about a legal problem. He gives her negligent advice and, as a result, she suffers a financial loss.

Gary and each partner in the firm is liable (jointly and separately) for Gary's professional negligence. This is because he was negligent in the course of carrying out the firm's business.

(e) Suing a Limited Liability Partnership

Limited Liability Partnerships are a type of partnership created by the Limited Liability Partnership Act 2000. Some accountants' and solicitors' firms are now LLPs. Each partner is liable for his own wrongful behaviour. However, instead of his co-partners being liable as described in (d) above for wrongs committed in the normal course of the firm's business, the firm itself is liable, much like a company would be.

(f) Claims involving unincorporated associations

There are many situations where people join together in an activity without forming a company or partnership. Examples may include a sports club or charity, association or club. Such clubs are made up of all the members, and under the law are only a collection of individuals. In other words, the association does not have a separate legal identity of its own. Care should be taken when deciding whom to sue – are all the members of the club individually liable, or only some of the members? If the wrongdoing in question was the fault of certain members acting on their own, then they should be sued as individuals. If, however, the wrongdoing was something that every member of the club would be held individually liable for, it would be unwieldy to name each and every one of them. In these circumstances, Civil Procedure Rules, Part 19.6 allows one or more of the members to act as representatives of the other members in order to defend the action on their behalf. If damages are awarded against the representatives, they may recover the money from other members. See page 98 for an explanation of representative orders.

Example 1: I slip on defective flooring on an ill-lit flight of stairs at a local badminton club. The club consists of 300 members and the building is owned by the members in the name of the captain Hugh MacKay.

I could sue each member of the club for their unsafe premises, including Mr MacKay, but such a claim would be costly, complicated and administratively unworkable (300 Defence Forms, 300 solicitors and 300 barristers in court, etc!). I could choose one or more individuals to pursue for damages, but that may become complicated if they decide to bring actions blaming each other. In the circumstances, I should make an application to the court for a representative order naming Hugh MacKay as a representative of all the members of the club. This is because the court will only make a person represent others if each and every person represented could defend the action in the same way (i.e. they have the same interest in the litigation as the representative). In this example, all the people represented would raise the same defence to the action.

Example 2: A leading member of a local political party and a few of his fellow members begin an anonymous campaign of harassment against me when I announce my intention to leave the party and join a rival group. Most of the party members were unaware of what was going on and only found out who was doing this when I did. This harassment causes me a great deal of anxiety and stress.

I should sue the individuals harassing me (if it had been a large number of them, I could obtain a representative order that one or two of them represent the others). This case is not appropriate for a representative order against all the members of the local party. Not all the members of the club have the same interest in the litigation; the harassment was committed by a few, not in the name of the other members, or as agents or employees of them, but in a personal capacity.

(g) Claims against children

A child can be sued for torts but not generally for breach of contract, or for misrepresenting his age in order to enter a contract (the tort of deceit). A suitable adult known as a 'litigation friend' conducts the litigation on his behalf (see above). It is worth remembering that children may not have any assets with which to pay any award of damages. Moreover, children, by virtue of their age and inexperience, are not expected to have the same awareness of danger or the consequences of their actions that adults have. A great deal will depend on what the child intended by his actions, and what a reasonably sensible child of the defendant's age would have known or realised.

3. The name of the defendant or claimant on the Claim Form is wrong; can it be corrected?

It is essential that the parties are named correctly. Bringing an action against the wrong person is a waste of time and money. Moreover, court orders must be obeyed by the persons they are addressed to (and the consequences of disobedience can be very serious). Happily, if the pre-action protocols have been observed by the parties, this sort of mistake will not happen (see below). The claimant must:

- identify the correct party (or parties);

- name them correctly in court papers.

If the defendant is correct but there has been a typing error (or similar mistake) in the court forms, an amendment can be made under the Civil Procedure Rules, Part 17. It is also possible to add or substitute defendants under the Civil Procedure Rules, Part 19. In both cases, the permission of the court is needed if the claim has already been served. If a person is wrongly named as the defendant, the claimant may apply to discontinue the claim against him under Part 38 of the Civil Procedure Rules, and start a new action against the correct one. Usually the claimant will be ordered to pay the legal costs of the other parties which arose from the need to amend.

The defendant should draw the claimant's attention to any inaccuracies of identification as soon as he realises the mistake.

Example 1: I am involved in a road traffic accident with Ian Reed, a lorry driver who works for a company. My Claim Form names Ian Reed and 'CAB Transport Ltd' (registered office in Leeds) as defendants. Ian Reed's defence documents deny that he works for CAB Transport Ltd, and state that he is employed by ABC Transport Ltd of Carlisle. CAB Transport Ltd's defence documents deny employing Ian Reed and deny all liability for damages.

It is clear that I have named the wrong party. I should discontinue the claim against CAB Transport Ltd and begin a fresh claim against ABC Transport Ltd.

Example 2: I am involved in a road traffic accident with a person whose name I take to be Sarah-Jane Mitchland, living at 14 Ormah Road, London. I name her as the defendant in my Claim Form and other court documents. It later becomes clear that her name is, in fact, Sarah-Joan Mitcham. She does indeed live at 14 Ormah Road, London and accepts the fact that she was involved in the accident, although she denies it was her fault.

This is a case of simply getting the name wrong. I should ask the court for permission to amend the Claim Form and the statement of case*.

GETTING WHAT YOU WANT WITHOUT GOING TO COURT

Using official complaints procedures

There are various official complaints procedures that can be used to obtain a successful resolution of a dispute (including payment of compensation) without the costs, delay and worry of going to court. These tend to be created by the larger institutions, such as the NHS Complaints Procedure, or by the government (the Criminal Injuries Compensation Board) or a particular industry in agreement with the government (such as the insurance industry by way of the Motor Insurers' Bureau).

1. The NHS Complaints Procedure

This is a non-adversarial system governed by the NHS Ombudsman. It provides a three-stage system:

1.   The local resolution of the complaint by the healthcare provider involved.

2.   If that fails, the complaint goes before a convener for consideration.

3.   Finally, a panel investigation of the complaint and decision.

The procedure does not apply where the complainant has indicated (orally or in writing) that he intends to litigate the matter. In this instance, the parties involved must comply with the pre-action protocol for the resolution of clinical disputes (see Appendix 4). Also, the complaints procedure is not appropriate for claims involving large amounts of money or complexity.

The complainant may be represented by a lawyer or lay advocate, although this is not necessary. In a claim which is borderline for qualifying for Community Legal Services Funding (the new form of Legal Aid), it is advisable for the complaints procedure to be attempted (and exhausted) first before litigation is embarked upon.

The outline of the scheme is as follows:

The local resolution stage is designed to be flexible and relatively informal, and the complaint should be resolved within 12 months of the incident complained about (or the date that the patient realised that the incident was 'significant'). Each healthcare provider provides its own complaints procedure and identifies a person responsible for receiving and investigating complaints. Look for the posters and leaflets in waiting rooms; there should also be details of any advocacy services that may be available. Healthcare providers have a duty to investigate (in a formal or informal way) and respond to complaints. The outcome of the investigation may be an apology (and details of how the matter will be avoided in the future), compensation to put the patient in the position he would have been in had the error not occurred (this will usually be for out of pocket expenses, not for pain and suffering, etc), or a recommendation for the patient to seek legal advice. If the patient is dissatisfied with the response, he should move to stage 2 of the scheme.

Within 28 days of the unsatisfactory outcome of the local dispute resolution stage, the patient should ask the convener to establish an independent review panel to look at his complaint. The convener considers this request and either refers the complaint back for further local dispute resolution, convenes an independent panel or reports the matter to an appropriate agency, such as the police, the General Medical Council or other professional regulatory body.

The third stage is the panel investigation by the convener, a lay chairman, and one other person. The panel cannot recommend disciplinary action against an NHS worker (in such cases the convener should have made the referral to the appropriate regulatory body or the police). However, it can recommend changes in NHS practice.

2. The Criminal Injuries Compensation Scheme

The current Criminal Injuries Compensation Scheme was set up by the government under the Criminal Injuries Compensation Act 1995. As the name suggests, it is a scheme that makes payments to the victims of crime from a central fund in order to compensate them for their injury. It is a system that is an alternative to the civil claim for damages which is covered by the rest of this book. Furthermore, it is a scheme that is designed for the layman – it is considered inappropriate for applicants to require lawyers and although, of course, applicants may hire lawyers for advice or representation, no legal costs will be paid by the scheme.

This section gives a brief overview of the scheme. More detailed guidance is set out in the Criminal Injuries Compensation Authority publication *A Guide to the Criminal Injuries Compensation Scheme*. Further guidance is given in the leaflet *Child Abuse and the Criminal Injuries Compensation Scheme*. Under the rules, any money paid out under the scheme must be repaid to the extent that the applicant later recovers money from the criminal or another government scheme in relation to the injury.

Note that the charity Action for Victims of Medical Accidents (AVMA) provides advice and support for victims of medical accdents (see their website at www.avma.org.uk).

Who qualifies?

Victims of crime and other persons seeking compensation in their own right

Persons who suffered a criminal injury on or after 1 August 1964, and who have not made an earlier application under the 1990 or other previous schemes, may apply for compensation. The exception to this general rule is that someone who was living with their assailant as a member of the same family may not be awarded compensation, unless the injury in question was sustained on or after 1 October 1979.

A criminal injury is described as a crime of violence (including physical attacks, some threats, sexual offences, arson and poisoning): trespass on a railway, an injury received as a consequence of apprehending a suspected offender, preventing an offence or assisting a constable who is doing any of those things. Each case will be taken on its own merits.

An 'injury' includes all physical injury and fatal injury. Mental injuries (medically recognised illnesses or conditions) may be compensated, but only if one of the following features also is present:

- The applicant victim's mental injury arises from a physical one.

- The crime put the applicant victim in reasonable fear of suffering immediate physical harm.

- The applicant had a close relationship of love and affection with the victim who suffered criminal injury and witnessed or was present when the victim was injured, or was closely involved in the aftermath (the applicant need not be the direct victim of the crime).

- The crime involved was a sexual offence to which the applicant victim did not in fact consent.

- The applicant was employed on the railways and witnessed and was present when another person was injured as a result of a criminal trespass on the railway (or was closely involved in its aftermath).

Claims by dependants and relatives of a dead victim of crime

Where the victim of a criminal injury dies, either as a result of the injuries or from another cause, the following people may apply for compensation under the scheme:

- The victim's husband or wife.

- The victim's long-term unmarried partner (of the opposite sex).

- The victim's parent.

- The victim's child, even if over the age of 18.

- The victim's former husband or wife who was financially supported by the victim.

There is provision for compensation to be paid to more than one eligible applicant. Awards, where the victim died as a result of the criminal injury, will be appropriately granted as follows:

- A 'fatal injury award' is a set amount: £10,000 where there is only one qualifying applicant, and £5,000 each where there is more than one (not including former dependent spouses).

- A 'dependency award' is designed to compensate the applicant who was financially dependent on the deceased. The claims officer looks at the earnings, etc of the victim before his death and calculates the amount of loss suffered by the descendant applicant. Where the victim died from separate causes, compensation is based upon the victim's loss of earnings and expenses suffered as a result of the criminal injury and not from the death.

- An 'award for loss of parental services' is currently £2,000 per year until the child's 18th birthday.

Claims by parents or guardians on behalf of injured children

Under the law, a child is someone who has not yet had his 18th birthday. A person who has parental responsibility for the child (including the local authority, where appropriate) may apply on behalf of the child for compensation. In the rare event of there being no such adult to act, the official solicitor may assist. Note that a copy of the child's birth certificate must be enclosed with the application form.

There are similar provisions for a suitable adult to represent a person who is unable, through a mental disorder, to manage his own affairs.

How to make an application

An application is made using a form supplied by the Criminal Injuries Compensation Authority. There are two forms available: Personal Injury and Fatal Injury which can be obtained from:

The Criminal Injuries Compensation Authority
Tay House
300 Bath Street
Glasgow G2 4JR

Tel: 0141 331 2726
Fax: 0141 331 2287

The application should be received by the Authority no longer than two years from the date of the injury. In certain circumstances, the time limit may be waived if the Authority is satisfied that:

(a) there has been a good reason for the delay; and

(b) it is in the interests of justice to do so.

The decision

The assessment process is conducted by claims officers. Applicants are expected to cooperate with the officer who undertakes an investigation. Enquiries may be made of the medical authorities, the police, employers and any other relevant bodies (the application form requires the applicant to state the relevant body with which they can discuss the otherwise confidential information). Further information may also be sought; for example, the applicant may be required to undergo a (further) medical examination.

Some factors that are taken into account upon assessment

General considerations:

(a) Whether the applicant failed to take all reasonable steps to report the relevant crime to the police.

(b) Whether the applicant failed to cooperate with the police or any other body trying to bring the assailant to justice.

(c) Whether the applicant has cooperated with the Criminal Injuries Compensation Authority.

(d) The conduct of the applicant before, during or after the incident (e.g. provocation or bad language, a history of violence with the assailant, etc).

(e) The criminal record of the applicant (except 'spent' convictions) which will attract penalty points leading to a percentage reduction of compensation at the appropriate level.

(f) Any other material before the claims officer which makes it inappropriate to make a full or reduced award.

(g) Whether an award will indirectly benefit the assailant (particularly where the assailant and victim are living in the same household).

(h) The amount the applicant has received from the compensation scheme of another country (or Northern Ireland), as well as civil damages and compensation awarded by a criminal court payable by the assailant.

(i) The maximum sum that may be awarded to a claimant is £500,000.

Considerations regarding the standard amount of compensation:

(a) Whether or not there is a single injury or multiple injuries to be considered.

(b) The nature of the injury.

Considerations regarding loss of earnings:

(a) Whether or not the applicant has lost earnings or his earning capacity for 28 weeks or more as a result of his injury (loss of earnings will not be compensated if the incapacity/inability to work has lasted for less than 28 weeks).

(b) The actual length of loss of earnings or earning capacity (if more than 28 weeks).

(c) Any salary fees or other payment from work received (or should have been received) by the applicant.

(d) Any changes to the applicant's pension rights.

(e) The amount of social security benefits received.

(f) Insurance payments received.

Considerations regarding special expenses:

(a) Whether or not the applicant has lost earnings or his earning capacity for longer than 28 weeks (special expenses will not be compensated if the incapacity/inability to work has lasted for less than 28 weeks).

(b) Loss or damage to equipment belonging to the applicant which he used as a physical aid (such as glasses, wheelchair, etc).

(c) NHS costs.

(d) Private medical costs, where it was reasonable to 'go private' and the amount charged is reasonable.

(e) Reasonable costs of special equipment, adaptations of accommodation, costs of care (whether or not at home or in a residential establishment).

(f) The loss of earnings, loss of earning capacity or additional costs of a relative or friend of the applicant who undertakes care of him free of charge, and the level of care provided.

(g) Whether such costs are ongoing and, if so, what figure is appropriate to cover future expenses.

The amount of the standard award: 'the tariff':

The standard award for the injury is worked out by referring to a table, known as 'the tariff'. Minor multiple injuries (defined in note 12 of the tariff as injuries, such as extensive bruising, a black eye, a bloody nose, etc which necessitate at least two visits to a GP within six weeks) attract a Level 1 award (currently £1,000). More serious separate multiple injuries are calculated as follows:

the full amount for the injury attracting the highest level of award

+

10 per cent of the amount attracting the next highest level of award

+

5 per cent of the amount attracting the third highest level of award

= the award

3. A claim to the Motor Insurers' Bureau for injuries caused in a hit-and-run accident (untraced drivers agreement)

Under an agreement with the government, the insurance industry, under the auspices of the Motor Insurers' Bureau (MIB), may pay compensation for people injured in hit-and-run accidents, where there is simply no one to name as the defendant. The scheme does not apply to vehicles owned or in the possession of either the Crown, a local authority, the police or NHS bodies, unless those vehicles are being driven for unauthorised purposes at the time of the accident. The MIB will not pay compensation where the untraced driver deliberately used the vehicle as a weapon against the complainant (see above for claims to the Criminal Injuries Compensation Board). Also, the MIB will not pay compensation to a claimant who allowed himself to become the defendant's passenger:

(a) in a vehicle which he knew was stolen, or was being used to commit a crime or to escape from lawful apprehension, etc;

(b) knowing that the defendant was uninsured.

Instead of bringing a claim in the court, an application is made directly to the MIB at the following address:

152 Silbury Boulevard
Central Milton Keynes MK9 1NB

Applications must be made within three years of the accident. The claimant must have reported the accident to the police within 14 days of the accident and cooperated with them in their investigations. As no court procedure is involved, apart from any payment for pain, suffering, loss of amenity and consequential losses, the MIB will only pay up to £150 and VAT towards any legal fees incurred by the claimant.

(The MIB also run a scheme paying damages awarded by the court against uninsured drivers – see chapter 5 for further information.)

Other methods

Contact your Citizens Advice Bureau for details of suitable alternatives to legal proceedings – mediation, complaints to Ombudsmen and professional bodies, as well as arbitration. A search on the Internet also produces a good deal of information about 'alternative dispute resolution' (a phrase describing various conciliation, mediation or 'mini-trial' schemes where disputes can be resolved without recourse to litigation), although do make sure that the site that you visit is applicable to the UK.

Settling a claim out of court

What is an 'out of court settlement'?

The parties involved in a dispute may agree to resolve the claim or potential claim between themselves without requiring the judge to decide the case at trial. The agreement is known as a 'settlement' or 'compromise'*. Once the subject matter has been settled between the parties, it cannot (except in very limited circumstances) be brought before the judge again (i.e. there is no appeal from a settlement). Note that settlements which involve child claimants or defendants must be approved by a judge under Part 21.10 of the Civil Procedure Rules (even if the settlement was agreed before a claim began in the courts).

When can a claim be settled?

A potential claim between parties may be settled at various stages:

1. In a contract before court proceedings begin.

2. In a compromise or settlement after proceedings have started, at any time before the judge has given judgment (thus a settlement may be reached even after the judge has heard all the evidence and closing speeches!).

The pre-action protocols are designed to promote early settlement and judges will often assist parties by giving them time to negotiate, if it looks as though there are real prospects of a deal being struck.

What are the advantages of an out of court settlement?

Whilst the rules of court and the pre-action protocols are designed to promote cooperation between the parties (and to stop tactical games), the English and Welsh system is still an adversarial one. The judge does not investigate facts in an attempt to uncover the truth; instead, the parties present the evidence supporting their version of events for him to decide which he prefers. A great deal will depend on how the witness performs on the day. A key witness may not attend (although it is possible to compel attendance by issuing a witness summons), he may fall apart under cross-examination or may simply be disbelieved. The other side's evidence may simply be stronger, clearer or more credible. Litigation is therefore unpredictable, expensive and stressful. Settlements, especially if they are made early on in the dispute, bypass the need for further litigation – the dispute is at an end and the parties have agreed on their own terms. As a result, a gamble on the outcome of the trial is replaced with certainty.

Settlements also enable the parties to arrive at a resolution earlier than they would have if they had awaited the court's process and final outcome. A case may take considerable time to go through the courts. The trial may occur some years after the accident. Even fast track trials, which are intended to have a timetable of 30 weeks (about seven months) between the court giving directions and the trial, are not particularly fast. Gathering evidence, complying with the pre-action protocols, and preparing for a trial may take considerable time (even when the parties are cooperating and reasonably efficient). Lastly, there is the matter of 'listing' the case for trial (finding a slot in the court timetable for the trial). A court may be very busy, and trial dates are often fixed far ahead, particularly if the case is to last more than one day in court.

Finally, the settlement of a case prevents further costs being incurred. If money is involved the payer need not incur any further interest on damages, and the payee receives his money earlier than he would otherwise do so.

How and when to negotiate

Settlement involves negotiation. Inevitably, most claims will be primarily about money compensation. Just as a claim (or counterclaim) has a value (i.e. what the judge is likely to award as damages), so do the risks of litigation. These risks must be assessed at every stage, especially as they may change as the case develops. A weak claim or defence has less value than a strong one. The weaker party has less to bargain with, whether he is the claimant or defendant, and may therefore have to settle for less. The purpose of negotiation is to find the 'magic sum' – in an ideal world, this is the highest a claimant can obtain and the least the defendant will pay. Similar concerns will affect the bargaining position of parties in claims that are not about money (i.e. claims seeking injunctions, declarations and other court orders).

Negotiations are not drawn to the court's attention until a deal is struck. Therefore all letters, faxes and emails that show a genuine aim by the parties to negotiate a settlement agreement are 'without prejudice'* and are usually marked clearly with this phrase. 'Without prejudice' is a phrase used by lawyers to signal that no admissions*, acceptance of liability or weakness in the case are being made – the discussions are aimed at settlement for argument's sake. Similarly, without prejudice negotiations may be conducted orally over the telephone or face to face. When you are negotiating you should make clear that all your discussions and correspondence are without prejudice to your case. If the negotiations break down, the parties continue towards trial in the normal way. There is nothing to stop negotiations beginning again later on. Often, judges will halt the beginning (or sometimes even the middle) of a trial to allow the parties time to negotiate where there seems a realistic prospect of a deal being struck.

Negotiation is a matter of personality, style and confidence. Some people (lawyers included!) are conciliatory in their approach; others are bullish or confrontational. Keep the following matters clearly in mind before entering negotiations:

1. What court order is sought (damages, injunction, etc). Do not forget interest and legal costs too!

2. The strengths and weaknesses of the evidence and legal arguments of your own case.

3. The strengths and weaknesses of the other party's case (as far as you know them).

The terms of the settlement

The settlement will bring the dispute to an end. It must tie up all loose ends, as generally it is not possible to go back to court with fresh issues, further complaints or new calculations.

The two main types of settlement are as follows:

1. The payment of money by the defendant to the claimant or an undertaking by him to do something or refrain from doing something (as appropriate), possibly on certain terms.

2. A 'walk away' deal where no money is paid and each party agrees to end the litigation, each giving up his right to pursue his claim or defence further.

A counterclaim can be settled in the same way as a claim may be. The parties may agree that the claimant (defendant to a counterclaim) pays the counterclaimant damages. Where the defendant has additionally agreed to pay damages in respect of the claim, the parties can agree to set off the two sums of money against each other, with one party paying the appropriate difference.

Settlements usually provide for the following matters:

1. The amount of damages and interest to be paid, by whom and to whom.

2. The date of the payment of the whole amount (or the dates of the agreed instalments).

3. The amount of legal costs to be paid by a party (unless each side is to bear his own).

Example consent order

IN THE BLANKTOWN COUNTY COURT

B E T W E E N

Harinda Singh

Claimant

and

John Brown

Defendant

ON this 13th day of January 2004
BEFORE His Honour Judge Lockhart
BY CONSENT IT IS ORDERED:

(1) The Defendant to pay the Claimant £15,500 by 7 April 2004

(2) [There be no order as to costs] [the Defendant to pay the Claimant's costs assessed at £4,501.02 by 7 April 2004] [the Defendant to pay the Claimant's costs to be subject to detailed assessment if not agreed between the parties]

The form of the settlement

1. Before court proceedings

Once a party makes an offer to settle the case on terms that are accepted by the other party, it is advisable for the terms to be contained or confirmed in writing and it is important to make it clear that the contract is 'in full and final settlement' of matters arising from the incident in question. Once agreed, the contract can be shown to the court as a defence in further proceedings arising from the incident in question. If a party fails to comply with the terms of the agreement, the other party may bring a fresh claim (within six years) for breach of contract.

2. After court proceedings have begun

The parties may come to an agreement at any time before the judge gives his judgment. A looming trial date concentrates minds wonderfully! It is advisable for the parties to put their agreement before the judge and ask him to make a consent order (see the example on the previous page). Where a child (someone who has not yet reached their 18th birthday) or a patient (someone who has a mental disorder within the meaning of the Mental Health Act 1983 and is incapable of managing his own affairs) is involved in the case, a settlement is not valid until it is approved by the court.

What is a 'payment into court' or 'Part 36 offer'?

Just as the pre-action protocol aims to promote settlement before the claim is issued at court, the rules of court (Civil Procedure Rules 1998) encourage parties to settle once the claim has begun.

1. Payments into court

The defendant may make a payment of money into court* in order to settle all or part of the claim. The court looks after the money and then pays it:

(a) to the claimant, upon him formally accepting the sum; or

(b) to the claimant, upon the judge making an award of damages in his favour; or

(c) to the defendant.

For the defendant who takes a view that the judge may order him to pay damages to the claimant, the procedure gives him some protection against having to pay for the claimant's subsequent legal costs and thus is a useful tool with which to pressurise the claimant.

The defendant must use Form N242A, Notice of Payment into Court, and the claimant will be informed of the payment. The claimant then has 21 days in which to accept or reject it. The offer cannot be withdrawn by the defendant unless the court gives permission. However, the defendant can increase the offer by paying more into court. The advantage to the defendant of offering to settle the action in this way is that if the claimant refuses the offer and then does not succeed at trial, or is not awarded damages in a larger sum than that paid into court, the claimant must bear the defendant's legal costs from the last date of possible acceptance of the payment. For the defendant who wishes to settle his case, therefore, the procedure gives him some protection for his costs and thus is a useful tool with which to pressurise the claimant.

2. Part 36 offers

Governed by Part 36 of the Civil Procedure Rules 1998, this is the procedure allowing the claimant to make an offer in writing to the defendant – usually that he will accept a specified sum of money to settle the case. The offer must remain open for 21 days. The consequences of the defendant rejecting the offer and then being found liable by the court for a greater sum are that the defendant will probably have to pay a considerable costs and interest bill.

The existence of rejected Part 36 payments and offers is not communicated to the trial judge until he has ruled on liability and the amount of damages (if any), and is considering costs. If the Part 36 offer* or payment is made less than 21 days before trial, the permission of the court is needed in order to accept the payment or offer (unless the parties agree between them who shall pay the legal costs). Note also that the cost consequences of Part 36 payments and offers do not apply to small claims track cases.

PRE-ACTION PROTOCOLS

Where do the pre-action protocols fit in the litigation process?

The pre-action protocols tell the parties how they are expected to deal with the dispute in the period between the incident complained of and the issuing of a claim in court. In this period the person with the grievance raises the complaint with the potential defendant(s), evidence is gathered and investigations undertaken.

What exactly are 'pre-action protocols'?

The protocols are lists of requirements that claimants and defendants are expected to fulfil before a claim is issued. The aim was to increase the likelihood of early settlement by promoting increased contact between the parties, better and earlier investigations of the claim, and an earlier and wider exchange of information between the parties about the claim. If these early discussions do not result in a resolution of the dispute, and litigation begins, hopefully the path to trial will be smooth and efficient.

Does a pre-action protocol apply to my case?

It depends on the type of case. If a protocol does not apply, the court still expects a significant degree of communication and information sharing between the potential parties in order to avoid trial (if possible) – see below. The following protocols have been issued for the following types of cases:

1. Fast track personal injury claims.

2. Clinical disputes.

3. Construction and engineering disputes.

4. Professional negligence claims.

5. Defamation and judicial review cases (which are not covered by this book).

No pre-action protocol applies; are there any guidelines or requirements?

Yes. The court still expects the parties to settle the dispute before a claim is made, where possible. The general guidelines can be found at Appendix 7. The parties' behaviour in conducting the litigation can be taken into account by the judge when he decides what costs order to make.

What happens if I (or my opponent) do not comply with the pre-action protocol?

The failure of a party to comply with either the whole of a relevant pre-action protocol or a particular requirement set by it can be taken into account by the judge when he is considering who should pay the legal costs of the claim, or whether to award interest. It is important to draw his attention to any such failure by the opposing party. Minor breaches are unlikely to attract much criticism, however. Where a party was disadvantaged by the other's failure to comply, the court may wish to penalise the wrongdoer (even if he has been successful in the actual litigation).

What do the protocols say?

The protocols and associated materials (sample letters, etc) are set out in the Appendices. Below is a brief overview of the protocols relevant to the types of case covered by this book.

1. The personal injury claims protocol

Step 1 The proposed claimant sends each proposed defendant two copies of a letter of claim (see Appendix 3 for a specimen letter), which should be adapted to fit the circumstances of the case and in particular should:

  (a)   set out a clear summary of the facts;

  (b)   give a brief indication of the nature of the injuries;

(c)   make an indication of the nature and amount of financial loss suffered; and

(d)   ask for details of the proposed defendant's insurer.

Step 2   Within 21 days (of the letter of claim's date of posting) the proposed defendant(s) should:

(a)   pass the letter of claim to his insurance company, if he has one;

(b)   write to the claimant acknowledging receipt of the letter of claim; and

(c)   give details of his insurers (if he has insurance for the particular type of case, e.g. compulsory road traffic insurance).

If the defendant fails to respond, the claimant may issue his claim.

NB: If the accident has occurred abroad or the defendant is based abroad, the period is 42 days.

Step 3   The proposed defendant has a maximum of three calendar months after his letter of acknowledgement to investigate the claim. By the end of that period he should send to the proposed claimant his letter of reply:

(a)   admitting the claim; or

(b)   denying liability (together with his reasons for doing so); or

(c)   admitting liability but asserting contributory negligence.

If liability is denied, the letter of reply should enclose any relevant documents which have a bearing on the case. If contributory negligence is asserted by the proposed defendant, he should specify his reasons in the letter of reply and enclose any relevant documentation. See Contributory negligence in chapter 1 and a discussion on the disclosure of documents at chapter 4 for further information.

NB: If the accident has occurred abroad or the defendant is based abroad, the period is six months.

Step 4   The proposed claimant should send to the proposed defendant a 'schedule of special damages' and copies of the supporting documents, if not before the proposed defendant has replied, then as soon as practicable after he has denied liability. A sample schedule of special damages can be found in chapter 4.

Step 5   The parties (particularly the claimant) will wish to instruct an expert witness to produce a report. Medical expert evidence will be necessary, but either party may wish to obtain evidence from other professionals (such as an engineer, employment specialist or occupational therapist). The protocol requires the parties to try to agree on which expert to instruct and agree the terms on which he is to produce a report.

Accordingly, the party wishing to obtain a particular type of expert should give the other party the name (or names) of suitable experts in that field. Within 14 days, the second party should agree to one or more of the names, or outline his objections to any of them. If there is no agreement as to whom should be instructed, each party may instruct their own expert and the court will later decide if the parties have acted reasonably in failing to agree on whom should be instructed. Note that the expert(s) will need to look at relevant documentation, such as medical records, and conduct an examination, such as a site view, or a medical examination of the claimant. If there are various types of professional evidence sought, the process will need to be repeated with each one.

Step 6   If there has been no settlement of the case by this stage, the claimant issues the claim (see Beginning a claim). Note that this must be within the limitation period (see Is it too late to sue? – it may be necessary to apply to the court for an extension of time).

2. The clinical disputes/negligence claims protocol

This protocol differs slightly from the personal injury protocol, because it is tailored to the particular circumstances out of which such disputes arise. At the heart of a clinical dispute is a broken professional relationship between the healthcare worker and the patient. There are also disciplinary issues and sensitivities, involving both hospital/health trust and the relevant professional body (such as the General Medical Council). The protocol tries to foster openness at an early stage, encourage early investigation, promote early disclosure of medical records, facilitate resolution and discourage weak claims or defences from dragging on.

The protocol is divided into two parts:

(a)   The initial stages which impose good practice commitments on the patient and the healthcare provider.

(b)   The protocol stages which outline a series of steps which are designed to achieve early resolution of the dispute and efficient preparation for trial.

Initial stages

(a)   The patient and his advisors should report any concerns and dissatisfactions to the healthcare provider, as soon as is reasonable in the circumstances. This enables the healthcare provider to offer clinical advice, if appropriate, and to advise (admit) if anything has gone wrong.

(b)   The healthcare provider should tell the patient (i.e. without being asked) if there has been a 'serious adverse outcome'. He should provide an oral or written explanation of what has happened and, where appropriate, offer further treatment to rectify the problem, an apology, changes in procedure and compensation.

(c) The patient and his advisors should consider all routes open to him: request for an explanation or a meeting, lodge a complaint, go down the route of alternative dispute resolution (see Settling a claim out of court) and negotiation, as well as litigation. The healthcare worker should advise the patient of the options available to him. See also the NHS Complaints Procedure which is discussed at Getting what you want without going to court.

Protocol steps

(a) The patient should ask to see copies of his medical records, being specific about which records are required (i.e. relating to a particular procedure) and giving an indication to the healthcare provider about what has gone wrong (see the approved specimen form for this request at Appendix 4). There is a charge for this – currently £10, plus photocopying and postage costs.

(b) The healthcare provider should provide the records within 40 days, explain promptly where there is a problem in complying and give details of how the problem is being resolved.

(c) If the healthcare provider fails to provide the records or an explanation described above, the patient may apply to the court for pre-action disclosure (see chapter 4).

(d) The patient and healthcare provider will need to consider whether or not to instruct expert(s) so that they can analyse:

- whether or not a healthcare worker has been negligent; and/or

- the patient's condition and prognosis; and/or

- the value of the claim (i.e. the likely damages).

The expert(s) may be instructed by each party, by one party with the agreement of the other, or jointly, as appropriate for the circumstances.

(e) Where there is no resolution of the dispute, the patient sends the healthcare provider a letter of claim. This should contain a clear summary of the facts relied upon:

- An indication of the negligence alleged.

- A description of the claimant's injuries, present condition and prognosis.

- An outline of the financial losses suffered and expected.

Relevant documents should be mentioned and copies included, and in complex cases (such as where various healthcare providers are involved) a chronology of events should be provided. A specimen letter, which should be adapted to fit the circumstances, is included in Appendix 3. No claim should be issued for three months (unless there is a limitation problem), to allow the healthcare provider time to make further investigations and consider its position.

    (f) The proposed defendant (the healthcare provider) should send to the patient an acknowledgement letter within 14 days of receiving it, identifying who is dealing with the matter.

    (g) The proposed defendant should send the patient a letter of response within three months. The letter of response should state (and give reasons):

- whether the claim is admitted;

- whether part of the claim is admitted;

- whether the claim is denied (specifying what issues are disputed).

    (h) If there has been no settlement by this stage, the claimant may issue his claim.

3. The construction and engineering disputes protocol

This protocol is simple in its structure, and unique in its provision for the proposed claimant and defendant to have a formal face-to-face meeting (in order to define the issues between them, and to explore the possible ways in which the dispute may be resolved). As with the other protocols, if the claimant has a limitation problem, the protocol does not have to be complied with before the issue of the claim. However, the judge should be asked to give the parties time to comply with the protocol before any further steps are taken towards trial.

Stage 1   The party with a grievance (the proposed claimant) sends the proposed defendant a letter of claim. This outlines the facts of the claim and gives other important information. A list of what the letter must contain is given in the protocol (please see Appendix 5).

Stage 2   Within 14 days of receiving the letter of claim, the defendant should send a letter of acknowledgement. This acknowledges receipt of the letter, and may include the defendant's insurance details. If the defendant does not do so, the claimant may go ahead and issue the claim at court.

Stage 3   28 days after the defendant received the letter of claim, he must sent the claimant the defendant's response. In this the defendant sets out his reply to the claim – challenging the jurisdiction of the English and Welsh courts to deal with the dispute; agreeing to certain facts, disputing others; alleging contributory negligence; or asserting a counterclaim, as the case may be.

Stage 4   The claimant must respond to the counterclaim (if one has been made by the defendant) within 28 days of the receipt of the defendant's response.

Stage 5   The pre-action meeting(s) should take place as soon as possible after stage 3 (or, where appropriate, stage 4) has been complied with. A discussion of what is expected to take place at the meeting is contained in the protocol – see

Appendix 5. Everything said in the meeting is without prejudice (i.e. will not be mentioned in court to the judge if the matter gets to trial).

Stage 6   Issue of the claim (if no settlement is agreed).

4. The professional negligence claims protocol

This protocol applies to claims against most professionals. For claims against architects, engineers and quantity surveyors, please see the construction and engineering disputes protocol above, and for claims against all doctors and other healthcare providers, see the protocol for the resolution of clinical disputes above. As with other protocols, if the claimant's limitation period is about to expire, he should first issue his claim, and then apply to the court for a stay of proceedings (so that no further steps are taken towards trial) until the protocol steps have been complied with.

Stage 1   The person with the grievance sends each potential defendant an open (rather than without prejudice) letter of claim. This outlines the case against him and the claim for compensation or other redress, and contains specific information – please see the list set out in the protocol at Appendix 6.

Stage 2   Within 21 days of receiving the letter of claim the defendant sends the claimant a letter of acknowledgement (acknowledging receipt).

Stage 3   The defendant(s) have three months (extendable by agreement between the parties) to conduct investigations into the claim.

Stage 4   The defendant(s) then respond with either an open letter of response or a without prejudice letter of settlement. The letter of response sets out the admissions or denials of the claim and asserts the defendant's case if he wishes to defend any action in court (for the list of required information, please see the protocol at Appendix 6). The letter of settlement is sent when the defendant wishes to settle the claim without the need for court proceedings. Settlements are discussed above. The protocol sets out what information should be included in the letter of settlement.

Stage 5   Having set out their positions, the parties should begin negotiations for settlement, whether the defendant has supplied a letter of response, or a letter of settlement. This period lasts six months (extendable by agreement between the parties).

Stage 6   If no settlement has been reached, the claimant may issue the claim.

The protocol also provides for the parties to agree to alternative dispute resolution at any time, to instruct expert witnesses and to notify that the claim is about to be issued.

IS ENGLAND & WALES THE CORRECT PLACE TO BRING A CLAIM?

Scotland and Northern Ireland

Claims arising from contract, tort and breach of statutory duty in circumstances which took place in either Scotland or Northern Ireland are governed by the Civil Jurisdiction and Judgments Act 1982. The rules are set out in schedule 4 of that Act. The claim should be brought in the area of the UK where the defendant is domiciled*, but alternatively may be brought in the part of the UK where the harm was suffered (tort and breaches of statutory duty) or where the contract was to be performed, if different. A contract is performed by the parties fulfilling promises made in the contract, such as the payment of money, the supplying of goods, or the performance of a service or piece of work.

Example: Katie lives in South London, but for her holiday attends a centre for rock climbing near Stirling, Scotland. The centre is owned and run by a company based in Carlisle, England. The company acts unlawfully and, as a result, she is injured.

Katie has a choice. She may bring a claim in Scotland for such compensation as she is entitled to under Scottish law (on the basis that she suffered harm in Scotland, and the contract was performed there). Alternatively, she may claim in England, where the defendant company is domiciled, relying on English law.

European countries

The countries in EFTA and the European Union (Austria, Belgium, Denmark, Finland, France, Germany, Greece, Iceland, Italy, Luxembourg, The Netherlands, Norway, Portugal, Republic of Ireland, Spain, Sweden, Switzerland and the United Kingdom) agreed to have common rules for deciding where a claim should be litigated. The rules are set down in the Brussels and Lugano Conventions.

Generally, claims based on negligence, breach of statutory duty, assault and battery, or other torts (or the local equivalent) should be brought in the country in which the defendant is domiciled, or the country where the harm (injury, financial loss or damage to property) occurred. A person is domiciled in a country if he lives there on more than just a temporary or transient basis. A company is domiciled in a country where it has its 'seat of business' (usually the place where it is incorporated and registered, or where its central management and control is situated).

Where a claim is founded upon a breach of contract (even if it also claims an alternative or additional claim in tort, or the local equivalent), it should be brought in the country where the contract was to be performed.

Anywhere else

It may be possible to bring a claim against a defendant in the English or Welsh courts (see chapter 5 for further information) for an incident that occurred outside the UK or against a member of the EU or EFTA. The claimant must serve the defendant with the Claim Form whilst the defendant is on English or Welsh soil. This may be straightforward if the defendant is a person or company domiciled in the UK but for someone based elsewhere the rule may present considerable practical difficulties. Even if the claim is served on the defendant, he may be able to persuade the court (at a later preliminary hearing) that England or Wales is not a convenient forum to hear the dispute.

CHAPTER 4

HOW DO I BRING OR DEFEND A CLAIM IN COURT?

BEGINNING A CLAIM; THE PAPERWORK

Which court shall I bring my claim in?

The High Court or County court?

Claims such as those covered by the book may begin in the High Court if the amount of the damages claimed is more than £15,000 (unless the claim includes a request for personal injury damages, in which case the claim must be for more than £50,000). Other claims should be started in the County court.

Which High Court or County court?

If the claim is to be brought in the County court, the claimant may issue his claim in any County court in England or Wales. If that particular court is not convenient (for the defendant, claimant or witnesses), the case may be transferred to another County court. Cases brought in the High Court should be brought in the local District Registry (branches of the High Court, manned by High Court Judges in the larger cities across England and Wales, often sharing a building with the local County court). If there is no local District Registry, the claim may be issued at the Royal Courts of Justice in London.

What is the 'Claim Form' and how is it used by the court?

The Claim Form is the form used by the claimant to tell the court the facts of his case, and to request a court order for damages (or other types of relief or remedy, such as injunctions or orders for possession), interest and costs. By issuing a Claim Form, the claimant begins the formal litigation process. The Claim Form and the Defence Form are types of document known as 'statements of case'. These documents assist the judge to learn quickly what the case is about; to realise at a quick glance what the heart of the dispute is; and to appreciate all the significant relevant facts. It is important to remember that a pre-action protocol may apply to your case (please chapter 3 for further information).

Which form do I use?

Claims that do not involve a substantial dispute of fact

If yours is a case that does not involve a substantial dispute of fact, the claim will be dealt with under Part 8 of the Civil Procedure Rules. An example of such a case would be where both parties agree about what has happened, but need a decision on the law applying to the situation. Another example may be where there isn't a dispute over the sum owed by the defendant to the claimant, but the sum simply has not been paid. In such cases, Form N208 should be used. Note that if the case would be more appropriately dealt with under Part 7 or any other procedure, the judge may give directions to this effect.

Claims including a claim for possession of land

Where a person is seeking a court order for the repossession of land (a possession claim), Forms N5, N5B or N6 should be used. N5B is for cases where the landlord wants to recover land (not damages) and legal costs from tenants who have an assured shorthold tenancy. This is known as the 'accelerated possession procedure' and possession may be granted by the judge without the parties attending a hearing. N6 is the form used by a landlord claiming that his tenants have forfeited their tenancy, or that he has some other right of re-entry. Form N5 is the form for other claims for all types of court orders which includes a claim for possession of land or a building.

All other claims

All other claims should be made on Form N1. They will be governed by Part 7 of the Civil Procedure Rules. The majority of all cases will be dealt with under this procedure.

Part 7 claims; how do I fill in the form?

The Claim Form (Form N1) can be obtained from the court or from the court service website (www.courtservice.gov.uk). It comes with comprehensive and easy to understand notes to help you fill it in. See example at Appendix 8.

What are the 'Particulars of Claim'?

The front page of the Claim Form asks the claimant for a brief statement about the type of claim, such as:

Example 1: A claim for damages for personal injury and damage to property arising from a road traffic accident

or

Example 2: A claim for damages for stress, anxiety and damage to property under the Protection from Harassment Act 1997.

The most important part of the claim, however, is the section called the 'Particulars of Claim'. The claimant uses this to identify all the key facts of his claim – to set out the legal justification for the case and to request for a particular remedy (such as damages, an injunction, interest and costs). Examples of Particulars of Claims for various types of cases are set out at Appendix 1.

The Particulars can be written in the box on the form, or written on separate sheets of paper and attached to the form. If the Particulars are on separate sheets of paper, remember to head the document with the claim number, the name of the court and the full names of each of the parties identified as claimant or defendant, etc. If you wish, the Particulars may be sent to the defendant to arrive within 14 days of the date of issue of the claim, in which case, write in the box on Form N1 'the Particulars of Claim will follow'.

Finally, the Claim Form (and the Particulars of Claim if they are contained on separate sheets of paper) must be verified by a statement of truth.

Are there any matters that must be included in the Particulars of Claim?

Below are checklists of statements that must be included in the Particulars of Claim in various types of cases.

All cases

- A statement as to the claimant's capacity if he is claiming as someone's representative, rather than for himself (such as an executor).

- A statement that the claimant seeks an award of interest on damages under section 69 of the County Courts Act 1984, or section 35A of the Supreme Court Act 1981 or a contract. Where the claim is for a specified amount, the claimant must also state the rate of interest (a percentage), the date from which interest is claimed, the date to which interest is claimed (this date cannot be later than the issue date) and, where applicable, the ongoing daily amount of interest. For further details on whether you can claim interest on damages, and how to calculate the figures, please see chapter 2.

- Any allegation of fraud, illegality or misrepresentation by the defendant or any other relied upon by the claimant in support of his claim, together with full details.

- Where the claimant relies upon an allegation that the defendant (or someone else) knew about a relevant fact or had notice of it, together with full details.

- Any facts proving that the claimant has mitigated his loss or damage.

- Where the defendant is the Crown, a statement of all the circumstances which gave rise to the liability of the Crown, and details of the officers of the Crown or government departments concerned. (NB: This book does not specifically cover the procedure in cases against the Crown. In the High Court, the case will be governed by Order 77 of the Rules of the Supreme Court (contained in schedule 1 of the Civil Procedure Rules 1998) and in the County court, County Court Rule 42 will apply (contained in schedule 2 of the Civil Procedure Rules 1998.))

Personal injury claims

- The claimant's date of birth.

- Brief details of the claimant's injuries.

- A schedule of past and future expenses or losses (sometimes known as 'special damages') that forms part of the Particulars of Claim. Please see the example on the following page.

Example schedule of special damages

CASE NO: 758FK947

IN THE ANYTOWN COUNTY COURT

BETWEEN

MISS HARRIET CHURCH — Claimant

and

MRS RACHEL GOLDSTEIN — Defendant

SCHEDULE OF SPECIAL DAMAGES

[List here all the expenses, e.g.

Analgesic tablets: 3 per week for 4 weeks at £1.89 each – £22.68

Four visits to the consultant at Anyshire County Hospital:

Round trip = 32 miles @ 36p per mile – £46.08

Net lost earnings: 1 week beginning 19 January 2004 – £75.00

Total £143.76]

- Where provisional damages are claimed, a statement that an award of provisional damages is claimed under section 51 of the County Courts Act 1984 (County court cases) or under section 32A of the Supreme Court Act 1981, as well as a statement that there is a chance that the claimant will suffer a serious disease or experience a serious deterioration in his physical or mental condition (and name the disease or type of deterioration) which may form the basis of a later application for damages.

- The report of a medical expert concerning the claimant's personal injuries.

- In clinical negligence claims, the words 'clinical negligence' should be written at the top of every statement of case, including the Particulars of Claim and the Claim Form.

Fatal accident claims

- A statement that the claim is brought under the Fatal Accidents Act 1976.

- A list of the dependants of the deceased for whom the claim is brought, together with the date of birth of each of them.

- Full details of the nature of the dependants' dependency on the deceased.

Relying on the defendant's conviction for an offence

- A statement on the type of conviction.

- The name of the court where the conviction took place.

- A statement as to which issue in the case the conviction is relevant to.

Where the claim relates to a contract or agreement

- If the contract was written (or partly contained in writing) a copy of the contract or the contractual documents, including any standard terms or conditions (or where bulky, a copy of the relevant portions).

- If the contract was made orally (or partly orally), details of exactly who said what to whom, when and where, as the parties formed the contract.

What other documents should I attach to the Claim Form?

- A schedule of past and future expenses and losses.

- Any contractual documents (see above).

- Any medical reports (see above).

- A notice of funding arrangement (Form N251) where a CFA is in place.

How many copies should I make?

- One for the court (the original).

- One for each defendant.

- At least one for your own records.

Part 8 claims; how do I fill in the Claim Form?

Are there any matters that must be included in the details of the claim?

The details of the claim is a section of the N208 Claim Form where the claimant must summarise the legal basis of his claim and request his remedy (damages, injunction, etc – please see chapter 2). The details should be typed or written on the form itself (it will not usually be necessary for you to use a separate sheet of paper). The following matters must also be included:

- A statement that 'Civil Procedure Rules 1998, Part 8 applies to this claim'.

- Any Act of Parliament that forms the basis of a claim.

- The capacity the claimant is suing in, if he is a representative for someone else.

- The capacity of the defendant, if he is being sued as someone else's representative.

What documents should I attach to the form?

Evidence (such as witness statements or affidavits* together with any exhibits) should be sent to the court with the Claim Form at the time of issue of the claim. Note that the claimant may also rely on the facts set out in the details of the claim as long as it is verified by a statement of truth. See chapter 3. Note that when the defendant has responded to the claim by filing his evidence, the claimant can (within 14 days of receiving it) send further evidence in reply to the court.

How many copies should I make?

- One for the court (the original).

- One for each defendant.

- At least one for your own records.

Possession claims; how do I fill in the Claim Form?

Which court shall I bring the claim in?

The High Court

Claims should only be brought in the High Court if the case involves complicated disputes of fact, points of law of general importance, or (in urgent cases against trespassers) where there is a substantial risk of public disturbance or serious harm to persons or property. A certificate (verified by a statement of truth) stating the reasons for bringing the claim in the High Court must accompany the Claim Form when it is submitted to the court for issue. Do not forget that the High Court sits not only at the Royal Courts of Justice in London, but also at District Registries in cities around the country. If the claim is wrongly started in the High Court, the judge may transfer it to the County court, or may strike out the case, leaving the claimant to begin again in the correct court (and probably leaving him out of pocket for his legal expenses).

The County court

All other claims which include a claim for possession of land should be started in the County court which covers the area where the land in question is situated.

Which form should I use?

Claims against assured shorthold tenants for possession only

Form N5B should be used for claims against the tenant of residential premises renting under an assured shorthold tenancy where only possession (not rent or damages) is sought. Such claims are dealt with in the special procedure known as the 'accelerated possession procedure'. For further information on assured shorthold tenancies, please see chapter 1.

Other claims for possession together with other remedies

Form N5 is used for other claims where possession of land or buildings is sought. The Particulars of Claim should be attached to the Claim Form – using either N119 (cases against tenants of rented residential premises based upon non-payment of rent) or Form N121 (cases against trespassers). See below for what information must be included in the Particulars of Claim.

How soon will the court hear my case (the situation is urgent)?

Note that where the case is urgent, and violence has or may be used against the landlord (or someone else), or there is a danger that the property will be damaged or further damaged, it is possible to apply for the court to grant an early appointment. Usually the hearing date will be a minimum of 28 days from the date the Claim Form was issued (or five days in the case of residential property in trespass cases, or two days where the land trespassed upon is not residential premises). The claimant in such cases should complete Application Notice Form N244 and submit it to the court with the Claim Form and the Particulars of Claim.

I do not know the names of the trespassers on my property; can I claim?

Yes. The defendants will be labelled 'persons unknown' and they are served with the claim documents by posting a copy through the letterbox to the property in a transparent envelope marked 'to the occupiers' and by attaching a further copy to the main door of the building (or other similar obvious place). Where non-residential property is occupied by trespassers, sufficient copies of the claim documents should be placed in transparent (weatherproof!) envelopes and attached to stakes driven into the land at suitably prominent places. Remember that you must give the court sufficient transparent envelopes and stakes to do this.

Are there any matters that must be included in the Particulars of Claim?

Below are checklists of information which must be included in the claimant's Particulars of Claim for the various types of cases.

All cases

- A statement that the claimant seeks an award of interest on damages under section 69 of the County Courts Act 1984, or section 35A of the Supreme Court Act 1981, or a contract. Where the claim is for a specified amount, the claimant must also state the rate of interest (a percentage), the date from which interest is claimed, the date to which interest is claimed (this date cannot be later than the issue date) and, where applicable, the ongoing daily amount of interest. For further details regarding whether you can claim interest on damages, and how to calculate the figures, please see chapter 2.

- Information identifying the land (or building) involved, such as the address.

- Confirmation that the land (or building) is residential property (if it is!).

- A statement of the legal ground on which possession is claimed.

- Full details of the relevant tenancy agreement (lease), with copies attached of any written agreement.

- Details of all those people known to be in possession of the property.

- A statement of truth should be included, signed and dated at the end of the Particulars of Claim saying, 'I believe that the facts stated in these Particulars of Claim are true'.

Claims against residential tenants

Form N119 sets out the information required in rent arrears cases. The form can be obtained from the court office or from www.courtservice.gov.uk. Do not forget to submit a 'rent statement' with the forms. This is a table setting out the following information:

- The date when each item of rent became due.

- The amount of each item of rent which became due.

- The dates and amounts of all payments made by the defendant.

- A running total of arrears.

- A statement of truth should be included, signed and dated at the end of the Particulars of Claim saying, 'I believe that the facts stated in these Particulars of Claim are true'.

Claims against trespassers

Form N121 sets out the information required in cases against trespassers and can be obtained from the court office or from www.courtservice.gov.uk. Witness statements supporting the case must be submitted to the court with the Claim Form.

A statement of truth should be included, signed and dated at the end of the Particulars of Claim saying, 'I believe that the facts stated in these Particulars of Claim are true'.

How many copies should I make?

- One for the court (the original).

- One for each defendant.

- At least one for your own records.

When do I have to send my evidence to the court and other party?

The general rule is that a claimant must deliver the witness statements he intends to rely on in support of his claim to the court and to the defendant so that they arrive at least two days before the hearing date. However, in claims against trespassers, the claimant must send his witness statements with the Claim Form.

How is the claim issued?

Retaining a copy of the Claim Form and enclosures, send or take the documents to the relevant court. Do not forget to pay the issue fee! The court will issue it by stamping its seal on the documents together with the day's date.

What is 'service' of the Claim Form and how is it done?

The court will send copies of the Claim Form as well as other documents and the relevant response forms to the defendants.

RESPONDING TO THE CLAIM

Choosing whether to admit or deny liability

What is the claimant's case? You will need to read the Claim Form carefully to discover what the claimant is claiming. If a pre-action protocol applies and has been followed, you will already know quite a lot about the claimant's case, and your own. Please refer to chapter 3 for further information on pre-action protocols.

Consider whether you have a defence to the claim (see Defences at chapter 1). If so, you will need to tell the court what is in the document known (imaginatively!) as a 'Defence'. The sample Defence paragraphs in Appendix 2 show you how to deal with parts of the Particulars of Claim that are agreed, 'not admitted', or denied. It is important to deal with each allegation separately as it helps clarity. The Defence should set out your version of events clearly.

Even if you deny liability for the claim, or dispute the amount of damages claimed, some facts will probably be agreed by both parties, for example, the date of an accident, the fact of an injury (although not necessarily the extent) or the terms of a contract.

Evidence of agreed matters does not need to be heard at trial – the parties simply tell the judge the facts that are agreed. The more that is agreed between the parties, the less there is for the judge to decide and the more focus there will be on the important issues that are really in dispute. It is thus possible to agree certain matters without prejudicing your defence generally. Moreover, the trial will consequently be shorter and the legal costs will be smaller.

Responding to Part 7 claims

What is the 'Response Pack'?

The 'Response Pack'* contains a number of forms and helpful explanatory notes. If the claim is for a specified amount, the pack will contain the Admission Form N9A, a Defence and Counterclaim Form N9B and an Acknowledgement of Service Form N9. If the claim is for an unspecified amount (where the claimant is asking the court to assess the amount of damages), then Admission Form N9C, Defence and Counterclaim Form N9D and an Acknowledgement of Service Form N9 will be included. Only one (or possibly two) of the forms will be relevant to your situation, so choose carefully. Do not ignore the Claim Form; it will not go away! If you do nothing, the claimant may apply to the court for a 'judgment in default' (see Cutting litigation short; avoiding a trial) and either order you to pay a sum or list the case for a hearing to decide what sum you will have to pay.

What are the options?

- To admit liability for the whole claim – complete the Admission Form (N9A or N9C).

- To deny liability (and/or to counterclaim against the claimant) – complete Defence Form N9B or N9D).

- To admit liability for part of the claim, but deny some of it – complete both the Admission Form (N9A or N9C) and the Defence and Counterclaim Form (N9B or N9D).

- To obtain a little more time to prepare your defence, return the Acknowledgement of Service Form N9. You must then send the court your defence to arrive 28 days after the date the Particulars of Claim was received (these may have been included on the Claim Form itself).

- Do nothing. The claimant may obtain a judgment against you (see below). A failure to obey court orders is punishable by the court.

How do I fill in the forms?

Read the notes accompanying the forms carefully. The forms themselves are designed to be user-friendly. If in doubt, seek legal advice from a solicitor, Citizens Advice Bureau or law centre (see chapter 3 for further information).

Wording the Defence

The Defence should be as carefully and clearly worded as the Particulars of Claim should be. The paragraph should set out the defendant's position in relation to every fact alleged by the claimant. Each fact may be 'admitted' (i.e. agreed), 'not-admitted' or denied. A fact should be 'not-admitted' when the defendant is not in a position to agree or deny it – he leaves it for the claimant to call evidence to prove it. Where the defendant denies a particular fact, he should also assert his version of events.

Example: Miss Green and Mr Blue have a road traffic accident which damages the two vehicles and injures Miss Green. Miss Green brings a claim against Mr Blue. She claims damages for repairs to her car that she has already paid for (special damages). She provides an original receipt from the garage showing that the repairs cost £3,005.74. Miss

Green also produces medical evidence that she has suffered from a whiplash injury to her neck. She wants to obtain damages for this injury (general damages).

Mr Blue does not accept that his driving caused the accident and instead blames Miss Green's driving. He therefore wishes to deny liability and wants to claim damages against Miss Green for the cost of repairs of his vehicle – estimated at £545. However, Mr Blue agrees that the damage to Miss Green's car was caused by the accident, it was reasonable of her to have her car repaired in the circumstances and the amount charged by the garage was also reasonable.

Mr Blue should complete the Defence and Counterclaim Form. The facts that he admits are: the date and time of and parties involved in the accident, and the cost of the repairs at £3005.74. The facts that he does not admit include the fact, extent and prognosis of her injury. The facts he denies include that he drove negligently and that his driving caused the accident. He should assert that Miss Green's driving was negligent, that she caused the accident, that the accident caused damage to his own car, and that the bill for repairing it will be £545.

The sample defence paragraphs in Appendix 2 show how to deal with parts of the Particulars of Claim that are agreed, or not admitted or denied.

Disputing the schedule of past and future expenses (known as 'special damages')

If a 'schedule of past and future losses and expenses' has been served and you wish to dispute some or all of the items, you should set out your responses in a counter-schedule. This follows the same pattern as the schedule of special damages and is designed for everyone to see at a glance what is agreed and what is still in dispute. You should make it clear if you agree or disagree with:

- the type of expense claimed – was it reasonably incurred?
- the amount of the expense, or the value of the loss (is it a reasonable amount in the circumstances?).

Wording the counterclaim

The counterclaim is the section of the form used by the defendant to assert his own claim for damages or other remedy against the claimant. It should be worded very carefully so as to be as clear and concise as possible. In fact, the most convenient style to use is that of the Particulars of Claim which it is equivalent to. Please see the discussion on making claims above and also the sample Particulars of Claim at Appendix 1.

Responding to Part 8 claims

What are the options?

- Not to contest the claim. Fill in the Acknowledgement of Service Form N210 and return it to the court office – the Notes for the Defendant (Part 8 Claims) enclosed with the court papers set out how the time limits are calculated. The hearing, in which you may also take part, will then go ahead and the judge will make the appropriate order.

- To contest the claim, complete the Acknowledgement of Service Form N210 and return it to the court office – the Notes for the Defendant (Part 8 Claims) enclosed with the court papers set out how the time limits are calculated. If you wish to rely on any written evidence (such as contracts and witness statements), attach them to the form and send it to the court. The case will be heard at the appointment given by the court, and the judge will make the appropriate order.

- To contest the jurisdiction of the court, complete the relevant section in the Acknowledgement of Service Form N210. The court will then set a date for hearing the application.

- To object to the use of the Part 8 procedure, complete the relevant section in the Acknowledgement of Service Form N210.

- To do nothing. The effect of ignoring the claim is that although you may attend any appointment or hearing in the case, you may not take part in it until the judge gives specific permission for you to do so.

Responding to possession actions

What are the options (possession claims against tenants)?

- Not to contest the claim. There is no requirement to fill in any forms.

- To contest the claim, complete the Defence Form N11 (or N11R if you are a tenant of residential premises being sued by your landlord).

- To do nothing. The hearing will go ahead at the appointed time. Although you may participate at the hearing (e.g. you can make submissions to the judge and call witnesses), your failure formally to let the claimant and court know of your defence may result in the hearing being adjourned with directions on how the case is to be conducted, and may result in you having to pay a percentage of the claimant's legal costs.

What are the options (accelerated procedure possession claims)?

- Not to contest the claim. There is no need to fill in any forms.

- To contest the claim, complete Form N11B.

- To do nothing. The hearing will go ahead at the appointed time. Although you may participate at the hearing (e.g. you can make submissions to the judge and call witnesses), your failure formally to let the claimant and court know of your defence may result in the hearing being adjourned with directions on how the case is to be conducted, and may result in you having to pay a percentage of the claimant's legal costs.

What are the options; claims against trespassers (including squatters)?

- Not to contest the claim.

- To contest the claim, complete the Defence Form N11.

- To do nothing. The hearing will go ahead at the appointed time. You may participate at the hearing (e.g. you can make submissions to the judge and call witnesses), although the hearing may have to be adjourned with directions.

WHAT HAPPENS NEXT?

Allocation of the case to a trial 'track'

Once a Defence has been filed at court, the court sends each party an allocation questionnaire*. This must be completed and returned within a particular time.

What is the 'small claims track', and when does it apply?

The court will allocate* the case to the most appropriate 'track'. The 'small claims track' is designed for cases where the claimant's claim is for less than £5,000. If the claim is a personal injury case, the only cases allocated to the small claims track will be where the damages for pain, suffering and loss of amenity are worth less than £1,000 and the total damages claimed are less than £5,000. Possession claims can only be allocated to the small claims track if all the parties agree. The pre-action protocols do not apply to this track. Many of the other rules are relaxed in relation to the small claims track and the procedure is designed to be used by those with no legal experience. The hearing is informal and there are strict limits on the costs that can be recovered (see below).

What is the 'fast track', and when does it apply?

The 'fast track' is most appropriate for claims that are worth up to £15,000 (including possession claims), where the trial is likely to take only one day in court (five hours), and where only two separate fields of expertise are to be considered by the court. In deciding whether to allocate a case to the fast track, the court will take into account the expert evidence the parties are proposing to bring, the amount of documentary evidence that will be disclosed and relied upon, and whether or not there is a counterclaim. Once allocated to the fast track, the court will issue directions which deal with the bureaucratic steps leading to trial. The aim is to hold the trial for not more than 30 weeks (about seven months) from the giving of directions. Some cases may be suitable for a case management conference* held at court or by telephone conference. This is a hearing at which the court will deal with administrative issues and give directions.

What is the 'multi-track', and when does it apply?

The 'multi-track' is the track suitable for cases that are not suitable for allocation to the small claims or fast track, and also for claims begun under the Part 8 procedure (see above). This will include cases that are worth more that £15,000 and those that involve a great deal of expert evidence, complex legal argument, or where the trial is likely to take more than one day. The court will give directions, usually at a case management conference. Unlike fast track cases, however, the court will not set a trial date at this stage.

Directions for trial

The court has wide powers to make directions for the preparation of the case for trial. It can make directions of its own initiative, or grant a direction sought by one of the parties. It is quite common that parties will be able to agree a timetable of steps. Unless one of the parties is being very controversial or is delaying, the court is usually happy to make the agreed order. This has the advantage that the timetable of directions will suit the needs of the parties from the outset and avoid the need of extensions of time which may imperil the readiness for trial.

Small claims directions

Usually standard directions are issued by the court and sent to the parties, although in unusual cases the court may make different directions. The parties may also ask for specific directions by filling in an Application Notice. The standard directions are various lists of requirements for use in:

- road traffic accident cases;
- building disputes;
- vehicle repairs and other contractual disputes;

- landlord and tenant disputes (the return of deposits and claims for damage caused by tenants);

- holiday and wedding claims.

There is also a list of standard directions for the court to issue when none of the above apply.

Fast and multi-track directions

Often it is possible (and it is certainly desirable) for the parties to agree between themselves what directions to suggest to the court. Such an agreement would, in some circumstances, avoid the parties having to come to court for a separate directions hearing. The court will usually order the:

- disclosure of documents;

- exchange of witness statements;

- exchange of experts' reports; and

- completion of listing questionnaires* (see below for further information).

Each party must write a list of all the documents in his possession that relate to the case. The list should comprise documents that form part of his case (e.g. his medical records or repair estimates), documents adverse to another party's case and documents adverse to his own case. The list of documents is sent to the other parties, who then may 'inspect' the documents listed (i.e. physically looking at the documents and making photocopies). It is becoming normal practice for a party to send photocopies of the documents mentioned in the list when the list is sent, which avoids the need of the receiving party formally inspecting them at the opponent's premises. Of course, if a pre-action protocol applies to the case, the parties are expected to have done a great deal of this information (sharing about their respective cases) before even the Claim Form was issued.

Directions in Part 8 claims

Part 8 claims are automatically allocated to the multi-track. A hearing date will be fixed by the court shortly after the claim is issued. At the hearing the judge may hear the evidence and the claimant's legal arguments, give his judgment and make orders; or he may give directions about the further management of the case and put off the trial until a later date.

Note that a summary judgment* (discussed below) is available for Part 8 claims. Judgments in default of defence* are not.

Witness statements

What are 'witness statements' and how are they used in court?

The general rule is that at trial, evidence is given orally. However, 'witness statements' are crucial to the preparation of trial. A fundamental principle in English law is that each party should know what case the other party will be putting, so that he has time to prepare to deal with it. Witness statements are therefore exchanged before the trial so that all the parties may examine the evidence brought by the other side. Additionally, written evidence in the form of witness statements will (usually) be read by the judge prior to the trial, which saves court time. Finally, when a witness goes into the box to give his evidence he will usually only be asked to confirm the contents of the statement. With the permission of the court he may make any clarifying points (hopefully not necessary) and bring the court up to date on any events or developments since the statement was signed. Apart from this 'introductory and clarificatory' evidence, almost all of the oral evidence given by a witness will be his cross-examination evidence. The witness statement should therefore be as detailed as possible.

What information should be included in the witness statement?

The witness statement should:

- identify the witness' name and address;

- tell the witness' own story (identifying those parts which are his own direct knowledge and those parts which he knows from another source ('hearsay'* – see below));

- be verified by a statement of truth;

- be signed and dated;

- 'exhibit' copies of documents mentioned in the witness statement in a separate document (see the sample witness statement below);

- give a page reference in the margin of the witness statement for any document mentioned;

- be in the following form: on A4 paper with a 3.5cm margin; typed only on one side of each page, bound together securely (i.e. by stapling the top left-hand corner – this does not interfere with filing), have the paragraphs and pages numbered, and have any corrections initialled.

What is 'hearsay'?

Usually one gives evidence of matters that one has experienced, for example, an eyewitness account of an accident. Sometimes, however, knowledge of a fact comes from a different source – an example may be an account of what one has read in a newspaper, or

Example witness statement

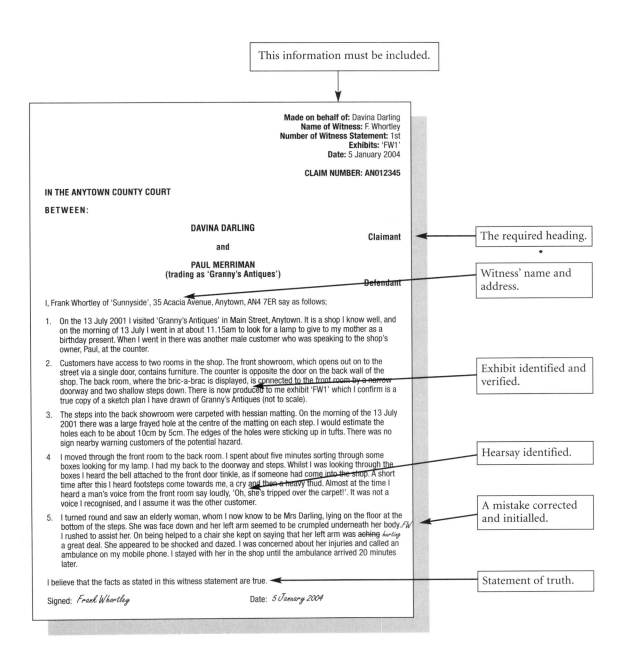

> This information must be included.

Made on behalf of: Davina Darling
Name of Witness: F. Whortley
Number of Witness Statement: 1st
Exhibits: 'FW1'
Date: 5 January 2004

CLAIM NUMBER: AN012345

IN THE ANYTOWN COUNTY COURT

BETWEEN:

DAVINA DARLING

Claimant

and

PAUL MERRIMAN
(trading as 'Granny's Antiques')

~~Defendant~~

> The required heading.

> Witness' name and address.

I, Frank Whortley of 'Sunnyside', 35 Acacia Avenue, Anytown, AN4 7ER say as follows;

1. On the 13 July 2001 I visited 'Granny's Antiques' in Main Street, Anytown. It is a shop I know well, and on the morning of 13 July I went in at about 11.15am to look for a lamp to give to my mother as a birthday present. When I went in there was another male customer who was speaking to the shop's owner, Paul, at the counter.

2. Customers have access to two rooms in the shop. The front showroom, which opens out on to the street via a single door, contains furniture. The counter is opposite the door on the back wall of the shop. The back room, where the bric-a-brac is displayed, is connected to the front room by a narrow doorway and two shallow steps down. There is now produced to me exhibit 'FW1' which I confirm is a true copy of a sketch plan I have drawn of Granny's Antiques (not to scale).

> Exhibit identified and verified.

3. The steps into the back showroom were carpeted with hessian matting. On the morning of the 13 July 2001 there was a large frayed hole at the centre of the matting on each step. I would estimate the holes each to be about 10cm by 5cm. The edges of the holes were sticking up in tufts. There was no sign nearby warning customers of the potential hazard.

4. I moved through the front room to the back room. I spent about five minutes sorting through some boxes looking for my lamp. I had my back to the doorway and steps. Whilst I was looking through the boxes I heard the bell attached to the front door tinkle, as if someone had come into the shop. A short time after this I heard footsteps come towards me, a cry and then a heavy thud. Almost at the time I heard a man's voice from the front room say loudly, 'Oh, she's tripped over the carpet!'. It was not a voice I recognised, and I assume it was the other customer.

> Hearsay identified.

5. I turned round and saw an elderly woman, whom I now know to be Mrs Darling, lying on the floor at the bottom of the steps. She was face down and her left arm seemed to be crumpled underneath her body. *FW* I rushed to assist her. On being helped to a chair she kept on saying that her left arm was ~~aching~~ *hurting* a great deal. She appeared to be shocked and dazed. I was concerned about her injuries and called an ambulance on my mobile phone. I stayed with her in the shop until the ambulance arrived 20 minutes later.

> A mistake corrected and initialled.

I believe that the facts as stated in this witness statement are true.

> Statement of truth.

Signed: *Frank Whortley*   Date: *5 January 2004*

Example witness statement (continued)

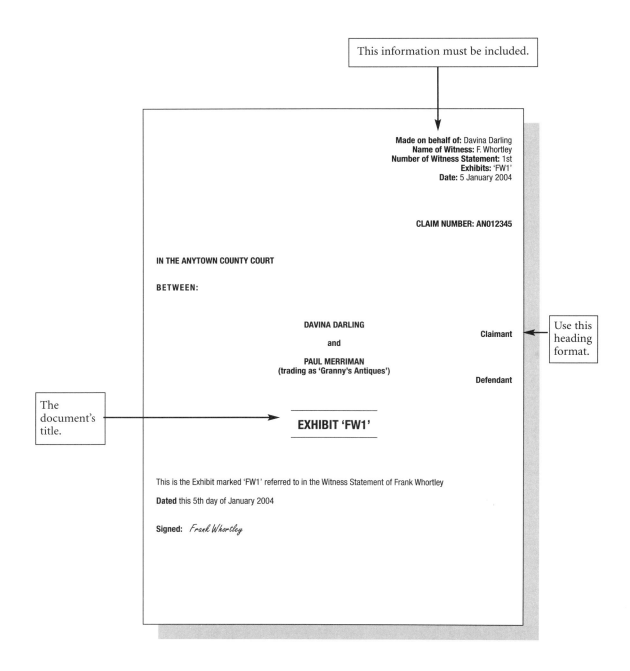

This information must be included.

Made on behalf of: Davina Darling
Name of Witness: F. Whortley
Number of Witness Statement: 1st
Exhibits: 'FW1'
Date: 5 January 2004

CLAIM NUMBER: AN012345

IN THE ANYTOWN COUNTY COURT

BETWEEN:

DAVINA DARLING

and

PAUL MERRIMAN
(trading as 'Granny's Antiques')

Claimant

Defendant

Use this heading format.

EXHIBIT 'FW1'

The document's title.

This is the Exhibit marked 'FW1' referred to in the Witness Statement of Frank Whortley

Dated this 5th day of January 2004

Signed: *Frank Whortley*

recounting what another person told one. This latter category is known as 'hearsay'. An example of hearsay evidence* is given in the sample witness statement on page 149.

The witness, Frank Whortley, gives evidence that he heard someone say, 'Oh, she's tripped over the carpet!' The fact that Frank heard someone speak the words is direct evidence – he heard the words spoken. However, it is only hearsay evidence of the fact that Mrs Darling actually tripped over the carpet. Frank cannot know that she tripped over the carpet because he did not see her do so. He is passing on the eyewitness evidence of another person. The only people who can give direct evidence of the fact that Mrs Darling tripped over the carpet are the customer and Mrs Darling herself. Frank's evidence is useful in that he can give direct evidence of the surrounding circumstances, particularly the position Mrs Darling was in after she had fallen.

The court can listen to hearsay evidence, but it may not attach a great deal of weight to it. First-hand evidence will always be preferable, partly because it can be tested by cross-examination (and is therefore fairer to other parties), but mainly because it is (perhaps) less likely to be distorted by being passed from person to person (as in the game of Chinese whispers). It is therefore important to identify the source of the information contained in a witness statement. It is also important to obtain as much direct or first-hand evidence as possible, rather than relying on hearsay evidence. Think carefully about what evidence needs to be given and who can give it.

As with other court documents, a witness statement should be verified by a statement of truth. If you sign a statement of truth without believing the facts are true, you are in contempt of court, for which you may be tried and punished with imprisonment.

What is 'expert evidence' and how is it used?

The court has a duty to restrict 'expert evidence' to that which is reasonably required to resolve the proceedings. Usually the matter of experts will be dealt with by the parties under the pre-action protocols, before the courts ever get involved (see chapter 3 for further information on pre-action protocols). In straightforward personal injury cases, only medical expert evidence is required. In other cases, various other professionals may be needed to assist the court. The expert's duty is first to the court. The report (which is equivalent to his witness statement) must contain a statement of truth and a declaration that he understands his primary duty to the court and that he has complied with that duty.

Sometimes a single expert will be jointly instructed by the parties. In other cases, each party may call an expert witness. In any case, the court's permission to rely on the expert must be sought. This will usually be given when the court gives directions.

The general rule is that an expert witness will not be required to attend the trial to give oral evidence. His report will stand as his evidence. Parties that wish to clarify a point made by another party's expert may ask him written questions about his report. This must be done within 28 days of receiving his report. The answers given are treated as part of the report. Sometimes the court will order two (or more) expert witnesses of the same field to conduct an experts' meeting (by telephone or face to face) in order to draw up a 'statement of agreed facts' or a 'statement of issues in dispute'. If an expert's report seems to be controversial or there is a dispute between the experts, it may be appropriate for the party wishing to cross-examine the other side's expert to ask the court to order that the expert attend the trial in order to give oral evidence.

What are 'listing questionnaires'?

The court may send out 'listing questionnaires' and parties will have a certain time in which to complete them. As the name implies, a listing questionnaire is a form that enables the administrative staff at the court to allocate resources to the case. It describes how many witnesses will be called by a party, whether any special facilities will be needed by any of them (e.g. an interpreter), how long the case is likely to last, the level of judge required and whether any further applications are likely to be made, etc.

APPLICATIONS IN THE PERIOD BEFORE TRIAL

There are many reasons why it will be necessary for a party to apply to the court for a particular order or permission. A party may want an extension of time to comply with a court order, or permission to rely on further evidence, or to vary directions made by the court. Where a party has failed to file a defence, the claimant may ask the court for a default judgment. Similarly, where either the claimant or the defendant feels that the other party has no reasonable prospects of success and there is no other reason why there should be a trial, he can apply to the court for a 'summary judgment'. All such applications are made on Form N244 (an Application Notice), which should be sent to the court where the claim is being dealt with. Further copies of the form and the evidence referred to in the form should be served on the other parties in the case.

Usually the court will consider whether or not it can deal with the application fairly without a hearing and, if a hearing is necessary, it will set a date and inform all the parties. The normal rule is that a respondent to an application should have three clear days' notice of the application before the hearing date. On rare emergency occasions, a party may go before the court and make his application without telling the other party. This is known as an 'application without notice'. If an order is made, the court will set a new date for a hearing where the application can be fully argued by both sides.

CUTTING LITIGATION SHORT; AVOIDING A TRIAL

The claim/defence is weak; do we have to wait for a full trial?

Once the claim and defences have been filed, the preparation for trial begins (see below). However, one shortcut to avoid full trial is available where the case put forward by one of the parties is so weak that it is bound to fail at trial. A party, either the claimant or defendant, can ask the court to look at the evidence filed and give judgment there and then at the preliminary hearing. This is known generally as a 'summary judgment' and is governed by Part 24 of the Civil Procedure Rules 1998.

How do I apply for a summary judgment?

An Application Notice (Form N244, available from the court office) should be completed and evidence, including a witness statement, may be attached. The other party may file evidence in response before the hearing.

At the hearing, the judge will read the statements of the case (the Claim Form, the Particulars of Claim and the Defence Form), the Application Notice and any witness statements. He will then decide (where the application is brought by the claimant) whether the defendant has a real prospect of successfully defending the claim and if there is any other reason for having a trial of the dispute. Where the application is made by the defendant, the judge must decide whether the claimant has a real prospect of succeeding on the claim.

The judge will not try to decide who is telling the truth; that is a decision which is only suitable for trial.

In some circumstances the judge may decide, without being asked, that the claim or defence should be struck out. This may be because the papers filed by the claimant or defendant do not show that there is a reason for bringing or defending the claim. Alternatively, a judge may decide that one of the parties is bound to fail at trial and there is no other reason for trial. In that case, the parties will be told to attend a hearing or take other steps (such as amend their statement of case, or provide more information).

The defendant has not filed a defence; what happens next?

Where the defendant fails to respond to the claim (by filing a Defence Form or an Acknowledgement of Service followed by a Defence Form within the time allowed – see What is the 'Response Pack'? above) the claimant can ask the court to 'enter judgment'. There is no need for a hearing of this application. The effect of obtaining a default judgment is that the defendant is held liable for the claim. The court will decide how much damages should be paid at a disposal hearing*. At such a hearing, only evidence as to the amount of damages will be heard or read. The court will not reopen the issue of liability at the hearing. Directions for the preparation of the disposal hearing will be given in the normal way. Default judgments are not available for Part 8 procedure claims, nor in possession cases.

How do I apply for a default judgment?

Use Form N205B (Notice of Issue (unspecified amount) and Request for Judgment), which the court will have sent you when your claim was issued. Alternatively, you can use Form N227 (Request for Default Judgment).

Note that if your claim is against a child, a patient or your spouse, you must apply for a default judgment by making an application to the court using an Application Notice Form N244 (see Applications in the period before trial, above). In these situations, there will be a hearing of the application for judgment.

THE TRIAL; WHAT TO EXPECT

Preparing for trial

Everyone, of course, will prepare for trial according to their own personality and ability. Just remember, you do not have to be Perry Mason – the aim should be to put your case simply and clearly to the judge. Notes, flow diagrams, checklists and sticky Post-it Notes may come in useful. A highlighter pen and a calculator may also be helpful.

Checklist

After the directions have been given

- Have all the directions been complied with?

- Are there any necessary applications to the court?

- Can the amount of damages be agreed with the other side, subject to the judge deciding who is at fault? (This will avoid the need to prove the amount of your losses.)

Once a trial date has been set

- Have all the directions been complied with?

- Have your witnesses been told the time and place of the trial?

- Have your witnesses confirmed that they will attend?

Preparing for the hearing

- Are there any applications that need to be made?

- List the issues in dispute. Has the amount of damages (if any) or liability been agreed? What parts of each of the witness' evidence are controversial? What parts are not disputed? It will save everyone time and money if you can tell the judge what areas of agreement and disagreement remain. This will enable the judge to focus on the areas he must adjudicate upon.

- Have you prepared the questions you wish to ask in cross-examination?

- What extra information (by way of clarification or updating) should the witnesses give to the court to supplement their witness statements?

- Are you ready to summarise the facts of the case for the judge?

On the day of the trial

- Arrive at court in plenty of time and report in to the usher.

- Read through your witness statement.

- Meet your witnesses (do not discuss their evidence with them, but give them a copy of their statements to read so that they can confirm the contents to the court).

- Are there any last-minute applications that need to be made to the judge? If so, let the other parties know what you are asking for.

During the trial

- It may be helpful to take a note of the evidence given by the witnesses, as well as the judgment delivered at the end.

- Jot down any weaknesses in the other side's case. When you spot any, you can draw the judge's attention to them when you summarise your case.

- Although the court will send out a copy of the order made at the end of the trial, this may take some weeks to be sent to you so it is wise to make a note of the judge's order (if necessary, ask him to read it out aloud at the end).

Arriving at court

Allow enough time and prepare for contingencies

Make sure that you arrive early enough for the hearing or trial. This will give you time to gather your thoughts and prepare yourself for the hearing. It will also give you an opportunity to speak to the other side before going in front of the judge. It may be possible to do a deal on the doorstep of the court. Alternatively, it may be an opportunity to discuss with the other party (especially if he is represented by a lawyer) exactly what issues you agree and disagree about. The more agreement there is, and the more pleasant cooperation between parties, the easier the hearing will be. Of course, this is a matter of personality (your own as well as your opponent's), but you may as well give yourself the opportunity of learning what stance your opponent is taking before the hearing.

Always leave plenty of time for a court hearing. Often a case that is listed for a morning hearing will end up being heard after lunch. This will involve you making appropriate contingency plans (parking, time off work, childcare arrangements, etc). On rare occasions, the judge may feel there is not enough time to hear the case and will adjourn it to another date. The usher and the judge will keep you informed.

Reporting in

The most important person in the whole legal system is the court usher. On arriving at court you must report in to the usher dealing with your particular court. You will first need to identify where your case will be heard. Many courts have a security guard at the door with a list of cases to be heard in each court who will direct parties to the correct courtroom. Otherwise, there will be a case list near the entrance, with lists of where cases will be heard.

The usher will introduce you to your opponents when they arrive and if you need any extra negotiation time, ask the usher to have a word with the judge. Do not leave the building without telling the usher; your case could be called whilst you are away and the case could go ahead without you. Finally, the usher will be able to tell you where to stand in court.

Where to stand and what to wear

There are no rules of court dress for litigants-in-person. Lawyers and judges will wear dark suits and in open court will usually be robed and be wearing wigs.

The trial

Small claims track hearings

The hearing will usually take place in the District Judge's office (known as 'chambers'). Technically, the hearing takes place in public and anyone may come and watch. Usually, only friends and relatives of the parties attend to give moral support and it is very unusual to have members of the public or press at such hearings. If lawyers attend for either party they will not wear robes (or wigs) and neither will the judge. The hearing will be conducted round a table, although in some courts the room may look more like a traditional courtroom. Everyone remains seated throughout.

The judge is addressed as 'Sir' or 'Madam', as appropriate, and has very wide powers to conduct the case as he or she thinks fit. The principal duty is to give each side a chance to put his case. The hearing may take the form of a series of questions from the judge to each side; or it may be more formal, with the claimant putting his case first and the defendant replying.

Witnesses, other than the claimant or defendant, may be asked to wait outside before they give evidence. This is so everyone can see that they have not been influenced by hearing other witnesses giving evidence. Witnesses will not usually give evidence on oath.

At the end of the hearing, the District Judge will give his judgment. He will usually outline the evidence put forward by each party, explain that the claimant (or counterclaimant) must prove the claim 'on the balance of probabilities', make findings of fact and make an order. A typical order where the claimant was successful may read:

1. Judgment for the claimant in the sum of £1,188.99 (damages and interest); payment within 21 days.

2. Defendant to pay to the claimant (sums specified for limited solicitors' costs (if used), witnesses' travel expenses, witnesses' loss of earnings (limited to £50)); payment within 21 days.

Fast track and multi-track trials

The principal differences between fast track and multi-track trials are the rules on legal costs that apply and the length of hearing. Cases that are expected to last only one day (five hours in court) or less will generally be allocated to the fast track.

The judge will be robed, as will any barrister or solicitor appearing. Circuit judges (full-time judges) and recorders (experienced barristers/solicitors who act as judges for a certain period each year) are addressed as 'Your Honour'. District Judges are addressed as 'Sir' or 'Madam'. Justice must be seen to be done and the trial will be conducted in public, which means that anyone may enter the courtroom during the hearing and there are no reporting restrictions. However, the judge may order the hearing to be in private in special circumstances.

After dealing with any applications or 'housekeeping matters' to do with the conduct of the trial, the judge will let the parties know how familiar he is with the papers. All judges are different. Some like to prepare meticulously in advance; many will not have had a chance to look at the papers beforehand (e.g. where the case has only just been assigned to his court). The judge may state clearly how he wants to run the case at the outset.

The running order of a normal trial is as follows:

- The claimant opens the case, briefly explaining the case for the judge.

- The claimant calls his evidence.

- The defendant calls his evidence.

- The defendant makes his closing speech.

- The claimant makes his closing speech.

- The judge gives his judgment there and then and makes the order OR the judge reserves judgment to be given with the appropriate order later.

The claimant's opening speech

Judges may not require the claimant to make an opening speech, especially if the dispute is straightforward. What follows, therefore, is a somewhat artificial example. However, it is better to be prepared and not to have to use it than the other way around!

1. An opening speech should give the judge an overview of the type of case:

   'Your Honour will see from the papers that this is my claim for personal injuries arising from a road traffic accident/an accident at work/contractual dispute arising from the fitting of a kitchen/possession claim, etc.'

2. It also helps to tell the judge what facts are agreed between the parties:

   'We both agree that the accident happened on 3 January 2001, at the junction of Easterhall Lane and Marketcross Avenue. There is no dispute that the accident happened in the dark and that it had just been raining. On that night I was a pedestrian, and the defendant was driving a Ford Fiesta, registration QWE 45T. Your Honour, only liability is in dispute. Special damages have been agreed in the sum of £856.23, and the medical evidence has been agreed.'

3. ...and what is disputed:

   'My case is that the defendant drove negligently, and knocked me over as I crossed the road. The defendant denies it, and says that she could not avoid the accident. She claims that I ran out in front of her.'

4. Lastly, give an overview of the evidence that will be called by both sides:

   'I will give evidence, as will my sister who was waiting for me on the other side of the road. Mr Smith, an independent witness who saw the accident from a parked car at the junction, will give evidence on my behalf. The defendant is giving evidence for himself, and will also call PC Constable who was called to the scene. The jointly instructed expert is not in court today, but his report is on page 5 of the bundle of papers in front of Your Honour.'

It may also be useful to refer the judge at this point to any documents (such as invoices, receipts, employment records, contracts, etc) relied upon by either party. Often there will be photographs or maps and the judge should be shown these, told whether the claimant or defendant relies upon them, and whether they are agreed on.

The judge SHOULD NOT be told about or shown any without prejudice discussions or letters. He does not find out about any payments into court (see Payments into court, and Part 36 offers) or attempts to settle the case.

The evidence

Witnesses will give evidence on oath (or 'affirmation'*, for those who prefer a secular promise) and will stand in the witness box. Having been asked to confirm their name and address and to verify their signature and the contents of the witness statement, the witness evidence will stand as their actual evidence. The judge may, if he has not had the opportunity to read it, do so at this point in silence, or ask the witness (or advocate) to read it aloud. Some witnesses may need to bring their statements up to date if there have been any developments or changes since they were made.

After a witness gives his evidence, the other party may cross-examine him. This is not an easy technique and advocates have many different styles and approaches. There are two main purposes of cross-examination:

- To challenge the other side's witness with the evidence that you rely on.

- To expose any contradictions, gaps or weaknesses in the other side's case.

Often minute discrepancies in observation or recall may make all the difference – witnesses may be unsure of certain parts of their evidence, or may have made assumptions about what happened that are not upheld by other evidence.

Closing arguments

This is an opportunity for both claimant and defendant to summarise the strengths of his own case and to highlight the weaknesses of the other side's. Any submissions on how the law applies to the case will be made at this stage, for example, references to relevant Acts of Parliament, Regulations, other codes (such as the Highway Code) and case law. Finally, tell the judge what order you are asking him to make (e.g. to dismiss the claim/defence/counterclaim, to award damages, etc).

Costs

The section How do I fund my claim? at chapter 3 discusses how to pay for legal costs from the beginning of the claim. This section sets out the rules used by the court to order one side to pay the other side's costs at the end of the trial.

After giving judgment, the judge will decide if either party should pay the legal costs of the other side. If the court makes no such order, each party simply bears his own costs. Usually the loser will be told to pay the other side's costs (legal and experts' fees, court fees and other expenses). The loser will probably have to pay:

- his own legal bill;

- the legal bill of the other side (after it has been assessed by the court);

- damages.

Of course, as with all costs, a party can only obtain an award for costs that he has incurred, or will incur under a CFA. Therefore, proof of costs by way of receipts, a 'schedule of costs' or a 'bill of costs' may be required by the court.

Small claims costs

The small claims track is designed for litigants who are not represented by a lawyer. As a result, neither party is expected to run up large legal bills and therefore a party may only recover very limited legal costs under the Civil Procedure Rules, Part 27:

Legal costs

- The fixed costs of issuing the claim (between £50 and £80 at present, depending on the size of the claim) if he has used a lawyer to issue the claim.

- Other legal costs where the judge has decided that the other side has behaved unreasonably in the conduct of the case.

Fees and expenses

- Court fees.

- A witness' or party's travel expenses (reasonably incurred) for attendance at the hearing.

- A witness' or party's loss of earnings incurred through attendance at the hearing (limited to £50 each at present).

- The fees of any expert witness (limited to £200 each at present).

Fast track and multi-track costs

The general rules for determining costs apply to both fast track and multi-track cases. The court has a discretion whether to award costs, how much to order a party to pay, and when the payment should be made. The recoverable fees of advocates (barristers or solicitors) attending fast track trials are fixed within certain limits, but, of course, this is only one element of a costs bill. The amount recoverable in respect of an advocate's fee for appearing at trial depends on the amount of the claim:

- Claim value up to £3,000   £350

- £3,000–£10,000   £500

- More than £10,000   £750

The court may, in certain circumstances, award less than the fixed amount (i.e. where there has been a successful counterclaim or where the receiving party has behaved improperly during the trial). The court may order the paying party to pay more than the fixed amount where he has acted improperly or unreasonably during the trial.

Where the party being awarded his costs by the court acted in person, the court may award him two-thirds of the appropriate fee had an advocate attended the trial (as above), if he proves financial loss arising from conducting his own claim. If he cannot prove financial loss, the court will award an amount in respect of the time reasonably spent doing the work, at certain specified rates.

In all multi-track cases and fast track cases where the litigant-in-person who is asking for a costs order is not able to prove financial loss in personally conducting the claim, the rules stipulate that the litigant-in-person can be paid:

1. his expenses (or 'disbursements' in legal speak), including travel expenses to court;

2. recompense for the financial loss involved in preparing the case and attending court (for which supporting documentary evidence should be served 24 hours before the hearing at which costs will be delivered) or £9.25 per hour (current rate covering both attendance at court and hours of preparation), but the sum allowed for this particular type of loss will only be two-thirds of the sum that he would be allowed if he had been represented by a legal representative;

3. the cost of obtaining occasional legal assistance (if incurred reasonably) from a solicitor or barrister, or a 'costs draftsman' (an expert who gives advice on solicitors' bills).

In short, the court will first consider if the other party should pay your costs. It will then consider the evidence of financial loss (e.g. your loss of earnings) during the time you prepared for the case, or attended court hearings. If there is no evidence of financial loss, it will decide that you will be paid at an hourly rate, currently £9.25. The judge will decide if the period you spent in preparing the case and attending court was reasonable, and state what period he thinks would have been reasonable. He will then decide what sum would have been payable if you had instructed solicitors and will not award more than two-thirds of that sum. Finally, the judge will look at all the expenses and disbursements you have incurred and award those. The court must decide whether or not it can assess the costs at the end of a trial (immediately after judgment is given), or whether the complexity of the case and the amount of costs incurred merits a separate hearing in front of a specialist 'costs judge', called a 'detailed assessment' of costs.

A litigant cannot be ordered to pay any costs that are unreasonable in amount or which have been unreasonably incurred. Usually only costs that are proportionate to the dispute will be awarded. Generally, therefore, the paying party will not be ordered to pay the full amount of the other side's costs. Put the other way around, a successful party rarely recoups all his legal costs.

Costs as a sanction against a party

Costs also may be used as a sanction or punishment against a party, for example, if earlier orders of the court or a pre-action protocol are not complied with. On rare occasions, a lawyer who has acted unconscionably or negligently may be ordered to pay any wasted costs personally. On the small claims track mere unreasonable conduct may result in a cost order (see above).

CHAPTER 5

HOW DOES THE COURT ENSURE ITS ORDERS ARE OBEYED?

ENFORCEMENT OF COURT ORDERS

The defendant has not complied with the court order; what can be done?

The court does not automatically compel a person to comply with court orders obtained against him. If the defendant does not do what he is ordered to do (whether pay money to the claimant, or vacate premises, etc) the claimant may obtain further orders from the court to put the original order into effect (by sending in the bailiffs, or putting a charge on the defendant's landed property, etc). To put this another way, the defendant will generally not be punished by the court, and nothing will happen to him when he disobeys a court order, unless the claimant decides to enforce the order by going back to court.

What is 'enforcement' and what are 'enforcement proceedings'?

'Enforcement' and 'enforcement proceedings' are the process by which the claimant obtains the further orders from the court that either compel the defendant to obey the original court order, take what is owed to the claimant or punish the defendant for his disobedience to the court.

What orders are available?

Orders to pay money	• Warrant of execution/writ of fieri facias • Charging order • Third party debt • Attachment of earnings order
Orders to vacate land (possession)	• Warrant or writ of possession
Injunctions and other orders	• Committal for contempt of court
Out of court settlements	• Claim for breach of contract (see chapter 1) • Enforce as other court orders (see Injunctions)

Enforcing orders to pay money (including damages, mesne profits and other judgment debts)

The court ensures the claimant gets his money by a variety of methods. Orders either bypass the judgment debtor's cooperation by seizing or limiting his use of the assets he owns, or require a third party to pay money to the claimant in satisfaction of the original order:

- A warrant of execution (issued by the County court) or writ of fieri facias (issued by the High Court) authorises the County court bailiff or High Court Sheriff to seize and sell goods belonging to the defendant to obtain the money (the judgment debt and the costs of execution) owed to the claimant.

- A charging order places a 'charge' over the defendant's property (such as land, securities or partnership property). This acts in the same way as a homeowner's mortgage; when the charged property is sold, the claimant gets his money from the purchase money. Once a charging order is obtained, the claimant may ask the court for a further order compelling the defendant to sell the property.

- An attachment of earnings order compels the judgment debtor's employer to pay the claimant from the defendant's wages.

- A third party debt order compels someone who owes the judgment debtor money (including a bank where he has a bank account in credit) to pay money to the claimant in satisfaction of the original order.

Warrants of execution and writs of fieri facias

These orders enable the court officer (bailiff or Sheriff) to seize certain goods belonging to the judgment debtor, sell them and pay the proceeds to the claimant to the value of the judgment debt and costs of execution. The Sheriff or bailiff may not force entry into the judgment debtor's premises (except to the outer door of a building or workshop which is not attached to the debtor's dwelling house). Additionally, the Sheriff or bailiff may not remove and sell items that are, broadly, the debtor's tools of trade, and those items (clothes, furniture, etc) that are necessary for his basic domestic requirements and those of his family (section 138(3A) of the Supreme Court Act 1981). Jointly owned items may be seized (although when they have been sold, the bailiff or Sheriff must give the co-owner his share of the proceeds of the sale).

Which order should I obtain?

The County court will issue a warrant of execution. The High Court will issue a writ of fieri facias de bonis ecclesiasticis (known generally as a 'writ of fi.fa.'). They are of identical effect.

In which court should I bring the enforcement proceedings?

Generally, where the sum the judgment creditor (i.e. the person awarded the damages, etc by the judge) is trying to enforce is less than £600, then it must be enforced in the County court. Where the sum is £5,000 or more, it must be enforced in the High Court (unless the case was about a Consumer Credit Act 1974 regulated agreement). Judgment debts worth between £600 and £4,999.99 may be enforced by either the County court or High Court. There are, additionally, some Acts of Parliament which specifically require transfer to the High Court for enforcement; a discussion of these is outside the scope of this book.

To transfer a claim for enforcement from the County court to the High Court the judgment creditor must first apply to transfer the case to the High Court (by filling in an Application Notice N244 and requesting the County court transfer the case to the High Court). Second, the claimant must request a certificate of the judgment from the County court. This is done by making the request in writing asking for the certificate, stating that it is required for the purpose of enforcing the judgment in the High Court and confirming that it is intended to enforce the judgment by execution 'against goods'. The County court will then transfer the case to the High Court.

To transfer a High Court case to the County court for enforcement, file a request for the issue of the warrant at the County court for the area in which the goods (to be seized) are. The County court will issue the warrant and tell the High Court it has done so; the transfer will then be made.

When can the request for a warrant or writ be made?

Usually the court will specify the date by which the judgment debt must be paid (e.g. within 14 days). The right to request a warrant or writ arises when that period has expired without payment. If the court is to assess damages or costs, the right arises when those have been done (and the time to pay has run out). If there is no such period or assessment, then the warrant or writ can be issued immediately.

Note that for County court warrants, if the judgment debt was payable in instalments, no warrant will be issued unless £50 at least is owed, and at least one-monthly or four-weekly instalments are unpaid.

Is there a time limit on asking for such an order?

Permission from the court is required to bring enforcement proceedings more than six years after the judgment was made. Such permission is sought by bringing an application under Part 23 of the Civil Procedure Rules (see chapter 4).

What forms do I fill in?

If the case needs to be transferred to a different court, please see the steps set out above, In which court should I bring the enforcement proceedings? For a County court warrant, use Form N323 (Request for Warrant of Execution). In the High Court, use Form PF86 (Praecipe for Writ of Fieri Facias).

How do I obtain the order?

Make any application to transfer proceedings if necessary (see above). If permission to issue is necessary, make an application to the court for permission (see above). In the County court, file the relevant request. The court officer will then issue the warrant and transfer it to another County court if appropriate. He will also notify the debtor. Execution by the County court bailiffs will not take place for seven days after issue.

In the High Court, file the relevant form at either the District Registry (High Court offices in cities around the country) or the Central Office of the Supreme Court which will issue the writ. The writ must then be taken to the under-Sheriff, or delivered to:

The Sheriffs Lodgement Centre
2 Serjeants Inn, Fleet Street

London EC4Y 1NX
Tel: 020 7353 3640.

Enforcement will then take place.

How long does the warrant/writ remain valid?

The warrant or writ remains valid for one year. After that, a fresh one must be obtained. Note that if the judgment is six years old or over, permission of the court is required before a warrant or writ may be issued.

Charging orders

A charging order is a method of securing a debt on tangible property, usually on land or funds paid into court by the defendant. The charge, once created, affects the owner's dealings with the property. Upon sale of the charged property, the charge entitles the claimant to obtain the money secured by the charge before the defendant gets any money from the proceeds of the sale. Because the court will generally impose a stop notice on the property at the same time as a charging order, the owner's ability to deal with the property (including to sell it) is severely curtailed. The court's powers come from the Charging Orders Act 1979. Such a method of enforcement is only feasible when the judgment debtor owns assets.

Which court should I use?

The general rule is that the application should be made to the court where the judgment itself was made, or to the court where the case has been transferred, or (if the application is to place a charging order on funds paid into court) to the court where the funds are held.

What forms do I fill in?

Form N379 is used to apply for a charging order over land, and Form N380 for a charging order over securities.

How is the application processed?

File the completed form at the relevant court. The form goes before the judge who may make an interim charging order without a hearing (i.e. without requiring the claimant to attend court). He will also set a date for a hearing in which he will decide whether or not to make a final order. The court will then serve copies of the application papers and interim charging order on the judgment debtor.

There will then be a hearing to decide if a final order is to be made. The judgment debtor may wish to oppose the making of such an order, in which case he must file at court (and send to the judgment creditor) a witness statement stating his objections so that they arrive at least seven days before the hearing date. At the hearing, the court will make a decision whether or not to make a final order. It may be necessary to adjourn the hearing to a later date in order to hear the evidence and make a decision on the disputed facts. The court will take all the circumstances into account and either make the interim order final (and impose a stop notice forbidding dealings with the property in question until further order of the court), or else discharge the interim order and dismiss the application.

How do I get my money once a charging order has been made?

Where the property charged under the order is land, it is essential to register the Interim Charge with either the Land Charges Department of HM Land Registry (Plymouth) (where the property in question is 'unregistered'), or with the HM Land Registry in London or the 22 district Registries around the country (registered land). Once there is a final charging order on the property, the claimant can ask the court to order the sale of the property. An application should be made under the Part 8 procedure (see chapter 4), requesting the order for sale, and enclosing a copy of the charging order. Note that if the property charged is owned partly by someone other than the judgment debtor, the law applying to an application for sale is sections 14 and 15 of the Trusts of Land and Appointment of Trustees Act 1996; this is because jointly owned property is held on a 'trust of land'.

Attachment of earnings orders

Attachment of earnings orders are available if the judgment debt still owing is more than £50. Orders are governed by the Attachment of Earnings Act 1971.

Which court do I use?

The County court for the area where the judgment debtor lives (even if the judgment was obtained in the High Court). If the judgment debtor does not live in England or Wales the order should be sought in the County court for the area where the original judgment was made.

What forms do I fill in?

Form N55, the Application for the Attachment of Earnings, which should be available from the court. This should be filed at the appropriate court (see above). If the judgment debtor's employer's details are known, fill in Form N338, which asks the employer for details of the defendant's earnings. These will be served on the judgment debtor with the court papers.

What is the procedure?

The court issues the completed forms, and sends a copy to the judgment debtor. The debtor then has eight days to complete the forms. If he responds and there is enough information about the debtor, the court officer or District Judge may grant the order without a hearing. Alternatively, the District Judge will fix an appointment for the hearing of the application. The hearing will take place and the judge will make the decision having considered the evidence. Either the application will be dismissed, or the order will be made.

If the judgment debtor fails to respond, the court can order him to give details of his employer and information about his financial situation. If he fails to comply, the court can bring proceedings to punish him for his disobedience (see Committal for contempt of court below).

Third party debt orders

Like obtaining charging orders, obtaining a third party debt order is a two-stage process. The order requires a third party (i.e. someone who had nothing to do with the litigation dispute and is not a party to the judgment) to pay money that it owes to the judgment debtor to the claimant instead. Such orders are usually made against a bank or building society with whom the judgment debtor has an account that is in credit (but not, it would seem, the National Savings Bank (*Civil Procedure 2003*, Volume 1, Paragraph 72.1.3, Sweet and Maxwell)). The bank in question must carry on business in England or Wales, or if the third party is a person, he must be within the jurisdiction at the time of the making of the interim order (see below).

Which court do I use?

The order should be sent to the court which gave the original judgment (or, where applicable, the court to which the case has been subsequently transferred).

Which forms do I fill in?

Form N349, Application for Third Party Debt Order.

What is the procedure for obtaining the order?

Give the completed form to the relevant court. The judge usually looks at the application and grants an interim third party debt order, and also sets a date for a hearing to decide if there should be a final third party debt order. He will also make an order forbidding the third party from making any payment of money which reduces the overall third party debt to less than the judgment debt until after the hearing. The interim order and the other documents will then be served upon the third party (at least 21 days before the date set for the hearing) and on the judgment debtor (at least seven days before the date set for the hearing). The decision on whether to make a final order will be taken after the hearing of the evidence and arguments at the hearing.

Can the third party or judgment debtor object to the making of a final order?

Yes. The judgment debtor may object to the making of a final order on the grounds that he objects in principle to the making of an order, that he is not owed money by the third party, or that there is someone else who has a claim to the money which is affected by the interim order (such as a joint account holder). If he intends to do so, he must file evidence to support his objection, such as a witness statement and documentation, at least three days before the hearing. Additionally, if the judgment debtor is in financial difficulties because the account has effectively been frozen until the hearing of the final order application, he may apply to the court for a hardship payment order for payment out of a frozen bank or building society account to meet his ordinary living expenses. Such an application would be made under the Civil Procedure Rules, Part 23 using Form N244.

Enforcing possession orders

Obtaining a warrant or writ of possession (of land)

Where the occupier of land (such as a squatter or sitting tenant) has disobeyed a possession order the claimant is entitled to obtain a warrant of possession (County court cases) or writ of possession (High Court cases). The warrant requests the court bailiff (County court) or Sheriff (High Court) to evict the unlawful occupier. The bailiff or Sheriff may use reasonable force to do so, and anyone found on the premises may also be evicted. Note that a warrant may only be obtained if the possession order has been disobeyed. If the original possession order has been stayed, suspended or has not yet come into effect, the court will not issue a warrant. If the possession order is more than six years old, the owner of the land must obtain the court's permission to the warrant.

In addition to enforcing possession of land, the warrant or writ may also give appropriate orders for the enforcement of money judgments.

Which court do I use?

The court where the possession order was granted.

What forms do I use?

In the County court, use Form N235. In the High Court, use either Form PF88 (Praecipe for Writ of Possession) or Form PF89 (Praecipe for Writ of Fieri Facias and Writ of Possession Combined). For more information as to writs of fieri facias and enforcing money judgments, see above at Enforcing orders to pay money (including damages, mesne profits and other judgment debts). Remember that if the possession order is more than six years old, the landowner who obtained it needs the permission of the court to issue a warrant.

What is the procedure?

In the County court the general rule is that the court, having received the application forms from the person who obtained the original possession order, will issue the warrant without a hearing. The bailiffs will then send the person against whom the order was made a Notice of Eviction, stating the date and time they propose to evict him.

Can the eviction be cancelled or delayed after the warrant has been granted?

In the High Court the court can really only stay the execution of the writ for a moderate period (generally only four to six weeks). In the County court the person who is about to be evicted may apply (urgently if necessary or otherwise with three days' notice) to the court on Form N245 or N244 for a stay or suspension of the warrant. The application may be without notice to the landowner or, which is preferable except in cases of real urgency, will give the landlord a copy of the application and apply to the court for permission to abridge retrospectively the usual notice period. If the court is persuaded to grant the stay or suspension, it may do so for the same periods it can stay or suspend a possession order (please see chapter 1). It may also impose terms or conditions on the person allowed to remain in the property. This may well happen in the case of a tenant, but will not happen in the case of a squatter or other trespasser.

If, after the warrant is executed and the property is vacated, the person evicted (or someone closely associated with him) goes back into the property unlawfully, the landowner may obtain a warrant of restitution (County court) or writ of restitution (High Court), rather than issuing fresh proceedings.

The process of the evicted person setting aside or appealing the making of a possession order is not within the ambit of this book, and reference should be made to specialist textbooks on the subject.

Enforcing injunctions, undertakings and other orders

Committal for contempt of court

A party to litigation may (at any time during the proceedings) apply to 'commit' a party who has disobeyed a court order for contempt of court. It is a draconian order, as the judge has the power to imprison or fine anyone he finds guilty, and therefore will not be used lightly. The court can of 'its own motion' (i.e. its own initiative) commit a disobedient party, but this section will deal only with committal applications in the context of enforcing injunctions and other orders. Committal for contempt is really a punishment rather than a strict enforcement procedure. However, it is primarily used to persuade the contemnor where possible to comply with the order originally made (known as 'purging a contempt').

Is committal available for all court orders?

No. The following factors must all be present:

- The injunction either requires a person to do a specific act within a time limit or generally forbids him to do a particular thing.

- A copy of the judgment or order imposing an injunction has been served personally on the person to whom it is addressed, or where a person made an undertaking to the court, a copy of it was served on him soon after it was made (by either a court officer handing it to him at court, posting it to him or handing it to him by another party).

- An injunction must be endorsed with a Penal Notice (standard Form N77 which warns of the consequences of disobedience).

- The application to commit for breach of an injunction together with any supporting evidence has been personally handed (not posted) to the contemnor.

Committal procedure

Where the case is ongoing, Form N244 should be used. If there is no existing case, use Form N208 and the Part 8 procedure. Once the court receives the paperwork, it will set a date for a hearing to 'show cause why an order committing you to prison should not be made' (known colloquially and somewhat inevitably as a 'show cause hearing'). The hearing will take the form of a mini-trial, and if a finding of guilt is made, the court will go on to make further orders.

Unless orders

Frequently, during the course of litigation, the court will require a party to take a particular action (such as to file or serve documents, for example). If the order is not obeyed, it is open for the other party (or the court itself) to make a further order that if the particular action is not taken, the party's statement of case (claim or defence) will be struck out*. This order is known as an 'unless order'. If the party fails to comply with the unless order, the other party may request judgment using Part 3.5 of the Civil Procedure Rules (where the claim is for money or the return of goods). In this circumstance, there will not be a trial of the merits of the claim or defence – it is akin to an automatic right to win the case on the basis that the claim or defence is unopposed.

However, there is no automatic right to a discretionary remedy such as a declaration (see chapter 2, Other remedies) or an injunction; and for those cases a request for judgment will be governed by the Civil Procedure Rules, Part 23. Discretionary remedies, historically, may only be granted if the judge, in his discretion, agrees that having proved the claim, the merits of the case also warrant such a remedy. On the other hand, damages and other common law remedies are available if the claimant's case is proved.

In circumstances where a negligent driver's insurance company cannot or will not pay, or where the driver is uninsured, the MIB will step into the breach and pay the full amount of the damages awarded. To make a claim, however, the claimant should follow strictly the procedure set out below. Note that all documents must be faxed or sent by recorded/ registered post (even hand-delivery or first-class post is not sufficient). The following checklist shows the steps that must be taken; they basically provide for the MIB to be told of each significant stage in the litigation.

When an uninsured driver won't pay the final sum

Before the claim is issued

1. The claimant must write a letter stating that he has been injured in a road traffic accident as a result of the negligent driving of the person who appears to be uninsured, giving details of the nature of the injuries, expenses and losses. The letter should enclose any police report of the accident and a completed MIB form (available from the Motor Insurers' Bureau, 152 Silbury Boulevard, Central Milton Keynes MK9 1NB).

After the claim has been issued

The claimant must give the following to the MIB:

2. A letter confirming that he has issued a claim against the defendant, enclosing a copy of the sealed (officially stamped) Claim Form and the Particulars of Claim together with all the documents attached to it, a copy of his motor insurance certificate and any correspondence between the claimant and the defendant's solicitors (if there are any) – within 14 days of the issue of the claim (see chapter 4, Beginning a claim).

3. A letter confirming the service of the proceedings on the defendant by the court – within seven days of receiving notice from the court that the proceedings have been served on the defendant (see chapter 4, What is 'service' of the Claim Form and how is it done?).

4. A letter confirming the filing of a defence by the defendant enclosing a copy of the defence – within seven days of it being filed (see chapter 4, Responding to the claim).

5. At least 35 days' notice in writing of the claimant's intention to ask the court for default judgment, where appropriate (see chapter 4, Cutting litigation short; avoiding a trial).

6. A letter informing the MIB of any amendments to the statements of case together with copies of the amended documents – within seven days of the amendments being agreed by the parties or authorised by the court.

7. A letter telling the MIB of the trial date – within seven days of it being given or set down.

After the trial or settlement (when damages have been awarded or agreed)

8. No more than seven days after the damages have become payable, the claimant must inform the MIB in writing that the defendant has not paid the judgment within the time allowed by the judge and request it to pay the sum. A copy of the sealed (officially stamped by the court) court order should be enclosed.

Note that if the MIB does not pay the award, the claimant may bring a fresh claim naming the MIB as the defendant.

APPENDICES CONTENTS

N11R   Defence Form (rented residential premises)
N227   Request for Judgment by Default
N244   Part 23 Applications

9 Questionnaires
N150   Allocation
N170   Listing

10 Forms (enforcement)
N225   Request for Judgment and Reply to Admission
N316   Application for Order that the Debtor Attend Court for Questioning
N323   Request for Warrant of Execution
N324   Request for Warrant of Delivery of Goods
N325   Request for Warrant of Possession of Land
N337   Request for Attachment of Earnings Order
N342   Request for Judgment Summons
N349   Application for Third Party Debt Order

11 Benefits recoverable from the defendant by the Department of Social Security
Employment safety legislation

Appendix 1
PARTICULARS OF CLAIM

Sample 1
Driver's claim for damages against another driver

IN THE ANYTOWN COUNTY COURT
B E T W E E N

MRS JOEY SILVER   Claimant
and
MR MARC DE TROP   Defendant

PARTICULARS OF CLAIM

1. The claimant was at all material times the *[owner]* and driver of a *[make, model, colour and registration number of the vehicle]*.

2. The defendant was at all material times the driver of a *[make, model, colour and registration number of the vehicle]*.

3. At about *[time]* on *[date]* the parties were involved in a collision at the *[describe the place of the accident by reference to road names, road numbers or other local references (such as the 'Dog-and-Duck' roundabout)]* in which the defendant's car collided with the *[rear, side, front, etc]* of the claimant's car.

4. The said collision was caused by the negligence of the defendant in that he:

PARTICULARS OF NEGLIGENCE[1]

[a]   drove too fast in all the circumstances
b)   failed to keep any or proper lookout
c)   overtook the claimant's vehicle when it was unsafe to do so
d)   crossed into the path of the claimant's correctly proceeding vehicle
e)   failed to observe the claimant's right of way and accord the claimant precedence
f)   failed to maintain lane discipline
g)   failed to stop, steer or otherwise control his vehicle so as to avoid colliding with the claimant's vehicle
h)   failed to comply with the [red light showing to him/stop sign/solid white line]
i)   reversed into the claimant's car
j)   failed to indicate his intention/the presence of his vehicle adequately or at all

---

[1] *The following is a list of sample allegations. Not all of them will apply to each case. They demonstrate how the claimant must analyse the accident in terms of precise allegations of wrongdoing. The Particulars of Claim must 'tell the story' of the accident and list the facts the court will hear.*

    k)   failed to heed the warning/indication given by the claimant's vehicle

    l)   drove a vehicle with defective breaks knowing that the said breaks were defective

    m) failed to cause the vehicle's breaks to be adequately maintained.]

5.   The claimant intends to place evidence before the court pursuant to section 11 of the Civil Evidence Act 1968 that the defendant was on *[date]* at *[name and address of the convicting court]* convicted of *[name of the offence]*. The said conviction is relevant to the issue of the defendant's liability for negligent driving as alleged above.[2]

6.   By reason of the above matters the claimant suffered injury loss and damage:

PARTICULARS OF INJURY

[Here give a brief description of the injuries suffered; listing the initial injury, past and anticipated future treatment, the level of care and assistance provided already and expected in the future, the loss of amenity (see section 5.1), the level of disruption to working life and the prognosis.]

The medical report of *[name]* is attached hereto.

PARTICULARS OF LOSS

See the Schedule of Special and General Damages attached hereto.

7.   And the claimant claims interest upon such damages as the court shall award at a rate and for such a period as the court thinks fit, pursuant to *[section 69 of the County Courts Act 1984] [section 35A of the Supreme Court Act].*[3]

AND the claimant claims

a)   Damages *[less than £5,000/more than £5,000 but less than £15,000/more than £15,000]*

b)   Interest as set out above.

STATEMENT OF TRUTH

I believe that the facts stated in these Particulars of Claim are true.

Full name
_____

Name and address of solicitors' firm
[if used]

_____

_____

Signed
_____

ADDRESS FOR SERVICE
OF DOCUMENTS
_____

[Address]

_____

_____

_____

---

[2] *Omit this paragraph if it does not apply to your case.*

[3] *If the case is brought in the High Court, the reference is to section 35A of the Supreme Court Act; in the County Court the power to award interest is created by section 69 of the County Courts Act; delete as applicable.*

Sample 2
Pedestrian's claim against a driver

IN THE ANYTOWN COUNTY COURT
B E T W E E N

MRS JOEY SILVER   Claimant
and
MR MARC DE TROP   Defendant

PARTICULARS OF CLAIM

1. The defendant was the driver of a *[make, model, colour and registration number of the vehicle]* at *[place]* on *[date]* at about *[time]*. The claimant was walking *[describe where]* when the defendant drove his vehicle into a collision with her, knocking her down.

PARTICULARS OF NEGLIGENCE[1]

[a) drove too fast in all the circumstances
b) failed to keep any or a proper lookout for pedestrians such as the claimant
c) overtook another vehicle within the zigzag lines of a pedestrian crossing
d) failed to accord the claimant precedence on the zebra crossing
e) failed to comply with the red light showing to him at the pelican/toucan/puffin crossing
f) failed to accord the claimant precedence on the pelican crossing [whilst the amber light was flashing] [when the amber light had finished flashing and a green light was showing whilst the claimant was still crossing]
g) failed to stop, steer or otherwise control his vehicle so as to avoid colliding with the claimant
h) reversed into the claimant
i) failed to indicate his intention/the presence of his vehicle adequately or at all
j) drove a vehicle with defective breaks knowing that the said breaks were defective
k) failed to cause his vehicle's breaks to be adequately maintained.]

2. The claimant intends to place evidence before the court pursuant to section 11 of the Civil Evidence Act 1968 that the defendant was on *[date]* at *[name and address of the convicting court]* convicted of *[name of the offence]*. The said conviction is relevant to the issue of the defendant's liability for negligent driving as alleged above.[2]

---

[1] *The following is a list of sample allegations. Not all of them will apply to each case. You may have to add appropriate allegations to describe how the defendant has been negligent. The claimant must analyse the accident and set out the precise allegations of wrongdoing. The Particulars must 'tell the story' of the accident and list all the facts the court will hear in evidence.*

[2] *Omit this paragraph if it is inapplicable to your case.*

3. By reason of the above matters the claimant suffered injury loss and damage:

PARTICULARS OF INJURY

[Here give a brief description of the injuries suffered; listing the initial injury, past and anticipated future treatment, the level of care and assistance provided already and expected in the future, the loss of amenity (see section 5.1), the level of disruption to working life and the prognosis.]

The medical report of *[name]* is attached hereto.

PARTICULARS OF LOSS

See the Schedule of Special and General Damages attached to this Particulars of Claim.

4. And the claimant claims interest upon such damages as the court shall award at a rate and for such a period as the court thinks fit, pursuant to *[section 69 of the County Courts Act 1984] [section 35A of the Supreme Court Act 1981].*[3]

AND the claimant claims

a) Damages *[less than £5,000/more than £5,000 but less than £15,000/more than £15,000]*

b) Interest as set out above.

STATEMENT OF TRUTH

I believe that the facts stated in these Particulars of Claim are true.

Full name _____

Name and address of solicitors' firm
[if used] _____

_____

Signed _____

ADDRESS FOR SERVICE
OF DOCUMENTS _____

[Address] _____

_____

---

[3] *If the case is brought in the High Court, the reference is to section 35A of the Supreme Court Act 1981; in the County Court the power to award interest is created by section 69 of the County Courts Act; delete as applicable.*

Sample 3
Bus passenger's claim against a bus company alleging negligence and breach of statutory duty

IN THE ANYTOWN COUNTY COURT
B E T W E E N

MRS JOEY SILVER   Claimant
and
THE ANYTOWN BUS COMPANY LIMITED   Defendant

PARTICULARS OF CLAIM

1. The defendant was at all relevant times the owner of a *[describe the bus by type or registration number]* ('the bus'[1]) which was travelling on Route *[number]* in *[town]* on *[date]* as a public service vehicle.

2. The Public Service Vehicles (Conduct of Drivers, Inspectors, Conductors and Passengers) Regulations 1990 ('the Regulations') applied to the bus driver *[and conductor]* who were the defendant's employees or agents.

3. On *[date]* the claimant, a paying passenger, *[lawfully boarded/attempted to board]* the bus when it stopped at a bus stop situated at *[road or place]*.

4. *[Describe what happened: what you did, what the driver and conductor did, the actions of any fellow passengers (if relevant) and what happened to the bus.]*

5. The claimant relies upon the fact of the accident as evidence of negligence on the part of the defendants, their employee(s) or agents. Alternatively, the defendants, their employee(s) or agents were in breach of statutory duty and/or negligent in that:

PARTICULARS OF NEGLIGENCE[2]

[a] *the defendant failed to instruct its driver [and/or conductor], adequately or at all, as to the proper procedure to be adopted at bus stops*

b) *the driver drove away from the bus stop before receiving any bell or other signal from the conductor*

c) *the driver failed to check whether the claimant had moved fully onto the bus before he operated the switch to close the door*

---

[1] *It is better to use a short description throughout, rather than repeated long-winded definitions. The short description should be identified and defined carefully at the outset. This example is perhaps over-careful, as in this set of circumstances there is only one bus. In some situations the facts may be much more complicated and in order to tell the story with clarity careful use of defining terminology is particularly important. In complex cases, therefore, you would expect to see terms such as 'the first incident', the 'second bus', the 'third payment', etc.*

[2] *These are samples, some (or even all) may not be relevant to your case; it is important to analyse the facts carefully and decide exactly who has failed in his duty of care, and how.*

d) the driver drove away from the bus stop without due regard for the people who were on, or in the act of boarding, the bus

e) the driver failed to give any or adequate warning that he was about to drive the bus away from the stop

f) the driver failed to pay any or sufficient regard to the fact that the bus had an open back

g) the conductor failed to give any or proper warning that the bus was about to move

h) the conductor failed to pay any or sufficient regard to the fact that the bus had an open back

i) the conductor failed to warn the driver, adequately or at all, that not everyone on, or in the act of boarding, the bus was in a safe position

j) the conductor failed to ensure that all the passengers had boarded the bus safely

k) the conductor failed to monitor and control, adequately or at all, the number of passengers standing in the rear doorway.]

PARTICULARS OF BREACH OF STATUTORY DUTY[3]

[l) the defendant's driver failed to take all reasonable precautions to ensure the safety of passengers on or entering the bus, including the claimant, contrary to regulation 5(1) of the Regulations

m) the defendant's conductor failed to take all reasonable precautions to ensure the safety of passengers on or entering the bus, including the claimant contrary to regulation 5(1) of the Regulations.]

6. By reason of all the matters complained of above, the claimant has suffered pain and injury and sustained loss and damage.

PARTICULARS OF INJURY

[Here give a brief description of the injuries suffered; listing the initial injury, past and anticipated future treatment, the level of care and assistance provided already and expected in the future, the loss of amenity (see section 5.1), the level of disruption to working life and the prognosis.]

The medical report of [name] is attached hereto.

PARTICULARS OF LOSS

See the Schedule of Special and General Damages attached to this Particulars of Claim.

7. The claimant is entitled to and claims interest on the amount found to be due to her, pursuant to [section 69 of the County Courts Act 1984/section 35A of the Supreme Court Act 1981].[4]

---

[3] This example only cites one regulation; in your case the bus company may have breached a different statutory duty. To identify the correct Regulation(s) from the outset always look at the Regulations before you draft your Particulars of Claim.

[4] Interest for County Court Cases may be awarded under the County Courts Act 1984; the High Court power to award interest is given by The Supreme Court Act 1981 – delete as applicable.

AND the claimant claims

a) Damages *[less than £5,000/more than £5,000 but less than £15,000/more than £15,000]*

b) Interest as set out above.

STATEMENT OF TRUTH

I believe that the facts stated in these Particulars of Claim are true.

Full name
_____

Name and address of solicitors' firm
[if used]
_____

_____

Signed
_____

ADDRESS FOR SERVICE
OF DOCUMENTS
_____

[Address]
_____

_____

_____

Sample 4
Pedestrian's claim against the Highway Authority for a tripping accident

IN THE ANYTOWN COUNTY COURT
B E T W E E N

MRS JOEY SILVER   Claimant
and
SMALLSHIRE DISTRICT COUNCIL   Defendant

PARTICULARS OF CLAIM[1]

1. The defendant was at the relevant time the Highway Authority responsible for the *[carriageway/pavement]* which is part of *[road or street name, town and county]*. That road is a highway within the meaning of the Highways Act 1980.

2. At *[time]* on *[date]* the claimant was *[walking/driving her car/riding her pushbike/motorbike/horse, etc.]* on the *[northern pavement/left-hand side of the carriageway/right-hand lane in accordance with the one-way system which operates at that point[1]]* travelling *[in the direction of the town centre/towards the junction of X Street with Y Road/in a westerly direction]*.

3. Whilst the claimant was thus travelling *[she/her car/motorbike/horse] [describe what happened. Include a measurement of the hole or other defect, and describe how deep or protruding the hazard was]*.

4. The accident was caused by the negligence and/or breach of statutory duty of the defendant, its employees or agents in that they:

PARTICULARS OF NEGLIGENCE

[a]   *allowed a [pothole/trench/uneven surface] in the [road/pavement] to continue in existence*

b)   *failed to [fill in the pothole/trench] [repair and make good the uneven surface] adequately [or at all]*

c)   *failed to resurface the road*

d)   *failed to warn users of the highway, such as the claimant, of the existence of the [pothole/trench/uneven surface] by way of signs, notices, bollards, lights or other appropriate means*

e)   *allowed the road to become or remain unsafe for road users including the claimant*

f)   *failed to cause road users, including the claimant, to avoid the danger created by the [pothole/trench/uneven surface] by way of signs, barriers, fencing, brightly coloured tape, bollards or otherwise directing them to keep clear of it*

---

[1] *The purpose of the Particulars of Claim is to paint a picture in words; you must identify exactly what you were doing just before the accident and describe very precisely where the accident happened.*

g)   *exposed the claimant to a danger or hazard and/or risk of injury.]*

PARTICULARS OF BREACH OF STATUTORY DUTY

[h)   *by reason of all the matters set out above, the defendant has failed to maintain the highway contrary to section 41 of the Highways Act 1980.]*

5.   As a result of the matters set out above the claimant, whose date of birth is *[date]* and was *[age]* at the time of the accident, suffered injury, loss and damage.

PARTICULARS OF INJURY

[Here give a brief description of the injuries suffered; listing the initial injury, past and anticipated future treatment, the level of care and assistance provided already and expected in the future, the loss of amenity (see section 5.1), the level of disruption to working life and the prognosis.]

The medical report of *[name]* is attached hereto.

PARTICULARS OF LOSS

See the Schedule of Special and General Damages attached to this Particulars of Claim.

6.   The claimant is entitled to and claims interest upon such damages as the court shall award at such a rate and for such a period as the court thinks fit, pursuant to *[section 69 of the County Courts Act 1984] [section 35A of the Supreme Court Act 1981].*[2]

AND the claimant claims

a)   Damages *[less than £5,000/more than £5,000 but less than £15,000/more than £15,000]*

b)   Interest as set out above.

STATEMENT OF TRUTH

I believe that the facts stated in these Particulars of Claim are true.

Full name
_____

Name and address of solicitors' firm
[if used]
_____

_____

Signed
_____

ADDRESS FOR SERVICE
OF DOCUMENTS
_____

[Address]
_____

_____

---

[2] *If the case is brought in the County court, the reference should be to section 69 County Courts Act 1984; for cases in the High Court the power to award interest is created by section 35A Supreme Court Act 1981; delete as appropriate.*

Sample 5
Tenant's claim against a landlord for injuries arising from defects in rented property (appearing after the tenant moved in)

IN THE ANYTOWN COUNTY COURT
B E T W E E N

MRS JOEY SILVER   Claimant
and
[name of landlord]   Defendant

PARTICULARS OF CLAIM

1. On *[date]* the defendant granted a lease of the dwelling house at *[full address of the property]* to the claimant. The terms of the lease included *[state how long the lease was to run, how much the rent was and how often it had to be paid]*.

2. It was an express term[1] of the lease that the landlord *[here quote the term making the landlord responsible for the relevant repairs]*. Additionally, or alternatively, a repairing covenant was implied into the lease by section 11 of the Landlord and Tenant Act 1985.[2] Additionally or alternatively, the lease gives the landlord the right to enter the premises in order to carry out maintenance or repair work.[3]

3. On *[say when the defect arose]* *[describe the nature of the defect]*. The claimant told the landlord of the existence of the defect on *[list each occasion the landlord was notified]* by *[letter/fax/email/telephone, etc]*.

4. In breach of the matter(s) set out in paragraph 2 above the defendant:

PARTICULARS OF NEGLIGENCE

[List here all the things the landlord has done to make the defect worse, and/or failed to do to in order to make things better.]

PARTICULARS OF BREACH OF STATUTORY DUTY

[List here all those factors which suggest the landlord has not taken reasonable care of the safety of people like you.]

---

[1] *i.e. openly agreed at the outset orally or listed as one of the agreed terms of the written tenancy agreement.*

[2] *Section 11 lays the responsibility for keeping the structure and exterior of the property and various installations in repair on the landlord. It is not relevant to the state of any other item or part of the building leased. Section 11 will also apply only if the property is residential (a 'dwelling house') and the length of the lease is less than seven years.*

[3] *If this clause is found in the lease (or was promised orally), section 4 of the Defective Premises Act 1972 places upon the landlord the duty to take such steps as are reasonable in the circumstances to make all those (such as the claimant) who may reasonably be affected by the disrepair reasonably safe.*

5. As a result of the matters set out above, the claimant, whose date of birth is *[date]*, suffered personal injury, loss and damage.

PARTICULARS OF INJURY

[Here give a brief description of the injuries suffered; listing the initial diagnosis, past and anticipated future treatment, the level of care and assistance provided already and expected in the future, the loss of amenity (see section 5.1), the level of disruption to working and home life and the prognosis.]

The medical report of *[name]* is attached hereto.

PARTICULARS OF LOSS

Please see the Schedule of Special and General Damages attached to this Particulars of Claim.

6. The claimant is entitled to and claims interest upon such damages as the court shall award at such a rate and for such a period as the court thinks fit, pursuant to *[section 69 of the County Courts Act 1984] [section 35A of the Supreme Court Act 1981]*.[4]

AND the claimant claims

a) Damages *[less than £5,000/more than £5,000 but less than £15,000/more than £15,000]*

b) Interest as set out above.

STATEMENT OF TRUTH

I believe that the facts stated in these Particulars of Claim are true.

Full name	ADDRESS FOR SERVICE OF DOCUMENTS
Name and address of solicitors' firm *[if used]*	*[Address]*
Signed	

---

[4] *If the case is brought in the County court, the reference should be to section 69 County Courts Act 1984; for cases in the High Court the power to award interest is created by section 35A Supreme Court Act 1981; delete as appropriate.*

Appendix 2
DEFENCES

How to use this Appendix

Form N9D should be returned to the court if you intend to defend the claim. If there is room, then write in the boxes provided and continue on a separate sheet with the claim number written clearly in the top right-hand corner. Alternatively, write the whole of your defence (and counterclaim if appropriate) on separate sheets of paper using the suggested layout below.

The defendant should attach any document he relies upon to the Defence. The following matters must be contained in the Defence itself (you may need to add further matters to make your position clear):

- Which facts you agree with.

- Which facts you neither admit nor deny but of which you have no knowledge.

- Which facts you deny AND your version of what happened.

- A 'counter-schedule of past and future losses and expenses' setting out which of the items in the claimant's schedule of past and future losses and expenses you agree with, do not admit or dispute.

- Whether you agree with the conclusions of the claimant's medical expert and if you disagree, why.

- Any medical report on the claimant by an expert instructed on your behalf which you want to rely on at trial.

- A statement that you intend to rely upon a limitation defence.

- A statement that the claimant was contributorily negligent AND a list of details to support your allegation.

- A statement of truth.

Below is a series of paragraphs which show examples of how to do so. The style is not as important as clarity; it is essential that you let the court know what your case will be, and to do that you must address every item of the claim. The contents of the counterclaim (also known as a Part 20 claim) are exactly like a claim; therefore for selected examples please refer to Appendix 1.

Specimen layout where the Defence Form is not used

IN THE ANYTOWN COUNTY COURT

BETWEEN

Claimant

JOSEPHINE BLOGGS

and

Defendant

JOHN SMITH

_____

DEFENCE

_____

1. [Paragraph]
2. [Paragraph]
3. [Paragraph]
4. [Paragraph]

_____

PARTICULARS OF NEGLIGENCE

_____

5. [Paragraph or sub-paragraphs]
6. [Paragraph]

_____

COUNTERCLAIM

_____

7. [Paragraph]
8. [Paragraph]
9. [Paragraph]

STATEMENT OF TRUTH
I believe that the facts stated in this Defence (and Counterclaim) are true.

Full name _____

Name and address of solicitors' firm [if used] _____

_____

Signed _____

ADDRESS FOR SERVICE OF DOCUMENTS
[Address]

Sample paragraphs

Defence

1. Asserting that the claimant has not established a cause of action[1]

Without prejudice to the following paragraphs, the defendant asserts that the facts set out in the Particulars of Claim do not amount to *[state the relevant cause of action[1]]* and furthermore, the defendant will argue that *[state the relevant section number and title of Act of Parliament or Regulation]* does not apply in the circumstances. *[The defendant intends to make an application for summary judgment/to strike out the Particulars of Claim].[2]*

2. Agreeing particular facts

The defendant admits the following: *[here list all the paragraphs you fully agree with, or simply recite all the relevant facts in a list].*

3. Not admitting a particular fact

The defendant does not have any knowledge of the following facts and therefore is unable to admit or deny them *[here set out all the facts alleged in a list].*

4. Denying certain facts and putting forward alternative facts

The defendant denies that *[set out the allegation].* The *[defendant/name of other witness]* will give evidence to show that *[set out your version of what happened].*

[Repeat for each allegation in dispute.]

5. Denying liability

In all the circumstances the defendant denies that he *[was negligent/in breach of a statutory duty/in breach of contract/assaulted the claimant/harassed the claimant]* as alleged in the Particulars of Claim or at all.

6. Asserting a statutory defence

The defendant at all times acted reasonably/took reasonable steps to ensure *[details]* in that he did: *[set out here].*

---

[1] *For a definition of 'cause of action' see the glossary.*

[2] *See chapter 4, Cutting litigation short; avoiding a trial.*

7. The counter-schedule of past losses and expenses

The defendant attaches to this document a counter-schedule of past and future expenses and losses.[3]

8. Disputing the medical report

The defendant disputes the medical report of *[name]* attached to the Particulars of Claim in the following ways: *[list]*.

9. Relying on your own expert evidence

The defendant disputes the medical report of *[name]* attached to the Particulars of Claim and seeks to rely on the report of *[name and qualifications]* which is attached to this Defence.

10. Relying on expiry of the relevant limitation period

The claimant's claim is barred by the *[section number of the Limitation Act 1980/other appropriate legislation]*.

11. Asserting that the claimant has been contributorily negligent

Further, and alternatively, to the matters set out above, in the circumstances the claimant was wholly or partly responsible for the accident.

Particulars of negligence

[Set out here a list of the ways in which the claimant failed to take reasonable care of his own safety; see the examples of Particulars of Negligence in Appendix 1.]

12. Counterclaiming (Part 20 claim)

The defendant relies on the matters set out below by way of set-off and counterclaim.

Counterclaim

[A counterclaim is set out in the same way as the Particulars of Claim, because in respect of the counterclaim the defendant has become the 'claimant' and the claimant is the 'defendant' to it.]

---

[3] *A counter-schedule of past and future losses must be included in the defence. It should be set out in the same way as the schedule of past and future losses and expenses, and, dealing with each item in term, set out whether he agrees with the amount suggested, has no knowledge of the cost of the item or disputes the cost. If he disputes the cost, he must put forward a suitable alternative figure.*

Appendix 3
EXTRACT FROM THE PERSONAL INJURY CLAIMS PRE-ACTION PROTOCOL (FAST TRACK)

Letter of claim

3.1   The claimant shall send to the proposed defendant two copies of a letter of claim, immediately sufficient information is available to substantiate a realistic claim and before issues of quantum are addressed in detail. One copy of the letter is for the defendants, the second for passing on to his insurers.

3.2   The letter shall contain a **clear summary of the facts** on which the claim is based together with an indication of the **nature of any injuries** suffered and of **any financial loss** incurred. In cases of road traffic accidents, the letter should provide the name and address of the hospital where treatment has been obtained and the claimant's hospital reference number.

3.3   Solicitors are recommended to use a **standard format** for such a letter – an example is at Annex A: this can be amended to suit the particular case.

3.4   The letter should ask for **details of the insurer** and that a copy should be sent by the proposed defendant to the insurer where appropriate. If the insurer is known, a copy shall be sent directly to the insurer. Details of the claimant's National Insurance number and date of birth should be supplied to the defendant's insurer once the defendant has responded to the letter of claim and confirmed the identity of the insurer. This information should not be supplied in the letter of claim.

3.5   **Sufficient information** should be given in order to enable the defendant's insurer/solicitor to commence investigations and at least put a broad valuation on the 'risk'.

3.6   The **defendant should reply within 21 calendar days** of the date of posting of the letter identifying the insurer (if any). If there has been no reply by the defendant or insurer within 21 days, the claimant will be entitled to issue proceedings.

3.7   The **defendant**('s insurers) will have a **maximum of three months** from the date of acknowledgement of the claim **to investigate**. No later than the end of that period the defendant (insurer) shall reply, stating whether liability is denied and, if so, giving reasons for their denial of liability.

3.8   Where the accident occurred outside England and Wales and/or where the defendant is outside the jurisdiction, the time periods of 21 days and three months should normally be extended up to 42 days and six months.

3.9   Where **liability is admitted**, the presumption is that the defendant will be bound by this admission for all claims with a total value of up to £15,000.

Documents

3.10   If the **defendant denies liability**, he should enclose with the letter of reply **documents** in his possession that are **material to the issues** between the parties, and which would be likely to be ordered to be disclosed by the court, either on an application for pre-action disclosure, or on disclosure during proceedings.

3.11   Attached at Annex B are **specimen**, but non-exhaustive, **lists** of documents likely to be material in different types of claim. Where the claimant's investigation of the case is well advanced, the letter of claim could indicate which classes of documents are considered relevant for early disclosure. Alternatively, these could be identified at a later stage.

3.12   Where the defendant admits primary liability, but alleges contributory negligence by the claimant, the defendant should give reasons supporting those allegations and disclose those documents from Annex B which are relevant to the issues in dispute. The claimant should respond to the allegations of contributory negligence before proceedings are issued.

Special damages

3.13   The claimant will send to the defendant as soon as practicable a Schedule of Special Damages with supporting documents, particularly where the defendant has admitted liability.

Experts

3.14   Before any party instructs an expert he should give the other party a list of the name(s) of **one or more experts** in the relevant speciality whom he considers are suitable to instruct.

3.15   Where a medical expert is to be instructed the claimant's solicitor will organise access to relevant medical records – see specimen letter of instruction at Annex C.

3.16   **Within 14 days** the other party may indicate an **objection** to one or more of the named experts. The first party should then instruct a mutually acceptable expert. It must be emphasised that if the claimant nominates an expert in the original letter of claim, the defendant has 14 days to object to one or more of the named experts after expiration of the period of 21 days within which he has to reply to the letter of claim, as set out in paragraph 3.6.

3.17   If the second party objects to all the listed experts, the parties may then instruct **experts of their own choice**. It would be for the court to decide subsequently, if proceedings are issued, whether either party had acted unreasonably.

3.18   If the **second party does not object to an expert nominated**, he shall not be entitled to rely on his own expert evidence within that particular speciality unless:

(a)   the first party agrees;

(b)   the court so directs; or

(c)   the first party's expert report has been amended and the first party is not prepared to disclose the original report.

3.19   **Either party may send to an agreed expert written questions** on the report, relevant to the issues, via the first party's solicitors. The expert should send answers to the questions separately and directly to each party.

3.20   The cost of a report from an agreed expert will usually be paid by the instructing first party: the costs of the expert replying to questions will usually be borne by the party which asks the questions.

3.21   Where the defendant admits liability in whole or in part, before proceedings are issued, any medical report obtained by agreement under this protocol should be disclosed to the other party. The claimant should delay issuing proceedings for 21 days from disclosure of the report, to enable the parties to consider whether the claim is capable of settlement. The Civil Procedure Rules Part 36 permit claimants and defendants to make offers to settle pre-proceedings. Parties should always consider before issuing if it is appropriate to make a Part 36 Offer. If such an offer is made, the party making the offer must always supply sufficient evidence and/or information to enable the offer to be properly considered.

Annex A
Specimen letter of claim

To

Defendant

Dear Sirs

Re: *[Claimant's full name]*
    [Claimant's full address]
    [Claimant's clock or works number]
    [Claimant's employer (name and address)]

We are instructed by the above named to claim damages in connection with an accident at work/road traffic accident/tripping accident on *[day]* of *[year]* at *[place of accident which must be sufficiently detailed to establish location]*.

Please confirm the identity of your insurers. Please note that the insurers will need to see this letter as soon as possible and it may affect your insurance cover and/or the conduct of any subsequent legal proceedings if you do not send this letter to them.

The circumstances of the accident are: *[brief outline]*.

The reason why we are alleging fault is: *[simple explanation, e.g. defective machine, broken ground]*.

A description of our client's injuries is as follows: *[brief outline]*.

[In cases of road traffic accidents] Our client *[state hospital reference number]* received treatment for the injuries at *[name and address of hospital]*.

He is employed as *[occupation]* and has had the following time off work *[dates of absence]*. His approximate weekly income is *[insert if known]*.

If you are our client's employers, please provide us with the usual earnings details which will enable us to calculate his financial loss.

We are obtaining a police report and will let you have a copy of the same upon your undertaking to meet half the fee.

We have also sent a letter of claim to *[name and address]* and a copy of that letter is attached. We understand their insurers are *[name, address and claims number if known]*.

At this stage of our enquiries we would expect the documents contained in parts *[insert appropriate parts of standard disclosure list]* to be relevant to this action.

A copy of this letter is attached for you to send to your insurers. Finally, we expect an acknowledgement of this letter within 21 days by yourselves or your insurers.

Yours faithfully

Annex B
Standard list of relevant documents for fast track trial disclosure

RTA cases

SECTION A

In all cases where liability is at issue:

(i)   Documents identifying nature, extent and location of damage to defendant's vehicle where there is any dispute about point of impact.

(ii)   MOT certificate where relevant.

(iii)   Maintenance records where vehicle defect is alleged or it is alleged by defendant that there was an unforeseen defect which caused or contributed to the accident.

SECTION B

Accident involving commercial vehicle as potential defendant:

(i)   Tachograph charts or entry from individual control book.

(ii)   Maintenance and repair records required for operators' licence where vehicle defect is alleged or it is alleged by defendants that there was an unforeseen defect which caused or contributed to the accident.

SECTION C

Cases against local authorities where highway design defect is alleged:

(i)   Documents produced to comply with section 39 of the Road Traffic Act 1988 in respect of the duty designed to promote road safety to include studies into road accidents in the relevant area and documents relating to measures recommended to prevent accidents in the relevant area.

Highway tripping claims

Documents from Highway Authority for a period of 12 months prior to the accident:

(i)   Records of inspection for the relevant stretch of highway.

(ii)   Maintenance records including records of independent contractors working in relevant area.

(iii)   Records of the minutes of Highway Authority meetings where maintenance or repair policy has been discussed or decided.

(iv)   Records of complaints about the state of highways.

(v)   Records of other accidents that have occurred on the relevant stretch of highway.

Workplace claims

(i)   Accident book entry.

(ii)   First aider report.

(iii)   Surgery record.

(iv)   Foreman/supervisor accident report.

(v)   Safety representatives accident report.

(vi)   RIDDOR report to HSE.

(vii)   Other communications between defendants and HSE.

(viii) Minutes of Health and Safety Committee meeting(s) where accident/matter considered.

(ix)   Report to DSS.

(x)   Documents listed above relative to any previous accident/matter identified by the claimant and relied upon as proof of negligence.

(xi)   Earnings information where defendant is employer.

Documents produced to comply with requirements of the Management of Health and Safety at Work Regulations 1992:

(i)   Pre-accident Risk Assessment required by Regulation 3.

(ii)   Post-accident Re-Assessment required by Regulation 3.

(iii)   Accident Investigation Report prepared in implementing the requirements of Regulations 4, 6 and 9.

(iv)   Health Surveillance Records in appropriate cases required by Regulation 5.

(v)   Information provided to employees under Regulation 8.

(vi)   Documents relating to the employees' health and safety training required by Regulation 11.

Workplace claims; disclosure where specific regulations apply

SECTION A – WORKPLACE (HEALTH SAFETY AND WELFARE) REGULATIONS 1992

(i)   Repair and maintenance records required by Regulation 5.

(ii)   Housekeeping records to comply with the requirements of Regulation 9.

(iii)   Hazard warning signs or notices to comply with Regulation 17 (Traffic Routes).

SECTION B – PROVISION AND USE OF WORK EQUIPMENT REGULATIONS 1992

(i)   Manufacturers' specifications and instructions in respect of relevant work equipment establishing its suitability to comply with Regulation 5.

(ii)   Maintenance log/maintenance records required to comply with Regulation 6.

(iii)   Documents providing information and instructions to employees to comply with Regulation 8.

(iv)   Documents provided to the employee in respect of training for use to comply with Regulation 9.

(v)   Any notice, sign or document relied upon as a defence to alleged breaches of Regulations 14 to 18 dealing with controls and control systems.

(vi)   Instruction/training documents issued to comply with the requirements of Regulation 22 insofar as it deals with maintenance operations where the machinery is not shut down.

(vii)   Copies of markings required to comply with Regulation 23.

(viii) Copies of warnings required to comply with Regulation 24.

SECTION C – PERSONAL PROTECTIVE EQUIPMENT AT WORK REGULATIONS 1992

(i)   Documents relating to the assessment of the Personal Protective Equipment to comply with Regulation 6.

(ii)   Documents relating to the maintenance and replacement of Personal Protective Equipment to comply with Regulation 7.

(iii)   Record of maintenance procedures for Personal Protective Equipment to comply with Regulation 7.

(iv)   Records of tests and examinations of Personal Protective Equipment to comply with Regulation 7.

(v)   Documents providing information, instruction and training in relation to the Personal Protective Equipment to comply with Regulation 9.

(vi)   Instructions for use of Personal Protective Equipment to include the manufacturers' instructions to comply with Regulation 10.

SECTION D – MANUAL HANDLING OPERATIONS REGULATIONS 1992

(i)   Manual Handling Risk Assessment carried out to comply with the requirements of Regulation 4(1)(b)(i).

(ii)   Re-assessment carried out post-accident to comply with requirements of Regulation 4(1)(b)(i).

(iii)   Documents showing the information provided to the employee to give general indications related to the load and precise indications on the weight of the load and the heaviest side of the load if the centre of gravity was not positioned centrally to comply with Regulation 4(1)(b)(iii).

(iv)   Documents relating to training in respect of manual handling operations and training records.

SECTION E – HEALTH AND SAFETY (DISPLAY SCREEN EQUIPMENT) REGULATIONS 1992

(i)   Analysis of work stations to assess and reduce risks carried out to comply with the requirements of Regulation 2.

(ii)   Re-assessment of analysis of work stations to assess and reduce risks following development of symptoms by the claimant.

(iii)   Documents detailing the provision of training including training records to comply with the requirements of Regulation 6.

(iv)   Documents providing information to employees to comply with the requirements of Regulation 7.

SECTION F – CONTROL OF SUBSTANCES HAZARDOUS TO HEALTH REGULATIONS 1988

(i)   Risk assessment carried out to comply with the requirements of Regulation 6.

(ii)   Reviewed risk assessment carried out to comply with the requirements of Regulation 6.

(iii)   Copy labels from containers used for storage handling and disposal of carcinogenics to comply with the requirements of Regulation 7(2A)(h).

(iv)   Warning signs identifying designation of areas and installations which may be contaminated by carcinogenics to comply with the requirements of Regulation 7(2A)(h).

(v)   Documents relating to the assessment of the Personal Protective Equipment to comply with Regulation 7(3A).

(vi)   Documents relating to the maintenance and replacement of Personal Protective Equipment to comply with Regulation 7(3A).

(vii)   Record of maintenance procedures for Personal Protective Equipment to comply with Regulation 7(3A).

(viii) Records of tests and examinations of Personal Protective Equipment to comply with Regulation 7(3A).

(ix)   Documents providing information, instruction and training in relation to the Personal Protective Equipment to comply with Regulation 7(3A).

(x)   Instructions for use of Personal Protective Equipment to include the manufacturers' instructions to comply with Regulation 7(3A).

(xi)   Air monitoring records for substances assigned a maximum exposure limit or occupational exposure standard to comply with the requirements of Regulation 7.

(xii)   Maintenance examination and test of control measures records to comply with Regulation 9.

(xiii) Monitoring records to comply with the requirements of Regulation 10.

(xiv)   Health surveillance records to comply with the requirements of Regulation 11.

(xv)   Documents detailing information, instruction and training including training records for employees to comply with the requirements of Regulation 12.

(xvi)   Labels and health and safety data sheets supplied to the employers to comply with the CHIP Regulations.

SECTION G – CONSTRUCTION (DESIGN AND MANAGEMENT) REGULATIONS 1994

(i)   Notification of a Project Form (HSE F10) to comply with the requirements of Regulation 7.

(ii)   Health and safety plan to comply with requirements of Regulation 15.

(iii)   Health and safety file to comply with the requirements of Regulations 12 and 14.

(iv)   Information and training records provided to comply with the requirements of Regulation 17.

(v)   Records of advice from and views of persons at work to comply with the requirements of Regulation 18.

SECTION H – PRESSURE SYSTEMS AND TRANSPORTABLE GAS CONTAINERS REGULATIONS 1989

(i)   Information and specimen markings provided to comply with the requirements of Regulation 5.

(ii)   Written statements specifying the safe operating limits of a system to comply with the requirements of Regulation 7.

(iii)   Copy of the written scheme of examination required to comply with the requirements of Regulation 8.

(iv)   Examination records required to comply with the requirements of Regulation 9.

(v)   Instructions provided for the use of operator to comply with Regulation 11.

(vi)   Records kept to comply with the requirements of Regulation 13.

(vii)   Records kept to comply with the requirements of Regulation 22.

SECTION I – LIFTING PLANT AND EQUIPMENT (RECORDS OF TEST AND EXAMINATION ETC) REGULATIONS 1992

(i)   Record kept to comply with the requirements of Regulation 6.

SECTION J – THE NOISE AT WORK REGULATIONS 1989

(i)   Any risk assessment records required to comply with the requirements of Regulations 4 and 5.

(ii)   Manufacturers' literature in respect of all ear protection made available to claimant to comply with the requirements of Regulation 8.

(iii)   All documents provided to the employee for the provision of information to comply with Regulation 11.

SECTION K – CONSTRUCTION (HEAD PROTECTION) REGULATIONS 1989

(i)   Pre-accident assessment of head protection required to comply with Regulation 3(4).

(ii)   Post-accident re-assessment required to comply with Regulation 3(5).

SECTION L – THE CONSTRUCTION (GENERAL PROVISIONS) REGULATIONS 1961

(i)   Report prepared following inspections and examinations of excavations, etc to comply with the requirements of Regulation 9.

(ii)   Report prepared following inspections and examinations of work in cofferdams and caissons to comply with the requirements of Regulations 17 and 18.

Annex C
Specimen letter of instruction to medical expert

Dear Sir

Re: *[Name and address]*

Date of birth:

Telephone no:

Date of accident:

We are acting for the above named in connection with injuries received in an accident which occurred on the above date. The main injuries appear to have been *[main injuries]*.

We should be obliged if you would examine our client and let us have a full and detailed report dealing with any relevant pre-accident medical history, the injuries sustained, treatment received and present condition, dealing in particular with the capacity for work and giving a prognosis.

It is central to our assessment of the extent of our client's injuries to establish the extent and duration of any continuing disability. Accordingly, in the prognosis section we would ask you to comment specifically on any areas of continuing complaint or disability or impact on daily living. If there is such continuing disability, you should comment upon the level of suffering or inconvenience caused and, if you are able, give your view as to when or if the complaint or disability is likely to resolve.

Please send our client an appointment direct for this purpose. Should you be able to offer a cancellation appointment please contact our client direct. We confirm we will be responsible for your reasonable fees.

We are obtaining the notes and records from our client's GP and hospitals attended, and will forward them to you when they are to hand/or please request the GP and hospital records direct and advise that any invoice for the provision of these records should be forwarded to us.

In order to comply with court rules we should be grateful if you would insert above your signature a statement that the contents are true to the best of your knowledge and belief.

In order to avoid further correspondence we can confirm that on the evidence we have there is no reason to suspect we may be pursuing a claim against the hospital or its staff.

We look forward to receiving your report within *[number of]* weeks. If you will not be able to prepare your report within this period, please telephone us upon receipt of these instructions.

When acknowledging these instructions it would assist if you could give an estimate as to the likely time scale for the provision of your report and also an indication as to your fee.

Yours faithfully

Appendix 4
EXTRACT FROM THE CLINICAL DISPUTES PRE-ACTION PROTOCOL

3.1   This protocol is not a comprehensive code governing all the steps in clinical disputes. Rather, it attempts to set out a **code of good practice** which parties should follow when litigation might be a possibility.

3.2   The **commitments** section of the protocol summarises the guiding principles which healthcare providers, and patients and their advisors are invited to endorse when dealing with patient dissatisfaction with treatment and its outcome, and with potential complaints and claims.

3.3   The **steps** section sets out in a more prescriptive form a recommended sequence of actions to be followed if litigation is a prospect.

Good practice commitments

3.4   **Healthcare providers** should:

(i)   ensure that **key staff**, including claims and litigation managers, are appropriately trained and have some knowledge of healthcare law, and of complaints procedures and civil litigation practice and procedure;

(ii)   develop an approach to **clinical governance** that ensures that clinical practice is delivered to commonly accepted standards and that this is routinely monitored through a system of clinical audit and clinical risk management (particularly adverse outcome investigation);

(iii)   set up **adverse outcome reporting systems** in all specialties to record and investigate unexpected serious adverse outcomes as soon as possible. Such systems can enable evidence to be gathered quickly, which makes it easier to provide an accurate explanation of what happened and to defend or settle any subsequent claims;

(iv)   use the results of **adverse incidents and complaints positively** as a guide to how to improve services to patients in the future;

(v)   ensure that **patients receive clear and comprehensible information** in an accessible form about how to raise their concerns or complaints;

(vi)   establish **efficient and effective systems of recording and storing patient records**, notes, diagnostic reports and X-rays, and to retain these in accordance with Department of Health guidance (currently for a minimum of eight years in the case of adults, and all obstetric and paediatric notes for children until they reach the age of 25);

(vii)   **advise patients** of a serious adverse outcome and provide on request to the patient or the patient's representative an oral or written explanation of what happened, information on further steps open to the patient, including where appropriate an offer of future treatment to rectify the problem, an apology, changes in procedure which will benefit patients and/or compensation.

3.5   **Patients and their advisors** should:

    (i)   **report any concerns and dissatisfaction** to the healthcare provider as soon as is reasonable to enable that provider to offer clinical advice where possible, to advise the patient if anything has gone wrong and take appropriate action;

    (ii)   consider the **full range of options** available following an adverse outcome with which a patient is dissatisfied, including a request for an explanation, a meeting, a complaint and other appropriate dispute resolution methods (including mediation) and negotiation, not only litigation;

    (iii)   **inform the healthcare provider when the patient is satisfied** that the matter has been concluded: legal advisors should notify the provider when they are no longer acting for the patient, particularly if proceedings have not started.

Protocol steps

3.6   The steps of this protocol which follow have been kept deliberately simple. An illustration of the likely sequence of events in a number of healthcare situations is at Annex A.

Obtaining health records

3.7   Any request for records by the **patient** or their advisor should:

    provide sufficient information to alert the healthcare provider where an adverse outcome has been serious or had serious consequences;

    be as **specific as possible** about the records which are required.

3.8   Requests for copies of the patient's clinical records should be made using the Law Society and Department of Health approved **standard forms** (enclosed at Annex B), adapted as necessary.

3.9   The copy records should be provided **within 40 days** of the request and for a cost not exceeding the charges permissible under the Access to Health Records Act 1990 (currently a maximum of £10 plus photocopying and postage).

3.10   In the rare circumstances that the healthcare provider is in difficulty in complying with the request within 40 days, the **problem should be explained** quickly and details given of what is being done to resolve it.

3.11   It will not be practicable for healthcare providers to investigate in detail each case when records are requested. But healthcare providers should **adopt a policy on**

which cases will be investigated (see paragraph 3.5 on clinical governance and adverse outcome reporting).

3.12 If the healthcare provider fails to provide the health records within 40 days, the patient or their advisor can then apply to the court for an **order for pre-action disclosure**. The new Civil Procedure Rules should make pre-action applications to the court easier. The court will also have the power to impose costs sanctions for unreasonable delay in providing records.

3.13 If either the patient or the healthcare provider considers **additional health records are required from a third party**, in the first instance these should be requested by or through the patient. Third party healthcare providers are expected to cooperate. The Civil Procedure Rules will enable patients and healthcare providers to apply to the court for pre-action disclosure by third parties.

Letter of claim

3.14 Annex C1 to this protocol provides a **template for the recommended contents of a letter of claim**; the level of detail will need to be varied to suit the particular circumstances.

3.15 If, following the receipt and analysis of the records, and the receipt of any further advice (including from experts if necessary – see section 4), the patient/advisor decides that there are grounds for a claim, they should then send, as soon as practicable, to the healthcare provider/potential defendant, a **letter of claim**.

3.16 This letter should contain a **clear summary of the facts** on which the claim is based, including the alleged adverse outcome, and the **main allegations** of negligence. It should also describe the **patient's injuries**, and present condition and prognosis. The financial loss incurred by the plaintiff should be outlined with an indication of the heads of damage to be claimed and the scale of the loss, unless this is impracticable.

3.17 In more complex cases a **chronology** of the relevant events should be provided, particularly if the patient has been treated by a number of different healthcare providers.

3.18 The letter of claim **should refer to any relevant documents**, including health records, and if possible enclose copies of any of those which will not already be in the potential defendant's possession, for example, any relevant general practitioner records if the plaintiff's claim is against a hospital.

3.19 **Sufficient information** must be given to enable the healthcare provider defendant to commence investigations and to put an initial valuation on the claim.

3.20 Letters of claim are **not** intended to have the same formal status as a pleading, nor should any sanctions necessarily apply if the letter of claim and any subsequent statement of claim in the proceedings differ.

3.21   **Proceedings should not be issued until after three months from the letter of claim**, unless there is a limitation problem and/or the patient's position needs to be protected by early issue.

3.22   The patient or their advisor may want to make an **offer to settle** the claim at this early stage by putting forward an amount of compensation which would be satisfactory (possibly including any costs incurred to date). If an offer to settle is made, generally this should be supported by a medical report which deals with the injuries, condition and prognosis, and by a schedule of loss and supporting documentation. The level of detail necessary will depend on the value of the claim. Medical reports may not be necessary where there is no significant continuing injury, and a detailed schedule may not be necessary in a low value case. The Civil Procedure Rules are expected to set out the legal and procedural requirements for making offers to settle.

The response

3.23   Attached at Annex C2 is a template for the suggested contents of the letter of response.

3.24   The healthcare provider should **acknowledge** the letter of claim within **14 days of receipt** and should identify who will be dealing with the matter.

3.25   The healthcare provider should, **within three months** of the letter of claim, provide a **reasoned answer**:

> if the **claim is admitted**, the healthcare provider should say so in clear terms;

> if only **part of the claim is admitted**, the healthcare provider should make clear which issues of breach of duty and/or causation are admitted and which are denied and why;

> if it is intended that any **admissions will be binding**;

> if the claim is denied, this should include specific comments on the allegations of negligence, and if a synopsis or chronology of relevant events has been provided and is disputed, the healthcare provider's version of those events;

> where additional documents are relied upon, for example, an internal protocol, copies should be provided.

3.26   If the patient has made an offer to settle, the healthcare provider should **respond to that offer** in the response letter, preferably with reasons. The provider may make its own offer to settle at this stage, either as a counter-offer to the patient's, or of its own accord, but should accompany any offer by any supporting medical evidence, and/or by any other evidence in relation to the value of the claim which is in the healthcare provider's possession.

3.27   If the parties reach agreement on liability, but time is needed to resolve the value of the claim, they should aim to agree a reasonable period.

Experts

4.1   In clinical negligence disputes **expert opinions** may be needed:

on breach of duty and causation;

on the patient's condition and prognosis;

to assist in valuing aspects of the claim.

4.2   The civil justice reforms and the new **Civil Procedure Rules** will encourage economy in the use of experts and a **less adversarial expert culture**. It is recognised that in clinical negligence disputes, the parties and their advisors will require flexibility in their approach to expert evidence. Decisions on whether experts might be instructed jointly, and on whether reports might be disclosed sequentially or by exchange, should rest with the parties and their advisors. Sharing expert evidence may be appropriate on issues relating to the value of the claim. However, this protocol does not attempt to be prescriptive on issues in relation to expert evidence.

4.3   Obtaining expert evidence will often be an expensive step and may take time, especially in specialised areas of medicine where there are limited numbers of suitable experts. Patients and healthcare providers, and their advisors, will therefore need to consider carefully how best to obtain any necessary expert help quickly and cost effectively. Assistance with locating a suitable expert is available from a number of sources.

Alternative approaches to settling disputes

5.1   It would not be practicable for this protocol to address in any detail how a patient or their advisor, or healthcare provider, might decide which method to adopt to resolve the particular problem. But the courts increasingly expect parties to try to settle their differences by agreement before issuing proceedings.

5.2   Most disputes are resolved by **discussion and negotiation**. Parties should bear in mind that carefully planned face-to-face meetings may be particularly helpful in exploring further treatment for the patient, in reaching understandings about what happened, and on both parties' positions, in narrowing the issues in dispute and, if the timing is right, in helping to settle the whole matter.

5.3   Summarised below are some other alternatives for resolving disputes:

The revised NHS Complaints Procedure, which was implemented in April 1996, is designed to provide patients with an explanation of what happened and an apology if appropriate. It is not designed to provide compensation for cases of negligence. However, patients might choose to use the procedure if their only, or main, goal is to obtain an explanation, or to obtain more information to help them decide what other action might be appropriate.

Mediation may be appropriate in some cases: this is a form of facilitated negotiation assisted by an independent neutral party. It is expected that the new Civil Procedure Rules will give the court the power to stay proceedings for one month for settlement discussions or mediation.

Other methods of resolving disputes include arbitration, determination by an expert and early neutral evaluation by a medical or legal expert. The Legal Services Commission has published a booklet on '**Alternatives to Court**', LSC August 2001, CLS information leaflet number 23, which lists a number of organisations that provide alternative dispute resolution services.

Annex A
Illustrative flowchart

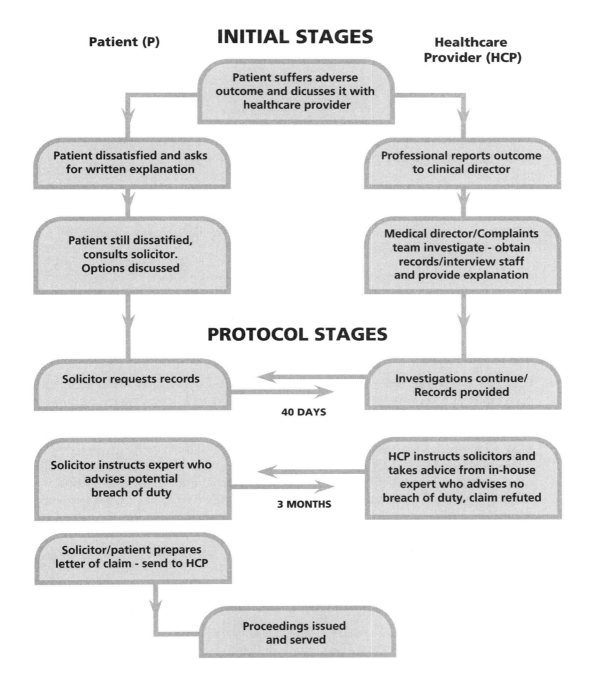

Annex B
Medical negligence and personal injury claims

A protocol for obtaining hospital medical records

Civil Litigation Committee
Revised edition
June 1998

APPLICATION ON BEHALF OF A PATIENT FOR HOSPITAL MEDICAL RECORDS
FOR USE WHEN COURT PROCEEDINGS ARE CONTEMPLATED

Purpose of the forms

This application form and response forms have been prepared by a working party of the Law Society's Civil Litigation Committee and approved by the Department of Health for use in NHS and Trust hospitals.

The purpose of the forms is to standardise and streamline the disclosure of medical records to a patient's solicitors, who are investigating pursuing a personal injury claim against a third party, or a medical negligence claim against the hospital to which the application is addressed and/or other hospitals or GPs.

Use of the forms

Use of the forms is entirely voluntary and does not prejudice any party's right under the Access to Health Records Act 1990, the Data Protection Act 1984, or sections 33 and 34 of the Supreme Court Act 1981. However, it is Department of Health policy that patients be permitted to see what has been written about them, and that healthcare providers should make arrangements to allow patients to see all their records, not only those covered by the Access to Health Records Act 1990. The aim of the forms is to save time and costs for all concerned for the benefit of the patient and the hospital and in the interests of justice. Use of the forms should make it unnecessary in most cases for there to be exchanges of letters or other enquiries. If there is any unusual matter not covered by the form, the patient's solicitor may write a separate letter at the outset.

Charges for the records

The Access to Health Records Act 1990 prescribes a maximum fee of £10. Photocopying and postage costs can be charged in addition. No other charges may be made.

The NHS Executive guidance makes it clear to healthcare providers that 'it is a perfectly proper use' of the 1990 Act to request records in that framework for the purpose of potential or actual litigation, whether against a third party or against the hospital or trust.

The 1990 Act does not permit differential rates of charges to be levied if the application is made by the patient, or by a solicitor on his behalf, or whether the response to the application is made by the healthcare provider directly (the medical records manager or a claims manager) or by a solicitor.

The NHS Executive guidance recommends that the same practice should be followed with regard to charges when the records are provided under a voluntary agreement as under the 1990 Act, except that in those circumstances the £10 access fee will not be appropriate.

The NHS Executive also advises:

> that the cost of photocopying may include 'the cost of staff time in making copies' and the costs of running the copier (but not costs of locating and sifting records);

> that the common practice of setting a standard rate for an application or charging an administration fee is not acceptable because there will be cases when this fails to comply with the 1990 Act.

Records: what might be included

X-rays and test results form part of the patient's records. Additional charges for copying X-rays are permissible. If there are large numbers of X-rays, the records officer should check with the patient/solicitor before arranging copying.

Reports on an 'adverse incident' and reports on the patient made for risk management and audit purposes may form part of the records and be disclosable; the exception will be any specific record or report made solely or mainly in connection with an actual or potential claim.

Records: quality standards

When copying records healthcare providers should ensure:

1. All documents are legible, and complete, if necessary by photocopying at less than 100% size.

2. Documents larger than A4 in the original, for example, ITU charts, should be reproduced in A3, or reduced to A4 where this retains readability.

3. Documents are copied only on one side of paper, unless the original is two sided.

4. Documents should not be unnecessarily shuffled or bound and holes should not be made in the copied papers.

Enquiries/further information

Any enquiries about the forms should be made initially to the solicitors making the request. Comments on the use and content of the forms should be made to the Secretary,

Civil Litigation Committee, The Law Society, 113 Chancery Lane, London WC2A 1PL, telephone 020 7320 5739, or to the NHS Management Executive, Quarry House, Quarry Hill, Leeds LS2 7UE.

The Law Society

May 1998

Application on behalf of a patient for hospital medical records for use when court proceedings are contemplated

This form should be completed as fully as possible

[Insert hospital name and address]

To: Medical Records Office   Hospital

1   a)   Full name of patient (including previous surname)

    b)   Address now

    c)   Address at start of treatment

    d)   Date of birth (and death, if applicable)

    e)   Hospital ref. no if available

    f)   NI Number if available

2   This application is made because patient is considering

    a)   a claim against your hospital as
        detailed in para 7 below   YES/NO

    b)   pursuing an action against someone else   YES/NO

3   Department(s) where treatment was received

4   Name(s) of consultant(s) at your hospital in charge of the treatment

5   Whether treatment at your hospital was private or NHS, wholly or in part

6   A description of the treatment received, with approximate dates

7   If the answer to Q2(a) is 'YES' details of

    a)   the likely nature of the claim

    b)   grounds for the claim

    c)   approximate dates of the events involved

8 If the answer to Q2(b) is 'YES' insert

    a)   the names of the proposed defendants

    b)   whether legal proceedings yet begun   YES/NO

    c)   if appropriate, details of the claim and action number

9 We confirm we will pay reasonable copying charges

10 We request prior details of

    a)   photocopying and administration
        charges for medical records   YES/NO

    b)   number of and cost of copying X-ray and scan films   YES/NO

11 Any other relevant information, particular requirements, or any particular documents not required (e.g. copies of computerised records)

Signature of solicitor

Name

Address

Ref.

Telephone number   Fax number

Signature of patient

Please print name beneath each signature. Signature by child over 12 but under 18 years also requires signature by parent.

Signature of parent or next friend if appropriate

Signature of personal representative where patient has died

First response to application for hospital records

Name of patient

Our ref.

Your ref.

1   Date of receipt of patient's application

2   We intend that copy medical records
will be dispatched within six weeks of that date   YES/NO

3   We require pre-payment of photocopying charges   YES/NO

4   If estimate of photocopying charges
requested or pre-payment required
the amount will be   £   /notified to you

5   The cost of X-ray and scan films will be   £   /notified to you

6   If there is any problem, we shall write to within those six weeks   YES/NO

7   Any other information

8   Please address further correspondence to

Signed

Direct telephone number   Direct fax number

Dated

Second response enclosing patient's hospital medical records

Address

Our ref.   Your ref.

Name of patient

1   We confirm that the enclosed copy medical records are
all those within the control of the hospital, relevant to
the application which you have made to the best of our
knowledge and belief, subject to paras 2–5 below   YES/NO

2   Details of any other documents that have not yet been located

3   Date by when it is expected that these will be supplied

4   Details of any records which we are not producing

5   The reasons for not doing so

6   An invoice for copying and administration
charges as attached   YES/NO

Signed

Dated

Annex C
Templates for letters of claim and response

Letter of claim

Essential contents

1. Client's name, address, date of birth, etc

2. Dates of allegedly negligent treatment

3. Events giving rise to the claim:

    an outline of what happened, including details of other relevant treatments to the client by other healthcare providers.

4. Allegation of negligence and causal link with injuries:

    an outline of the allegations or a more detailed list in a complex case;

    an outline of the causal link between allegations and the injuries complained of.

5. The client's injuries, condition and future prognosis

6. Request for clinical records (if not previously provided):

    use the Law Society form if appropriate or adapt;

    specify the records required;

    if other records are held by other providers, and may be relevant, say so;

    state what investigations have been carried out to date, for example, information from client and witnesses, any complaint and the outcome, if any clinical records have been seen or experts' advice obtained.

7. The likely value of the claim:

    an outline of the main heads of damage, or, in straightforward cases, the details of loss.

Optional information

What investigations have been carried out

An offer to settle without supporting evidence

Suggestions for obtaining expert evidence

Suggestions for meetings, negotiations, discussion or mediation

Possible enclosures

Chronology

Clinical records request form and client's authorisation

Expert report(s)

Schedules of loss and supporting evidence

Letter of response

Essential contents

1. Provide **requested records** and invoice for copying:

    explain if records are incomplete or extensive records are held and ask for further instructions;

    request additional records from third parties.

2. **Comments on events and/or chronology:**

    if events are disputed or the healthcare provider has further information or documents on which it wishes to rely, these should be provided, for example, internal protocol;

    details of any further information needed from the patient or a third party should be provided.

3. **If breach of duty and causation are accepted:**

    suggestions might be made for resolving the claim and/or requests for further information;

    a response should be made to any offer to settle.

4. **If breach of duty and/or causation are denied:**

    a bare denial will not be sufficient. If the healthcare provider has other explanations for what happened, these should be given at least in outline;

    suggestions might be made for the next steps, for example, further investigations, obtaining expert evidence, meetings/negotiations or mediation, or an invitation to issue proceedings.

Optional matters

An offer to settle if the patient has not made one, or a counter-offer to the patient's with supporting evidence

Possible enclosures

Clinical records

Annotated chronology

Expert reports

Annex D
Lord Woolf's recommendations

1. Lord Woolf in his Access to Justice Report in July 1996, following a detailed review of the problems of medical negligence claims, identified that one of the major sources of **costs and delay** is at the **pre-litigation stage** because:

    (a) Inadequate incident reporting and record keeping in hospitals, and mobility of staff, make it difficult to establish facts, often several years after the event.

    (b) Claimants must incur the cost of an expert in order to establish whether they have a viable claim.

    (c) There is often a long delay before a claim is made.

    (d) Defendants do not have sufficient resources to carry out a full investigation of every incident, and do not consider it worthwhile to start an investigation as soon as they receive a request for records, because many cases do not proceed beyond that stage.

    (e) Patients often give the defendant little or no notice of a firm intention to pursue a claim. Consequently, many incidents are not investigated by the defendants until after proceedings have started.

    (f) Doctors and other clinical staff are traditionally reluctant to admit negligence or apologise to, or negotiate with, claimants for fear of damage to their professional reputations or career prospects.

2. Lord Woolf acknowledged that under the present arrangements **healthcare providers**, faced with possible medical negligence claims, have a number of **practical problems** to contend with:

    (a) Difficulties of finding patients' records and tracing former staff, which can be exacerbated by late notification and by the healthcare provider's own failure to identify adverse incidents.

    (b) The healthcare provider may have treated the patient for only a limited time or for a specific complaint: the patient's previous history may be relevant but the records may be in the possession of one of several other healthcare providers.

(c)   The large number of potential claims which do not proceed beyond the stage of a request for medical records, or an explanation; and that it is difficult for healthcare providers to investigate fully every case whenever a patient asks to see the records.

Annex E
How to contact the forum

The Clinical Disputes Forum

Chairman
Dr Alastair Scotland
Medical Director and Chief Officer
National Clinical Assessment Authority
9th Floor, Market Towers
London SW8 5NQ
Tel: 020 7273 0850

Secretary
Sarah Leigh
c/o Margaret Dangoor
3 Clydesdale Gardens
Richmond
Surrey TW10 5EG
Tel: 020 8408 1012

Appendix 5
EXTRACT FROM THE CONSTRUCTION AND ENGINEERING DISPUTES PRE-ACTION PROTOCOL

Letter of claim

3.   Prior to commencing proceedings, the claimant or his solicitor shall send to each proposed defendant (if appropriate to his registered address) a copy of a letter of claim which shall contain the following information:

(i)   the claimant's full name and address;

(ii)   the full name and address of each proposed defendant;

(iii)   a clear summary of the facts on which each claim is based;

(iv)   the basis on which each claim is made, identifying the principal contractual terms and statutory provisions relied on;

(v)   the nature of the relief claimed: if damages are claimed, a breakdown showing how the damages have been quantified; if a sum is claimed pursuant to a contract, how it has been calculated; if an extension of time is claimed, the period claimed;

(vi)   where a claim has been made previously and rejected by a defendant, and the claimant is able to identify the reason(s) for such rejection, the claimant's grounds of belief as to why the claim was wrongly rejected;

(vii)   the names of any experts already instructed by the claimant on whose evidence he intends to rely, identifying the issues to which that evidence will be directed.

Defendant's response

Defendant's acknowledgement

4.1   Within 14 calendar days of receipt of the letter of claim, the defendant should acknowledge its receipt in writing and may give the name and address of his insurer (if any). If there has been no acknowledgement by or on behalf of the defendant within 14 days, the claimant will be entitled to commence proceedings without further compliance with this protocol.

Objections to the court's jurisdiction or the named defendant

4.2.1   If the defendant intends to take any objection to all or any part of the claimant's claim on the grounds that (i) the court lacks jurisdiction, (ii) the matter should be referred to arbitration, or (iii) the defendant named in the letter of claim is the wrong defendant, that objection should be raised by the defendant within 28 days after receipt of the letter of claim. The letter of objection shall specify the parts of the claim to which the objection relates, setting out the grounds relied on, and, where appropriate, shall identify the correct defendant (if known). Any failure to take such objection shall not prejudice the defendant's rights to do so in any subsequent proceedings, but the court may take such failure into account when considering the question of costs.

4.2.2   Where such notice of objection is given, the defendant is not required to send a letter of response in accordance with paragraph 4.3.1 in relation to the claim or those parts of it to which the objection relates (as the case may be).

4.2.3   If at any stage before the claimant commences proceedings the defendant withdraws his objection, then paragraph 4.3 and the remaining part of this protocol will apply to the claim or those parts of it to which the objection related as if the letter of claim had been received on the date on which notice of withdrawal of the objection had been given.

Defendant's response

4.3.1   Within 28 days from the date of receipt of the letter of claim, or such other period as the parties may reasonably agree (up to a maximum of four months), the defendant shall send a letter of response to the claimant which shall contain the following information:

(i)   the facts set out in the letter of claim which are agreed or not agreed, and if not agreed, the basis of the disagreement;

(ii)   which claims are accepted and which are rejected, and if rejected, the basis of the rejection;

(iii)   if a claim is accepted in whole or in part, whether the damages, sums or extensions of time claimed are accepted or rejected, and if rejected, the basis of the rejection;

(iv)   if contributory negligence is alleged against the claimant, a summary of the facts relied on;

(v)   whether the defendant intends to make a counterclaim, and if so, giving the information which is required to be given in a letter of claim by paragraph 3(iii) to (vi) above;

(vi)   the names of any experts already instructed on whose evidence it is intended to rely, identifying the issues to which that evidence will be directed;

4.3.2   If no response is received by the claimant within the period of 28 days (or such other period as has been agreed between the parties), the claimant shall be entitled to commence proceedings without further compliance with this protocol.

Claimant's response to counterclaim

4.4   The claimant shall provide a response to any counterclaim within the equivalent period allowed to the defendant to respond to the letter of claim under paragraph 4.3.1 above.

Pre-action meeting

5.1   As soon as possible after receipt by the claimant of the defendant's letter of response, or (if the claimant intends to respond to the counterclaim) after receipt by the defendant of the claimant's letter of response to the counterclaim, the parties should normally meet.

5.2   The aim of the meeting is for the parties to agree what are the main issues in the case, to identify the root cause of disagreement in respect of each issue, and to consider (i) whether, and if so how, the issues might be resolved without recourse to litigation, and (ii) if litigation is unavoidable, what steps should be taken to ensure that it is conducted in accordance with the overriding objective as defined in Part 1.1 of the Civil Practice Rules.

5.3   In some circumstances, it may be necessary to convene more than one meeting. It is not intended by this protocol to prescribe in detail the manner in which the meetings should be conducted. But the court will normally expect that those attending will include:

   (i)   where the party is an individual, that individual, and where the party is a corporate body, a representative of that body who has authority to settle or recommend settlement of the dispute;

   (ii)   a legal representative of each party (if one has been instructed);

   (iii)   where the involvement of insurers has been disclosed, a representative of the insurer (who may be its legal representative); and

   (iv)   where a claim is made or defended on behalf of some other party (such as, for example, a claim made by a main contractor pursuant to a contractual obligation to pass on subcontractor claims), the party on whose behalf the claim is made or defended and/or his legal representatives.

5.4   In respect of each agreed issue or the dispute as a whole, the parties should consider whether some form of alternative dispute resolution procedure would be more suitable than litigation, and if so, endeavour to agree which form to adopt.

5.5   If the parties are unable to agree on a means of resolving the dispute other than by litigation, they should use their best endeavours to agree:

(i)   whether, if there is any area where expert evidence is likely to be required, a joint expert may be appointed, and if so, who that should be; and (so far as is practicable)

(ii)   the extent of disclosure of documents with a view to saving costs; and

(iii)   the conduct of the litigation with the aim of minimising cost and delay.

5.6   Any party who attended any pre-action meeting shall be at liberty to disclose to the court:

(i)   that the meeting took place, when and who attended;

(ii)   the identity of any party who refused to attend, and the grounds for such refusal;

(iii)   if the meeting did not take place, why not; and

(iv)   any agreements concluded between the parties.

5.7   Except as provided in paragraph 5.6, everything said at a pre-action meeting shall be treated as 'without prejudice'.

Limitation of action

6.   If by reason of complying with any part of this protocol a claimant's claim may be time-barred under any provision of the Limitation Act 1980, or any other legislation that imposes a time limit for bringing an action, the claimant may commence proceedings without complying with this protocol. In such circumstances, a claimant who commences proceedings without complying with all, or any part, of this protocol must apply to the court on notice for directions as to the timetable and form of procedure to be adopted, at the same time as he requests the court to issue proceedings. The court will consider whether to order a stay of the whole or part of the proceedings pending compliance with this protocol.

Appendix 6
EXTRACT FROM THE PROFESSIONAL NEGLIGENCE CLAIMS PRE-ACTION PROTOCOL

Preliminary Notice (see also Guidance note C3.1)

B1.1   As soon as the claimant decides there is a reasonable chance that he will bring a claim against a professional, the claimant is encouraged to notify the professional in writing.

B1.2   This letter should contain the following information:

(a)   the identity of the claimant and any other parties;

(b)   a brief outline of the claimant's grievance against the professional;

(c)   if possible, a general indication of the financial value of the potential claim.

B1.3   This letter should be addressed to the professional and should ask the professional to inform his professional indemnity insurers, if any, immediately.

B1.4   The professional should acknowledge receipt of the claimant's letter within 21 days of receiving it. Other than this acknowledgement, the protocol places no obligation upon either party to take any further action.

Letter of claim

B2.1   As soon as the claimant decides there are grounds for a claim against the professional, the claimant should write a detailed letter of claim to the professional.

B2.2   The letter of claim will normally be an open letter (as opposed to being 'without prejudice') and should include the following:

(a)   The identity of any other parties involved in the dispute or a related dispute.

(b)   A clear chronological summary (including key dates) of the facts on which the claim is based. Key documents should be identified, copied and enclosed.

(c)   The allegations against the professional. What has he done wrong? What has he failed to do?

(d)   An explanation of how the alleged error has caused the loss claimed.

(e)   An estimate of the financial loss suffered by the claimant and how it is calculated. Supporting documents should be identified, copied and enclosed. If details of the financial loss cannot be supplied, the claimant should explain why and should state when he will be in a position to provide the details. This information should be sent to the professional as soon as reasonably possible.

> If the claimant is seeking some form of non-financial redress, this should be made clear.

(f) Confirmation whether or not an expert has been appointed. If so, providing the identity and discipline of the expert, together with the date upon which the expert was appointed.

(g) A request that a copy of the letter of claim be forwarded immediately to the professional's insurers, if any.

B2.3 The letter of claim is not intended to have the same formal status as a Statement of Case. If, however, the letter of claim differs materially from the Statement of Case in subsequent proceedings, the court may decide, in its discretion, to impose sanctions.

B2.4 If the claimant has sent other letters of claim (or equivalent) to any other party in relation to this dispute or related dispute, those letters should be copied to the professional. (If the claimant is claiming against someone else to whom this protocol does not apply, please see Guidance note C4.)

Letter of acknowledgement

B3.1 The professional should acknowledge receipt of the letter of claim within 21 days of receiving it.

Investigations

B4.1 The professional will have three months from the date of the letter of acknowledgement to investigate.

B4.2 If the professional is in difficulty in complying with the three-month time period, the problem should be explained to the claimant as soon as possible. The professional should explain what is being done to resolve the problem and when the professional expects to complete the investigations. The claimant should agree to any reasonable request for an extension of the three-month period.

B4.3 The parties should supply promptly, at this stage and throughout, whatever relevant information or documentation is reasonably requested. (Please see Guidance note C5.)

(If the professional intends to claim against someone who is not currently a party to the dispute, please see Guidance note C4.)

Letter of response and letter of settlement

B5.1 As soon as the professional has completed his investigations, the professional should send to the claimant:

(a)   a letter of response; or

(b)   a letter of settlement; or

(c)   both.

The letters of response and settlement can be contained within a single letter.

Letter of response

B5.2 The letter of response will normally be an open letter (as opposed to being 'without prejudice') and should be a reasoned answer to the claimant's allegations:

(a)   If the claim is admitted, the professional should say so in clear terms.

(b)   If only part of the claim is admitted, the professional should make clear which parts of the claim are admitted and which are denied.

(c)   If the claim is denied in whole or in part, the letter of response should include specific comments on the allegations against the professional and, if the claimant's version of events is disputed, the professional should provide his version of events.

(d)   If the professional is unable to admit or deny the claim, the professional should identify any further information which is required.

(e)   If the professional disputes the estimate of the claimant's financial loss, the letter of response should set out the professional's estimate. If an estimate cannot be provided, the professional should explain why and should state when he will be in a position to provide an estimate. This information should be sent to the claimant as soon as reasonably possible.

(f)   Where additional documents are relied upon, copies should be provided.

B5.3 The letter of response is not intended to have the same formal status as a Defence. If, however, the letter of response differs materially from the Defence in subsequent proceedings, the court may decide, in its discretion, to impose sanctions.

Letter of settlement

B5.4 The letter of settlement will normally be a without prejudice letter and should be sent if the professional intends to make proposals for settlement. It should:

(a)   set out the professional's views to date on the claim identifying those issues which the professional believes are likely to remain in dispute and those which are not (this information is unnecessary, however, if the professional has sent a letter of response);

(b)   make a settlement proposal or identify any further information which is required before the professional can formulate its proposals;

(c)   provide copies where additional documents are relied upon.

Effect of letter of response and/or letter of settlement

B5.5   If the letter of response denies the claim in its entirety and there is no letter of settlement, it is open to the claimant to commence proceedings.

B5.6   In any other circumstance, the professional and the claimant should commence negotiations with the aim of concluding those negotiations within six months of the date of the letter of acknowledgement (NOT from the date of the letter of response).

B5.7   If the claim cannot be resolved within this period:

(a)   The parties should agree within 14 days of the end of the period whether the period should be extended and, if so, by how long.

(b)   The parties should seek to identify those issues which are still in dispute and those which can be agreed.

(c)   If an extension of time is not agreed, it will then be open to the claimant to commence proceedings.

Alternative dispute resolution

B6.1   The parties can agree at any stage to take the dispute (or any part of the dispute) to mediation or some other form of alternative dispute resolution (ADR).

B6.2   In addition, any party at any stage can refer the dispute (or any part of the dispute) to an ADR agency for mediation or some other form of ADR.

B6.3   When approached by a party or an ADR agency with a proposal that ADR be used, the other party or parties should respond within 14 days stating that:

(a)   they agree to the proposal; or

(b)   they agree that ADR will be or may be appropriate, but they believe it has been suggested prematurely. They should state when they anticipate it would or may become appropriate; or

(c)   they agree that ADR is appropriate, but not the form of ADR proposed (if any). They should state the form of ADR which they believe to be appropriate; or

(d) they do not accept that any form of ADR is appropriate. They should state their reasons.

This letter should be copied to the other party or parties and can be disclosed to the court on the issue of costs.

B6.4 It is expressly recognised that no party can or should be forced to mediate or enter into any other form of ADR.

Experts

(The following provisions apply where the claim raises an issue of professional expertise whose resolution requires expert evidence.)

B7.1 If the claimant has obtained expert evidence prior to sending the letter of claim, the professional will have equal right to obtain expert evidence prior to sending the letter of response/letter of settlement.

B7.2 If the claimant has not obtained expert evidence prior to sending the letter of claim, the parties are encouraged to appoint a joint expert. If they agree to do so, they should seek to agree the identity of the expert and the terms of the expert's appointment.

B7.3 If agreement about a joint expert cannot be reached, all parties are free to appoint their own experts.

(For further details on experts see Guidance note C6.)

Proceedings

B8.1 Unless it is necessary (e.g. to obtain protection against the expiry of a relevant limitation period) the claimant should not start court proceedings until:

(a) the letter of response denies the claim in its entirety and there is no letter of settlement (see paragraph B5.5 above); or

(b) the end of the negotiation period (see paragraphs B5.6 and B5.7 above).

(For further discussion of statutory time limits for the commencement of litigation, please see Guidance note C7.)

B8.2 Where possible 14 days' written notice should be given to the professional before proceedings are started, indicating the court within which the claimant is intending to commence litigation.

B8.3 Proceedings should be served on the professional, unless the professional's solicitor has notified the claimant in writing that he is authorised to accept service on behalf of the professional.

GUIDANCE NOTES

Introduction

C1.1   The protocol has been kept simple to promote ease of use and general acceptability. The guidance notes which follow relate particularly to issues on which further guidance may be required.

C1.2   The Woolf reforms envisage that parties will act reasonably in the pre-action period. Accordingly, in the event that the protocol and the guidelines do not specifically address a problem, the parties should comply with the spirit of the protocol by acting reasonably.

Scope of protocol

C2.1   The protocol is specifically designed for claims of negligence against professionals. This will include claims in which the allegation against a professional is that he has breached a contractual term to take reasonable skill and care. The protocol is also appropriate for claims of breach of fiduciary duty against professionals.

C2.2   The protocol is not intended to apply to claims:

     (a)   against architects, engineers and quantity surveyors – parties should use the Construction and Engineering Disputes (CED) protocol;

     (b)   against healthcare providers – parties should use the pre-action protocol for the Resolution of Clinical Disputes;

     (c)   concerning defamation – parties should use the pre-action protocol for defamation claims.

C2.3   'Professional' is deliberately left undefined in the protocol. If it becomes an issue as to whether a defendant is or is not a professional, parties are reminded of the overriding need to act reasonably (see paragraphs A4 and C1.2 above). Rather than argue about the definition of 'professional', therefore, the parties are invited to use this protocol, adapting it where appropriate.

C2.4   The protocol may not be suitable for disputes with professionals concerning intellectual property claims, etc. Until specific protocols are created for those claims, however, parties are invited to use this protocol, adapting it where necessary.

C2.5   Allegations of professional negligence are sometimes made in response to an attempt by the professional to recover outstanding fees. Where possible these allegations should be raised before litigation has commenced, in which case the parties should comply with the protocol before either party commences litigation. If litigation has already commenced, it will be a matter for the court whether sanctions should be imposed against either party. In any event, the parties are encouraged to consider applying to the court for a stay to allow the protocol to be followed.

Interaction with other pre-action methods of dispute resolution

C3.1 There are a growing number of methods by which disputes can be resolved without the need for litigation, for example, internal complaints procedures, the Surveyors and Valuers Arbitration Scheme, and so on. The Preliminary Notice procedure of the protocol (see paragraph B1) is designed to enable both parties to take stock at an early stage and to decide before work starts on preparing a letter of claim whether the grievance should be referred to one of these other dispute resolution procedures. (For the avoidance of doubt, however, there is no obligation on either party under the protocol to take any action at this stage other than giving the acknowledgement provided for in paragraph B1.4.)

C3.2 Accordingly, parties are free to use (and are encouraged to use) any of the available pre-action procedures in an attempt to resolve their dispute. If appropriate, the parties can agree to suspend the protocol timetable whilst the other method of dispute resolution is used.

C3.3 If these methods fail to resolve the dispute, however, the protocol should be used before litigation is commenced. Because there has already been an attempt to resolve the dispute, it may be appropriate to adjust the protocol's requirements. In particular, unless the parties agree otherwise, there is unlikely to be any benefit in duplicating a stage which has in effect already been undertaken. However, if the protocol adds anything to the earlier method of dispute resolution, it should be used, adapting it where appropriate. Once again, the parties are expected to act reasonably.

Multi-party disputes

C4.1 Paragraph B2.2 (a) of the protocol requires a claimant to identify any other parties involved in the dispute or a related dispute. This is intended to ensure that all relevant parties are identified as soon as possible.

C4.2 If the dispute involves more than two parties, there are a number of potential problems. It is possible that different protocols will apply to different defendants. It is possible that defendants will claim against each other. It is possible that other parties will be drawn into the dispute. It is possible that the protocol timetable against one party will not be synchronised with the protocol timetable against a different party. How will these problems be resolved?

C4.3 As stated in paragraph C1.2 above, the parties are expected to act reasonably. What is 'reasonable' will, of course, depend upon the specific facts of each case. Accordingly, it would be inappropriate for the protocol to set down generalised rules. Whenever a problem arises, the parties are encouraged to discuss how it can be overcome. In doing so, parties are reminded of the protocol's aims which include the aim to resolve the dispute without the need for litigation (paragraph A2 above).

Investigations

C5.1   Paragraph B4.3 is intended to encourage the early exchange of relevant information, so that issues in the dispute can be clarified or resolved. It should not be used as a 'fishing expedition' by either party. No party is obliged under paragraph B4.3 to disclose any document which a court could not order them to disclose in the pre-action period.

C5.2   This protocol does not alter the parties' duties to disclose documents under any professional regulation or under general law.

Experts

C6.1   Expert evidence is not always needed, although the use and role of experts in professional negligence claims is often crucial. However, the way in which expert evidence is used in, say, an insurance brokers' negligence case, is not necessarily the same as in, say, an accountants' case. Similarly, the approach to be adopted in a £10,000 case does not necessarily compare with the approach in a £10 million case. The protocol therefore is designed to be flexible and does not dictate a standard approach. On the contrary, it envisages that the parties will bear the responsibility for agreeing how best to use experts.

C6.2   If a joint expert is used, therefore, the parties are left to decide issues such as: the payment of the expert, whether joint or separate instructions are used, how and to whom the expert is to report, how questions may be addressed to the expert and how the expert should respond, whether an agreed statement of facts is required, and so on.

C6.3   If separate experts are used, the parties are left to decide issues such as: whether the expert's reports should be exchanged, whether there should be an expert's meeting, and so on.

C6.4   Even if a joint expert is appointed, it is possible that parties will still want to instruct their own experts. The protocol does not prohibit this.

Proceedings

C7.1   This protocol does not alter the statutory time limits for starting court proceedings. A claimant is required to start proceedings within those time limits.

C7.2   If proceedings are for any reason started before the parties have followed the procedures in this protocol, the parties are encouraged to agree to apply to the court for a stay whilst the protocol is followed.

(*Note: A complete outline of the pre-action protocols mentioned in this book can be found at the Department for Constitutional Affairs' website at www.dca.gov.uk/civil/procrules_fin/menus/protocol.htm.*)

Appendix 7
PRE-ACTION MATERIALS WHERE NO PROTOCOL APPLIES

The courts expect litigants to comply with the following steps before the claim is issued. The court will take into account a party's failure to comply with these guidelines (and the reasons for his failure) when considering whether to make a party pay for the other's legal costs. The requirements are set out in a practice direction supplementing the Civil Procedure Rules 1998.

General guidance

The court expects parties to 'act reasonably in exchanging information and documents relevant to the claim and generally in trying to avoid the necessity for the start of legal proceedings'. The timescales given are guidelines only; in some circumstances, less time may be appropriate, and in others more may be reasonable. Readers should also look through the pre-action protocols; material and procedures from them may be used from them, if appropriate to the case (such as adapted sample letters, or a pre-action meeting similar to that required by the pre-action protocol for construction and engineering disputes).

Step one

The (potential) claimant writes a letter of claim to the (potential) defendant. The letter should give enough details for the defendant to start investigating the circumstances without asking for much more information. The essential documents that the claimant relies upon (such as a contract, etc) should be enclosed. The claimant should ask for an acknowledgement and detailed response within one month (or other suitable time period), and state that a claim will be issued if no full response is given. If further documents belonging to the defendant are required, they should be asked for (see chapter 4 for a discussion of disclosure of documents). An example letter of claim containing this and other suggested information is set out below.

Step two

The defendant sends a letter of acknowledgement within 21 days of receiving the letter of claim, acknowledging that he has received the letter of claim

Step three

The defendant sends the claimant his full response to the letter of claim. This sets out his position: either admitting the whole claim in principle (and if possible making proposals for settlement), admitting part of the claim and denying part (and if possible making proposals for settlement) or denying the claim. Detailed reasons should be given for each item denied, and matters that are agreed should be identified clearly (e.g. the date of an accident, the identity of the parties involved, the place of the accident, and so on).

Copies of documents requested by the claimant should be enclosed where possible and if there is a legitimate reason for not doing so, that reason should be given (such as the document in question being 'legally privileged' – see chapter 4 for an explantation of disclosure of documents). The defendant may also ask the claimant to send him copies of essential documents that he does not have.

Step four

The courts expect the parties to try to negotiate promptly a settlement of the dispute. See the discussion of this topic generally at chapter 3.

Step five

(This of course may occur at any stage in the dispute prior to issue of the claim, and will not necessarily be at 'stage five' in the pre-action conduct of the dispute.) The parties should, where possible, try to instruct a suitable expert jointly. See the discussion about instructing a joint expert in chapter 3.

Specimen letter of claim

> 12 Barings Road
> Estreham
> Norfolk
>
> 20 February 2004
>
> Mr J Snooks
> 108 Innerwick Close
> Northfields
> Suffolk
>
> Dear Mr Snooks
>
> *[One phrase describing the subject matter of the complaint]*
>
> I am writing to claim damages from you arising from the *[here state the date and nature of the incident such as 'my purchase from you of a pedigree spaniel puppy on 9 November 2003' or 'the trespass to 12 Barings Road, Estreham, Norfolk that occurred on 20 January 2004'].*
>
> My claim is based upon the following facts: *[here set out what happened, giving details of dates, times, places, persons involved, details of the negligence or deliberate intention of the defendant or other relevant persons, any employment relationship relied upon, etc.].*
>
> I enclose the following documents in support of my claim: *[list].*
>
> My loss/damage is as follows: *[here give a brief outline of the loss, expense and damage, giving figures where possible for special damages, and listing the types of loss or damage that attract general damages].*
>
> The following documents are relevant to this claim, and are in your possession. Please could you send me copies when you acknowledge this letter: *[list the documents].*
>
> Please acknowledge receipt of this letter promptly, and fully respond in writing to the above within *[one month, or other suitable period].*
>
> *[I am willing to consider mediation/other alternative method of dispute resolution.]*
>
> Please note that the court has the power to impose sanctions for failure to comply with the practice direction on pre-action protocols; please seek legal advice from a solicitor or Citizens Advice Bureau.
>
> Yours sincerely
>
> *Mr Smith*

Specimen letter of instruction to expert (non-personal injury cases)

12 Barings Road
Estreham
Norfolk

20 February 2004

Dorrit, Chuzzlewit & Twist
Gartmore House
1747 Finlarich Road
London W1

Dear Mr Chuzzlewit

Re: *[identify date, time and nature of incident]*

I am seeking compensation from *[name]* for loss and damage arising from *[incident or nature of behaviour complained of]*/We are potential parties to litigation arising from *[incident or nature of behaviour complained of]*.

I/We would be grateful if you could arrange to examine *[state the item, premises or documents which are to be examined]* and produce a full and detailed report for possible use in court.

The report should deal with the following matters: *[list here the matters which the expert must deal with; e.g. liability (who is legally to blame), causation, the amount of damages (also known as 'quantum'). In most circumstances it is helpful to ask the expert to deal with specific questions, especially where the claimant and defendant have a significant factual dispute. One way to deal with this is to ask the expert to venture an opinion on different factual scenarios – 'please consider the effect on (liability, causation or quantum) in the following circumstances – x, y or z'].*

I/We enclose the following documents for your information; they were produced *[state how, when and by whom, if relevant]*: *[list]*.

I/We confirm that we will be jointly responsible for your reasonable fees for producing the report and if necessary attendance at court.

Please could you confirm the date you will be able to produce the report by, by telephoning *[number]* or in writing as soon as you receive this letter of instruction.

Yours sincerely

Mr Smith

Appendix 8

FORMS

N1 Claim Form
(Part 7 claims)

Where: If you are suing in the High Court, you should bring the claim in your local District Registry, or if there is not one, the Royal Courts of Justice in London. If you are suing in the County court, you may begin in any County court but the case may be transferred to a more convenient court.

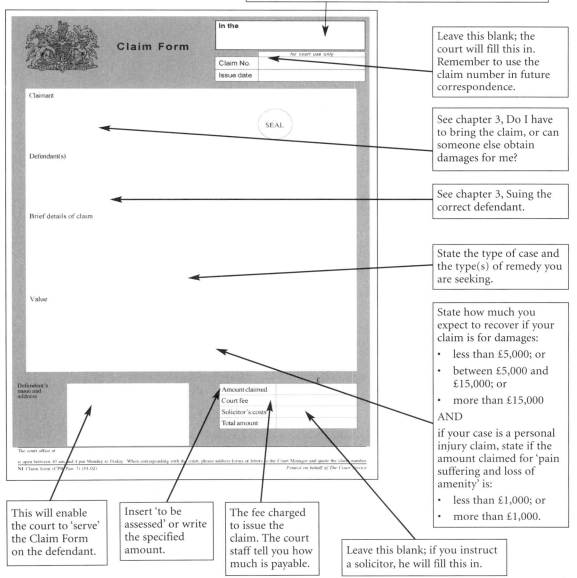

Leave this blank; the court will fill this in. Remember to use the claim number in future correspondence.

See chapter 3, Do I have to bring the claim, or can someone else obtain damages for me?

See chapter 3, Suing the correct defendant.

State the type of case and the type(s) of remedy you are seeking.

State how much you expect to recover if your claim is for damages:
- less than £5,000; or
- between £5,000 and £15,000; or
- more than £15,000

AND

if your case is a personal injury claim, state if the amount claimed for 'pain suffering and loss of amenity' is:
- less than £1,000; or
- more than £1,000.

This will enable the court to 'serve' the Claim Form on the defendant.

Insert 'to be assessed' or write the specified amount.

The fee charged to issue the claim. The court staff tell you how much is payable.

Leave this blank; if you instruct a solicitor, he will fill this in.

PERSONAL INJURY & MONEY CLAIMS

N1 Claim Form
(Part 7 claims) (continued)

For sample Particulars of Claim, please see Appendix 1.

You can:

(a) write your Particulars in the box; or

(b) attach your Particulars to the Claim Form on a separate piece of paper (with a heading that shows: the claim number; the name of the court; the names of the parties; or

(c) state that the Particulars will follow and send the defendant(s) the Particulars separately (they must arrive within 14 days of the date of issue of the Claim Form).

If you sign a statement of truth without believing the facts are true, you are committing a 'contempt of court' for which you may be tried and punished.

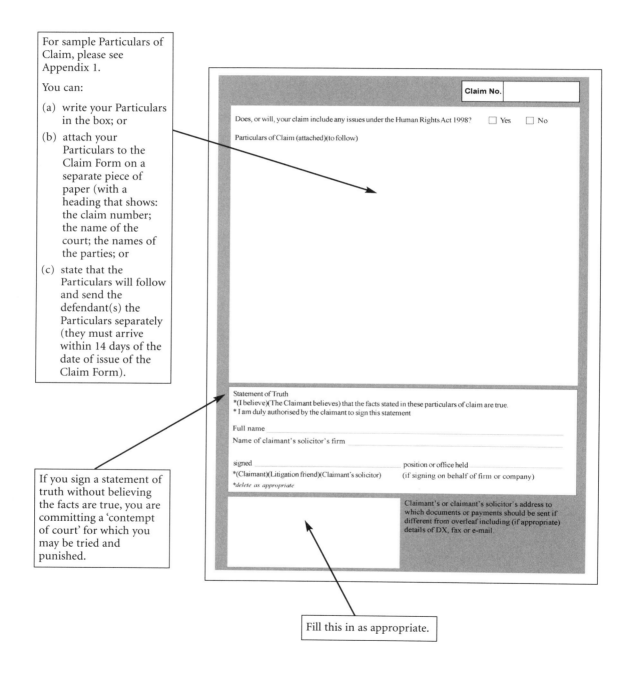

Claim No.

Does, or will, your claim include any issues under the Human Rights Act 1998?   ☐ Yes   ☐ No

Particulars of Claim (attached)(to follow)

Statement of Truth
*(I believe)(The Claimant believes) that the facts stated in these particulars of claim are true.
* I am duly authorised by the claimant to sign this statement

Full name

Name of claimant's solicitor's firm

signed   position or office held
*(Claimant)(Litigation friend)(Claimant's solicitor)   (if signing on behalf of firm or company)
*delete as appropriate

Claimant's or claimant's solicitor's address to which documents or payments should be sent if different from overleaf including (if appropriate) details of DX, fax or e-mail.

Fill this in as appropriate.

N208 Claim Form
(Part 8 claims)

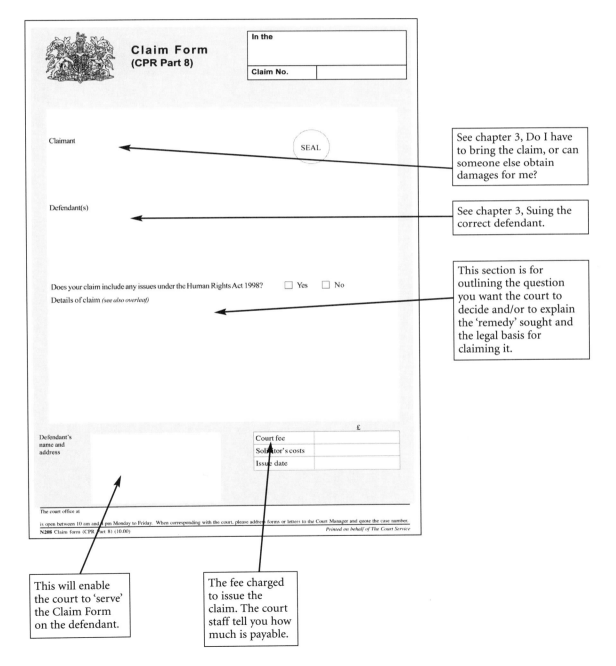

Claim Form
(CPR Part 8)

In the

Claim No.

Claimant

SEAL

See chapter 3, Do I have to bring the claim, or can someone else obtain damages for me?

Defendant(s)

See chapter 3, Suing the correct defendant.

Does your claim include any issues under the Human Rights Act 1998?   ☐ Yes   ☐ No

Details of claim *(see also overleaf)*

This section is for outlining the question you want the court to decide and/or to explain the 'remedy' sought and the legal basis for claiming it.

£

Defendant's name and address		Court fee	
		Solicitor's costs	
		Issue date	

The court office at

is open between 10 am and 4 pm Monday to Friday. When corresponding with the court, please address forms or letters to the Court Manager and quote the case number.
N208 Claim form (CPR Part 8) (10.00)   *Printed on behalf of The Court Service*

This will enable the court to 'serve' the Claim Form on the defendant.

The fee charged to issue the claim. The court staff tell you how much is payable.

N208 Claim Form
(Part 8 claims) (continued)

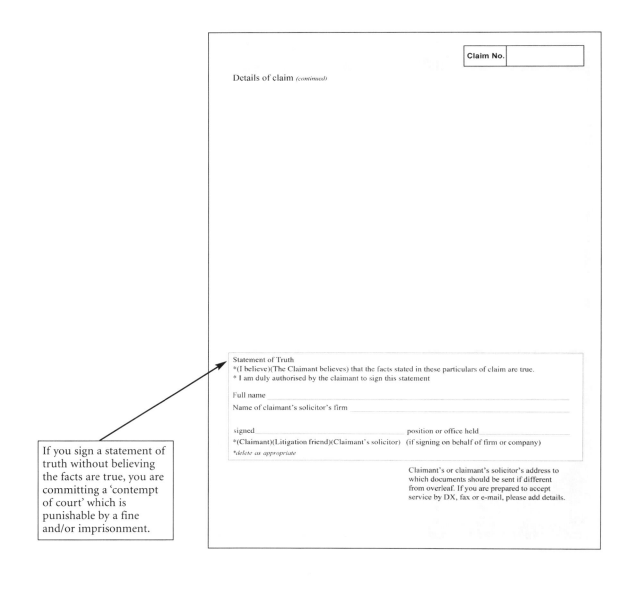

Claim No.

Details of claim *(continued)*

Statement of Truth
*(I believe)(The Claimant believes) that the facts stated in these particulars of claim are true.
* I am duly authorised by the claimant to sign this statement

Full name

Name of claimant's solicitor's firm

signed   position or office held
*(Claimant)(Litigation friend)(Claimant's solicitor) (if signing on behalf of firm or company)
*delete as appropriate

Claimant's or claimant's solicitor's address to
which documents should be sent if different
from overleaf. If you are prepared to accept
service by DX, fax or e-mail, please add details.

If you sign a statement of truth without believing the facts are true, you are committing a 'contempt of court' which is punishable by a fine and/or imprisonment.

N208C Notes for Defendant
(Part 8 Claim Form)

Notes for defendant (Part 8 claim form)

Please read these notes carefully - they will help you to decide what to do about this claim.

- You have 14 days* from the date on which you were served with the claim form to respond to the claim
- If you **do not return** the acknowledgment of service, you will be allowed to attend any hearing of this claim but you will **not** be allowed to take part in the hearing unless the court gives you permission to do so
- Court staff can tell you about procedures but they cannot give legal advice. If you need legal advice, you should contact a solicitor or Citizens Advice Bureau immediately

Time for responding

The completed acknowledgment of service must be returned to the court office within 14 days* of the date on which the claim form was served on you. If the claim form was:

- sent by post, the 14 days* begins 2 days from the date of the postmark on the envelope.
- delivered or left at your address, the 14 days* begins the day after it was delivered.
- handed to you personally, the 14 days* begins on the day it was given to you.

Completing the acknowledgment of service

You should complete sections A- E as appropriate. In **all** cases you must complete sections F and G.

Section A - not contesting the claim

If you do **not** wish to contest the remedy sought by the claimant in the claim form, you should complete section A. In some cases the claimant may only be seeking the court's directions as to how to act, rather than seeking a specific order. In these circumstances, if you wish the court to direct the claimant to act in a certain way, give brief details.

Section B - contesting the claim

If you do wish to contest the remedy sought by the claimant in the claim form, you should complete section B. If you seek a remedy different from that sought by the claimant, you should give brief details in the space provided.

Section C - disputing the court's jurisdiction

You should indicate your intention by completing section B and filing an application disputing the court's jurisdiction within 14 days of filing your acknowledgment of service at the court. The court will arrange a hearing date for the application and tell you and the claimant when and where to attend.

Section D - objecting to use of procedure

If you believe that the claimant should not have issued the claim under Part 8 because:

- there **is** a substantial dispute of fact involved; and
- you do not agree that the rule or practice direction stated does provide for the claimant to use this procedure

you should complete section C setting out your reasons in the space provided.

Section E - written evidence

Complete this section if you wish to rely on written evidence. You must send your written evidence to the court with your acknowledgment of service. It must be verified by a statement of truth or the court may disallow it. If you have agreed with the other party(ies) an extension of time for filing your written evidence,

a copy of your written agreement must be filed with your acknowledgment of service. Please note that the agreement can only extend time by 14 days from the date you file your acknowledgment of service.

Claims under section 1 of the Inheritance (Provision for Family and Dependants) Act 1975

A defendant who is a personal representative of the deceased must file and serve written evidence which must state to the best of that person's ability:

- full details of the value of the deceased's net estate, as defined in section 25 of the Act;
- the person or classes of person beneficially interested in the estate, and
  - the names and (unless they are parties to the claim) addresses of all living beneficiaries; and
  - the value of their interests in the estate so far as they are known;
- whether any living beneficiary (and if so, naming him) is a child or patient within the meaning of Rule 21.1(2); and
- any facts which might affect the exercise of the court's powers under the Act.

Section F - name of defendant

Print your full name, or the full name of the defendant on whose behalf you are completing this form.

Serving other parties

You must send to any other party named on the claim form, copies of both the acknowledgment of service and any written evidence, at the same time as you file them with the court.

What happens next

The claimant may, within 14 days of receiving any written evidence from you, file further evidence in reply. On receipt of your acknowledgment of service, the court file will be referred to the judge for directions for the disposal of the claim. The court will contact you and tell you what to do next.

Statement of truth

This must be signed by you, by your solicitor or your litigation friend, as appropriate.

Where the defendant is a registered company or a corporation the statement must be signed by either the director, treasurer, secretary, chief executive, manager or other officer of the company or (in the case of a corporation) the mayor, chairman, president or town clerk.

For claims under the Inheritance (Provision for Family and Dependants) Act 1975 the period is 21 days.

N208C Notes for defendant (CPR Part 8) (12.02)

Printed on behalf of The Court Service

N9A Admission
(specified amount)

Admission (specified amount)

- You have a limited number of days to complete and return this form
- Before completing this form, please read the notes for guidance attached to the claim form

When to fill in this form
Only fill in this form if:
- you are admitting all of the claim **and** you are asking for time to pay; or
- you are admitting part of the claim. (You should also complete form N9B)

How to fill in this form
- Tick the correct boxes and give as much information as you can. **Then sign and date the form.** If necessary provide details on a separate sheet, add the claim number and attach it to this form.
- Make your offer of payment in box 11 on the back of this form. **If you make no offer the claimant will decide how much and when you should pay.**
- If you are not an individual, you should ensure that you provide sufficient details about the assets and liabilities of your firm, company or corporation to support any offer of payment made in box 11.
- You can get help to complete this form at **any** county court office or Citizens Advice Bureau.

Where to send this form
- **If you admit the claim in full**
Send the completed form to the address shown on the claim form as one to which documents should be sent.
- **If you admit only part of the claim**
Send the form **to the court** at the address given on the claim form, together with the defence form (N9B).

How much of the claim do you admit?
☐ I admit the full amount claimed as shown on the claim form **or**

☐ I admit the amount of £ _____

1 Personal details

Surname	
Forename	

☐ Mr   ☐ Mrs   ☐ Miss   ☐ Ms

☐ Married   ☐ Single   ☐ Other *(specify)* _____

Age	

Address

Postcode _____

Tel. no. _____

In the

Claim No.	
Claimant (including ref)	
Defendant	

2 Dependants *(people you look after financially)*

Number of children in each age group

under 11 ☐   11-15 ☐   16-17 ☐   18 & over ☐

Other dependants *(give details)* _____

3 Employment

☐ **I am employed as a** _____
My employer is _____

Jobs other than main job *(give details)* _____

☐ **I am self employed as a** _____
Annual turnover is........................ £ _____

☐ **I am not** in arrears with my national insurance contributions, income tax and VAT

☐ **I am** in arrears and I owe........... £ _____

Give details of:
(a) contracts and other work in hand _____
(b) any sums due for work done _____

☐ **I have been unemployed for** ____ years ____ months

☐ **I am a pensioner**

4 Bank account and savings

☐ **I have a bank account**
☐ The account is in credit by........ £ _____
☐ The account is overdrawn by.... £ _____

☐ **I have a savings or building society account**
The amount in the account is.......... £ _____

5 Residence

I live in ☐ my own house   ☐ lodgings
☐ my jointly owned house   ☐ council accommodation
☐ rented accommodation

242

N9A Admission
(specified amount) (continued)

6 Income

	£	per
My usual take home pay (including overtime, commission, bonuses etc)	£	per
Income support	£	per
Child benefit(s)	£	per
Other state benefit(s)	£	per
My pension(s)	£	per
Others living in my home give me	£	per
Other income (give details below)		
	£	per
	£	per
	£	per
Total income	**£**	**per**

7 Expenses

(Do not include any payments made by other members of the household out of their own income)

I have regular expenses as follows:

	£	per
Mortgage (including second mortgage)	£	per
Rent	£	per
Council tax	£	per
Gas	£	per
Electricity	£	per
Water charges	£	per
TV rental and licence	£	per
HP repayments	£	per
Mail order	£	per
Housekeeping, food, school meals	£	per
Travelling expenses	£	per
Children's clothing	£	per
Maintenance payments	£	per
Others (not court orders or credit debts listed in boxes 9 and 10)		
	£	per
	£	per
	£	per
Total expenses	**£**	**per**

8 Priority debts

(This section is for arrears only. Do not include regular expenses listed in box 7.)

	£	per
Rent arrears	£	per
Mortgage arrears	£	per
Council tax/Community Charge arrears	£	per
Water charges arrears	£	per
Fuel debts: Gas	£	per
Electricity	£	per
Other	£	per
Maintenance arrears	£	per
Others (give details below)		
	£	per
	£	per
Total priority debts	**£**	**per**

9 Court orders

Court	Claim No.	£	per

Total court order instalments	**£**	**per**

Of the payments above, I am behind with payments to (please list)

10 Credit debts

Loans and credit card debts (please list)

	£	per
	£	per
	£	per

Of the payments above, I am behind with payments to (please list)

11 Offer of payment

☐ I can pay the amount admitted on _____

or

☐ I can pay by monthly instalments of £ _____

If you cannot pay immediately, please give brief reasons below

12 Declaration

I declare that the details I have given above are true to the best of my knowledge

Signed _____

Date _____

Position or office held (if signing on behalf of firm or company) _____

N9B Defence and Counterclaim
(specified amount)

<table>
<tr>
<td>

Defence and Counterclaim (specified amount)

- Fill in this form if you wish to dispute all or part of the claim and/or make a claim against the claimant (counterclaim).
- You have a limited number of days to complete and return this form to the court.
- Before completing this form, please read the notes for guidance attached to the claim form.
- Please ensure that all boxes at the top right of this form are completed. You can obtain the correct names and number from the claim form. The court cannot trace your case without this information.

How to fill in this form
- Complete sections 1 and 2. Tick the correct boxes and give the other details asked for.
- Set out your defence in section 3. If necessary continue on a separate piece of paper making sure that the claim number is clearly shown on it. In your defence you must state which allegations in the particulars of claim you deny and your reasons for doing so. **If you fail to deny an allegation it may be taken that you admit it.**
- If you dispute only some of the allegations you must
  - specify which you admit and which you deny; and
  - give your own version of events if different from the claimant's.

</td>
<td>

In the

Claim No.

Claimant
(including ref)

Defendant

- If you wish to make a claim against the claimant (a counterclaim) complete section 4.
- Complete and sign section 5 before sending this form to the court. Keep a copy of the claim form and this form.

Community Legal Service Fund (CLSF)
You may qualify for assistance from the CLSF (this used to be called 'legal aid') to meet some or all of your legal costs. Ask about the CLSF at any county court office or any information or help point which displays this logo.

</td>
</tr>
</table>

1. How much of the claim do you dispute?

☐ I dispute the full amount claimed as shown on the claim form

or

☐ I admit the amount of £ [   ]

If you dispute only part of the claim you must **either**:
- pay the amount admitted to the person named at the address for payment on the claim form (see How to Pay in the notes on the back of, or attached to, the claim form). Then send this defence to the court

or

- complete the admission form **and** this defence form and send them to the court.

☐ I paid the amount admitted on (*date*) [   ]

or

☐ I enclose the completed form of admission
(*go to section 2*)

2. Do you dispute this claim because you have already paid it? *Tick whichever applies*

☐ **No** (*go to section 3*)

☐ **Yes** I paid £ [   ] to the claimant
on [   ] *(before the claim form was issued)*

Give details of where and how you paid it in the box below *(then go to section 5)*

3. Defence

N9B Defence and Counterclaim
(specified amount) (continued)

Defence (continued)

Claim No. [   ]

4. If you wish to make a claim against the claimant (a counterclaim)

If your claim is for a specific sum of money, how much are you claiming? £ [   ]

- To start your counterclaim, you will have to pay a fee. Court staff can tell you how much you have to pay.

I enclose the counterclaim fee of £ [   ]

- You may not be able to make a counterclaim where the claimant is the Crown (e.g. a Government Department). Ask at your local county court office for further information.

My claim is for *(please specify nature of claim)*

[   ]

What are your reasons for making the counterclaim?
If you need to continue on a separate sheet put the claim number in the top right hand corner

[   ]

5. Signed
(To be signed by you or by your solicitor or litigation friend)

*(I believe)(The defendant believes) that the facts stated in this form are true. *I am duly authorised by the defendant to sign this statement

*delete as appropriate

Position or office held
(if signing on behalf of firm or company)

Date [   ]

Give an address to which notices about this case can be sent to you

Postcode

Tel. no.

if applicable

fax no.

DX no.

e-mail

N9C Admission
(unspecified amount and non-money claims)

Admission (unspecified amount, non-money and return of goods claims)

- Before completing this form please read the notes for guidance attached to the claim form. If necessary provide details on a separate sheet, add the claim number and attach it to this form.
- If you are not an individual, you should ensure that you provide sufficient details about the assets and liabilities of your firm, company or corporation to support any offer of payment made.

In the

Claim No.

Claimant (including ref.)

Defendant

In non-money claims only
☐ I admit liability for the whole claim (Complete section 11)

In return of goods cases only
Are the goods still in your possession?
☐ Yes   ☐ No

Part A   Response to claim (tick one box only)
☐ I admit liability for the whole claim but want the court to decide the amount I should pay / value of the goods
OR
☐ I admit liability for the claim and offer to pay _____ in satisfaction of the claim (Complete part B and sections 1-11)

Part B   How are you going to pay the amount you have admitted? (tick one box only)
☐ I offer to pay on (date) _____
OR
☐ I cannot pay the amount immediately because (state reason)
_____
AND
I offer to pay by instalments of £ _____ per (week)(month)
starting (date) _____

1   Personal details
Surname _____
Forename _____
☐ Mr ☐ Mrs ☐ Miss ☐ Ms
☐ Married ☐ Single ☐ Other (specify) _____
Age _____
Address _____
Postcode _____
Tel. no. _____

N9C - w3 Admission (unspecified amount and non-money claims) (8.99)

2   Dependants (people you look after financially)
Number of children in each age group
under 11 ____ 11-15 ____ 16-17 ____ 18 & over ____
Other dependants _____ (give details)

3   Employment
☐ I am employed as a _____
My employer is _____
Jobs other than main job (give details) _____
☐ I am self employed as a _____
Annual turnover is.............. £ _____
☐ I am not in arrears with my national insurance contributions, income tax and VAT
☐ I am in arrears and I owe.......... £ _____
Give details of:
(a) contracts and other work in hand
(b) any sums due for work done
☐ I have been unemployed for ____ years ____ months
☐ I am a pensioner

4   Bank account and savings
☐ I have a bank account
☐ The account is in credit by........ £ _____
☐ The account is overdrawn by.... £ _____
☐ I have a savings or building society account
The amount in the account is......... £ _____

5   Residence
I live in
☐ my own property ☐ lodgings
☐ jointly owned house ☐ rented property
☐ council accommodation

Printed on behalf of The Court Service

Tick this box if you admit liability but want the court to decide at a hearing how much the damages and costs will be.

Tick this box if you admit liability and want to offer to pay the claim. If the claimant does not accept the amount, a hearing will be fixed so that the court can decide how much you should pay.

Parts B1–11 need only be filled in if you are offering to settle.

N9C Admission
(unspecified amount and non-money claims) (continued)

Parts B1–11 need only be filled in if you are offering to settle.

6 Income

My usual take home pay *(including overtime, commission, bonuses etc)*	£	per
Income support	£	per
Child benefit(s)	£	per
Other state benefit(s)	£	per
My pension(s)	£	per
Others living in my home give me	£	per
Other income *(give details below)*		
	£	per
	£	per
	£	per
Total income	**£**	**per**

7 Expenses

(Do not include any payments made by other members of the household out of their own income)

I have regular expenses as follows:

Mortgate *(including second mortgage)*	£	per
Rent	£	per
Council tax	£	per
Gas	£	per
Electricity	£	per
Water charges	£	per
TV rental and licence	£	per
HP repayments	£	per
Mail order	£	per
Housekeeping, food, school meals	£	per
Travelling expenses	£	per
Children's clothing	£	per
Maintenance payments	£	per
Others *(not court orders or credit debts listed in sections 9 and 10)*		
	£	per
	£	per
	£	per
Total expenses	**£**	**per**

8 Priority debts

(This section is for arrears only. Do not include regular expenses listed in section 7)

Rent arrears	£	per
Mortgage arrears	£	per
Council tax/Community Charge arrears	£	per
Water charges arrears	£	per
Fuel debts: Gas	£	per
Electricity	£	per
Other	£	per
Maintenance arrears	£	per
Others *(give details below)*		
	£	per
	£	per
Total priority debts	**£**	**per**

9 Court orders

Court	Claim No.	£	per

Total court order instalments	**£**	**per**

Of the payments above, I am behind with payments to *(please list)*

10 Credit debts

Loans and credit card debts *(please list)*

	£	per
	£	per
	£	per

Of the payments above, I am behind with payments to *(please list)*

11 Declaration

I declare that the details I have given above are true to the best of my knowledge

Signed

Date

Position or office held *(if signing on behalf of firm or company)*

You must fill in this box. However, making a declaration of truth without an honest belief in the truth of the statements in the document is a contempt of court, which is punishable by imprisonment.

PERSONAL INJURY & MONEY CLAIMS

N9D Defence and Counterclaim
(unspecified amount and non-money claims)

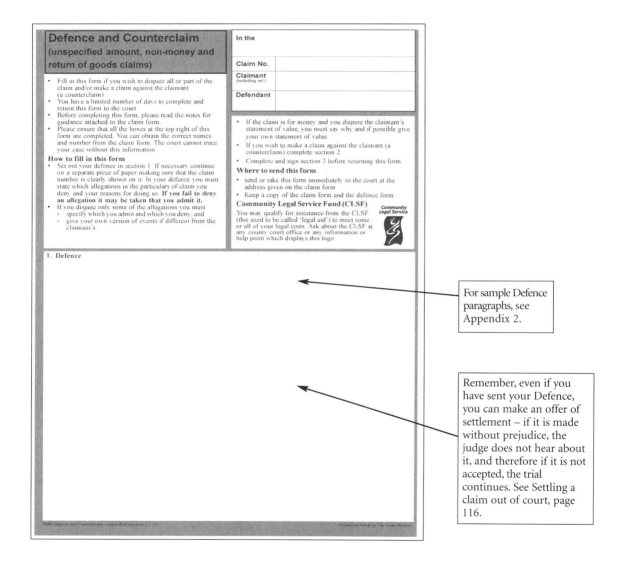

For sample Defence paragraphs, see Appendix 2.

Remember, even if you have sent your Defence, you can make an offer of settlement – if it is made without prejudice, the judge does not hear about it, and therefore if it is not accepted, the trial continues. See Settling a claim out of court, page 116.

N9D Defence and Counterclaim
(unspecified amount and non-money claims) (continued)

Defence (continued)   Claim No. [   ]

A counterclaim works in the same way a claim does. If you have suffered a personal injury, you will be asking for an unspecified amount. Therefore leave this blank.

2. If you wish to make a claim against the claimant (a counterclaim)

If your claim is for a specific sum of money, how much are you claiming? £ [   ]

I enclose the counterclaim fee of £ [   ]

My claim is for *(please specify)*

- To start your counterclaim, you will have to pay a fee. Court staff can tell you how much you have to pay.

- You may not be able to make a counterclaim where the claimant is the Crown (e.g. a Government Department). Ask at your local county court office for further information.

What are your reasons for making the counterclaim?
If you need to continue on a separate sheet put the claim number in the top right hand corner

For example, 'damages for personal injuries and consequential losses arising from a car accident'. See chapter 1 for sample brief details of claim arising in various situations.

3. Signed
(To be signed by you or by your solicitor or litigation friend)

*(I believe)(The defendant believes) that the facts stated in this form are true. *I am duly authorised by the defendant to sign this statement

Position or office held (if signing on behalf of firm or company)

*delete as appropriate

Date

Give an address to which notices about this case can be sent to you

Postcode

Tel. no.

if applicable

fax no.

DX no.

e-mail

If you sign this, not believing that the facts stated are true, you will be in contempt of court which is punishable by, amongst other things, imprisonment.

N11 Defence Form

Defence form

In the

Claim No.

Claimant

Defendant(s)

I dispute the claimant's claim because:-

Statement of Truth

*(I believe)(The defendant(s) believe(s)) that the facts stated in this defence form (and any continuation sheets) are true.
* I am duly authorised by the defendant(s) to sign this reply form.

signed _____ date _____

(Defendant(s))(Litigation friend(where the defendant is a child or a patient)*)(Defendant's solicitor)
delete as appropriate

Full name _____

Name of defendant's solicitor's firm _____

position or office held _____
(if signing on behalf of firm or company)

Defendant's or defendant's solicitor's address to which documents should be sent.

Postcode

	if applicable
Ref. no.	
fax no.	
DX no.	
e-mail	
Tel. no.	

N11 Defence form (10.01)

Printed on behalf The Court Service

N11B Defence Form
(accelerated procession procedure) (assured shorthold tenancy)

Defence form
(accelerated possession
procedure)
(assured shorthold
tenancy)

In the	Claim No.
County Court	
	Claimant
	Defendant(s)

To the Defendant
Please read the notes on the back page of the claim form before completing this form.
Some of the questions in this form refer to numbered sections in the claim form. You will find it helpful to have that open as you answer them.
You **must** complete and sign the statement of truth.
Please write clearly and in black ink. If there is not enough room for an answer, continue on the last page.

1   Are you the tenant(s) named in the tenancy agreement, marked 'A' (or 'A1'), attached to the claim form?   ☐ Yes   ☐ No

Does that tenancy agreement (or do both) set out the present terms of your tenancy (except for any changes in the rent or the length of the tenancy)?   ☐ Yes   ☐ No

If not, say what terms have changed and what the changes are:

2   Do you agree the date, in section 2 of the claim form, when the claimant says the tenancy began?   ☐ Yes   ☐ No

If not, on what date did it begin?   on

3   If the claimant has completed section 3 of the claim form, do you agree with what is said there?   ☐ Yes   ☐ No

If not, what do you disagree with and why?

N11B Defence form (accelerated possession procedure)(assured shorthold tenancy) (10.01)   *Printed on behalf The Court Service*

N11B Defence Form
(accelerated procession procedure) (assured shorthold tenancy) (continued)

4	If the claimant has completed section 4 of the claim form, did you receive the notice (a copy of which is attached to the claim form and marked 'B') and, if so, when?	☐ Yes	☐ No
		If Yes, give date _____	
	Do you agree with the rest of what is said in section 4? If not, what do you disagree with and why?	☐ Yes	☐ No
5	If the claimant has not deleted section 5 of the claim form, do you agree that what is said there is correct?	☐ Yes	☐ No
	If not, what do you disagree with and why?		
6	Did you receive the notice referred to in section 6 of the claim form, (a copy of which is attached to the claim form and marked 'C') and, if so, when?	☐ Yes	☐ No
		If Yes, give date _____	
7	If the claimant has put any additional information in section 7 of the claim form, do you agree that what is said there is correct?	☐ Yes	☐ No
	If not, what do you disagree with and why?		
8	If there is some other reason, not covered above, why you say the claimant is not entitled to recover possession of the property, please explain it here.		

N11B Defence Form
(accelerated procession procedure) (assured shorthold tenancy)
(continued)

Postponement of possession

| 9 | Are you asking the court, if it makes a possession order, to allow you longer than 14 days to leave the premises because you would suffer exceptional hardship? | ☐ Yes | ☐ No |

If so, explain why the hardship you would suffer would be exceptional.

Say how long you wish to be allowed to remain in the premises. (The court cannot allow more than 42 days after the order is made.)

up to _____ 20 _____

Payment of costs

| 10 | If the court orders you to pay the claimant's costs, do you ask it to allow you more than 14 days to pay? | ☐ Yes | ☐ No |

If so, give details of your means
(continue onto last page if necessary)

Statement of Truth

*(I believe)(The defendant(s) believe(s)) that the facts stated in this defence form (and any attached sheets) are true.
* I am duly authorised by the defendant(s) to sign this statement.

signed_____ date

(Defendant)(Litigation friend(where defendant is a child or a patient)*)(Defendant's solicitor)
delete as appropriate

Full name _____

Name of defendant's solicitor's firm _____

position or office held _____
(if signing on behalf of firm or company)

Defendant's or defendant's solicitor's address to which documents should be sent.		*if applicable*	
		Ref. no.	
		fax no.	
		DX no.	
		e-mail	
	Postcode	Tel. no.	

N11B Defence Form
(accelerated procession procedure) (assured shorthold tenancy)
(continued)

	Claim No.

Additional Information
(Include the number of the section which is being continued or to which the information relates)

Signed .... Date ....

(Continue on a separate sheet if necessary, remembering to sign and date it and heading it with the Claim Number)

N11R Defence Form
(rented residential premises)

Defence form
(rented residential
premises)

In the

Claim No.

Claimant

Defendant(s)

Date of hearing

Personal details

1. Please give your:

   Forename(s)

   Surname

   Address *(if different from the address on the claim form)*

   post code

Disputing the claim

2. Do you agree with what is said about the premises and the tenancy agreement? ☐ Yes ☐ No

   If No, set out your reasons below:

3. Did you receive the notice from the claimant referred to at paragraph 5 of the particulars of claim? ☐ Yes ☐ No

   If Yes, when:

N11R Defence form (rented residential premises) (10.01)

Printed on behalf of The Court Service

N11R Defence Form
(rented residential premises) (continued)

4. Do you agree that there are arrears of rent as stated in the particulars of claim?   ☐ Yes   ☐ No

If No, state how much the arrears are: £_____   ☐ None

5. If the particulars of claim give any reasons for possession other than rent arrears, do you agree with what is said?   ☐ Yes   ☐ No

If No, give details below:

6. Do you have a money or other claim (a counterclaim) against your landlord?   ☐ Yes   ☐ No

If Yes, give details:

Arrears

7. Have you paid any money to your landlord since the claim was issued?   ☐ Yes   ☐ No

If Yes, state how much you have paid and when: £_____   date_____

8. Have you come to any agreement with your landlord about repaying the arrears since the claim was issued?   ☐ Yes   ☐ No

I have agreed to pay £_____ each (week)(month)

9. If you have not reached an agreement with your landlord, do you want the court to consider allowing you to pay the arrears by instalments?   ☐ Yes   ☐ No

10. How much can you afford to pay in addition to the current rent?   £_____ per (week)(month)

N11R Defence Form
(rented residential premises) (continued)

About yourself
State benefits

11. Are you receiving Income Support?   ☐ Yes   ☐ No

12. Have you applied for Income Support?   ☐ Yes   ☐ No

    If Yes, when did you apply?   _____

13. Are you receiving housing benefit?   ☐ Yes   ☐ No

    If Yes, how much are you receiving?   £ _____ per (week)(month)

14. Have you applied for housing benefit?   ☐ Yes   ☐ No

    If Yes, when did you apply?   _____

15. Is the housing benefit paid   ☐ to you   ☐ to your landlord

Dependants *(people you look after financially)*

16. Have you any dependant children?   ☐ Yes   ☐ No

    If Yes, give the number in each age group below:

    ☐ under 11   ☐ 11-15   ☐ 16-17   ☐ 18 and over

Other dependants

17. Give details of any other dependants for whom you are
    financially responsible:

Other residents

18. Give details of any other people living at the premises for
    whom you are not financially responsible:

N11R Defence Form
(rented residential premises) (continued)

			Weekly	Monthly
Money you receive				
19. Usual take-home pay or income if self-employed *including overtime, commission. bonuses*	£_____		☐	☐
Job Seekers allowance	£_____		☐	☐
Pension	£_____		☐	☐
Child benefit	£_____		☐	☐
Other benefits and allowances	£_____		☐	☐
Others living in my home give me	£_____		☐	☐
I am paid maintenance for myself (or children) of	£_____		☐	☐
Other income	£_____		☐	☐
Total income	£_____		☐	☐

Bank accounts and savings

20. Do you have a current bank or building society account? ☐ Yes ☐ No

If Yes, is it

    ☐ in credit? If so, by how much? £

    ☐ overdrawn? If so, by how much? £_____

21. Do you have a savings or deposit account? ☐ Yes ☐ No

If Yes, what is the balance? £_____

Money you pay out

22. Do you have to pay any court orders or fines?

Court	Claim/Case number	Balance owing	Instalments paid
		Total Instalments paid £	per month

23. Give details if you are in arrears with any of the court payments or fines:

N11R Defence Form
(rented residential premises) (continued)

24. Do you have any loan or credit debts?   ☐ Yes   ☐ No

Loan/credit from	Balance owing	Instalments paid
	Total Instalments £	per month

25. Give details if you are in arrears with any loan / credit repayments:

Regular expenses

(Do not include any payments made by other members of the household out of their own income)

26. What regular expenses do you have? *(List below)*

		Weekly	Monthly
Council tax	£_____	☐	☐
Gas	£_____	☐	☐
Electricity	£_____	☐	☐
Water charges	£_____	☐	☐
TV rental & licence	£_____	☐	☐
Telephone	£_____	☐	☐
Credit repayments	£_____	☐	☐
Mail order	£_____	☐	☐
Housekeeping, food, school meals	£_____	☐	☐
Travelling expenses	£_____	☐	☐
Clothing	£_____	☐	☐
Maintenance payments	£_____	☐	☐
Other	£	☐	☐
Total expenses	£	☐	☐

N11R Defence Form
(rented residential premises) (continued)

Priority debts

27. This section is for **arrears** only. **Do not**
include regular expenses listed at Question 26.

		Weekly	Monthly
Council tax arrears	£	☐	☐
Water charges arrears	£	☐	☐
Gas account	£	☐	☐
Electricity account	£	☐	☐
Maintenance arrears	£	☐	☐
Others *(give details below)*			
	£	☐	☐
	£	☐	☐
	£	☐	☐

28. If an order for possession were to be made, would you have   ☐ Yes   ☐ No
somewhere else to live?

    If Yes, say when you would be able to move in:

29. Give details of any events or circumstances which have led to your being in arrears of rent *(for example divorce, separation, redundancy, bereavement, illness, bankruptcy)* or any other particular circumstances affecting your case. If there are any reasons why the date any possession order takes effect should be delayed, give them here. If you believe you would suffer exceptional hardship by being ordered to leave the property immediately, say why.

Statement of Truth

*(I believe)(The defendant(s) believe(s)) that the facts stated in this defence form are true.
* I am duly authorised by the defendant(s) to sign this statement.

signed _____ date

(Defendant)(Litigation friend(where defendant is a child or a patient)*)(Defendant's solicitor)
*delete as appropriate

Full name _____

Name of defendant's solicitor's firm _____

position or office held _____
                    (if signing on behalf of firm or company)

N227 Request for Judgment by Default

Request for judgment by default
(amount to be decided by the court)

In the	
Claim No.	
Claimant (including ref)	
Defendant	

To the court

The defendant has not filed (an acknowledgment of service) (a defence) to my claim and the time for doing so has expired.

I request judgment to be entered against the defendant for an amount to be decided by the court and costs.

Signed _____

(Claimant) (Claimant's solicitor) (Litigation friend)

Position or office held _____
(if signing on behalf of firm or company)

Date _____

Note: The court will enter judgment and refer the court file to a judge who will give directions for the management of the case including its allocation to track.

The Court Manager

The court office at

is open between 10 am and 4 pm Monday to Friday. When corresponding with the court, please address forms or letters to the Court Manager and quote the claim number.

N227 - w3 Request for judgment by default (amount to be decided by the court) (4.99)   *Printed on behalf of The Court Service*

N244 Part 23 Applications

Application Notice

In the

You should provide this information for listing the application

1. How do you wish to have your application dealt with

   a) at a hearing? ☐ } *complete all questions below*

   b) at a telephone conference? ☐

   c) without a hearing? ☐   *complete Qs 5 and 6 below*

2. Give a time estimate for the hearing/conference
_____ (hours) _____ (mins)

3. Is this agreed by all parties? ☐ Yes   ☐ No

4. Give dates of any trial period or fixed trial date _____

5. Level of judge _____

6. Parties to be served _____

Claim no.	
Warrant no. (If applicable)	
Claimant (including ref.)	
Defendant(s) (including ref.)	
Date	

Note You must complete Parts A **and** B, **and** Part C if applicable. Send any relevant fee and the completed application to the court with any draft order, witness statement or other evidence; and sufficient copies for service on each respondent.

        Part A

1. Enter your full name, or name of solicitor

I (We)[1]   (on behalf of)(the claimant)(the defendant)

2. State clearly what order you are seeking and if possible attach a draft

intend to apply for an order (a draft of which is attached) that[2]

because[3]

3. Briefly set out why you are seeking the order. Include the material facts on which you rely, identifying any rule or statutory provision

        Part B

I (We) wish to rely on: *tick one box*

             the attached (witness statement)(affidavit) ☐   my statement of case ☐

4. If you are not already a party to the proceedings, you must provide an address for service of documents

             evidence in Part C in support of my application ☐

Signed _____   **Position or office held** _____

    (Applicant)('s Solicitor)('s litigation friend)   (if signing on behalf of firm or company)

Address to which documents about this claim should be sent (including reference if appropriate)[4]

	if applicable
	fax no.
	DX no.
Tel. no. Postcode	e-mail

The court office at

is open from 10am to 4pm Monday to Friday. When corresponding with the court please address forms or letters to the Court Manager and quote the claim number.

N244 Application Notice (4.00)   *Printed on behalf of The Court Service*

Guidance notes provided.

N244 Part 23 Applications (continued)

Part C   Claim No. [   ]

I (We) wish to rely on the following evidence in support of this application:

Statement of Truth

*(I believe) *(The applicant believes) that the facts stated in Part C are true
*delete as appropriate

Signed [   ]   **Position or office held** [   ]

(Applicant)('s Solicitor)('s litigation friend)   (if signing on behalf of firm or company)

Date [   ]

Appendix 9
QUESTIONNAIRES

N150 Allocation

Allocation questionnaire

To be completed by, or on behalf of,

who is [1ˢᵗ][2ⁿᵈ][3ʳᵈ][ ][Claimant][Defendant]
[Part 20 claimant] in this claim

In the

Claim No.	
Last date for filing with court office	

Please read the notes on page five before completing the questionnaire.

You should note the date by which it must be returned and the name of the court it should be returned to since this may be different from the court where the proceedings were issued.

If you have settled this claim (or if you settle it on a future date) and do not need to have it heard or tried, you must let the court know immediately.

Have you sent a copy of this completed form to the other party(ies)? ☐ Yes ☐ No

---

A Settlement

Do you wish there to be a one month stay to attempt to settle the claim, either by informal discussion or by alternative dispute resolution? ☐ Yes ☐ No

---

B Location of trial

Is there any reason why your claim needs to be heard at a particular court? ☐ Yes ☐ No

If Yes, say which court and why?

C Pre-action protocols

If an approved pre-action protocol applies to this claim, complete **Part 1** only. If not, complete **Part 2** only. If you answer 'No' to the question in either Part 1 or 2, please explain the reasons why on a separate sheet and attach it to this questionnaire.

Part 1
*please say which protocol

The* [_____] protocol applies to this claim.

Have you complied with it? ☐ Yes ☐ No

Part 2

No pre-action protocol applies to this claim.

Have you exchanged information and/or documents (evidence) with the other party in order to assist in settling the claim? ☐ Yes ☐ No

---

N150 Allocation questionnaire (10.01)   I   *Printed on behalf of The Court Service*

N150 Allocation (continued)

D   Case management information

What amount of the claim is in dispute?   £ _____

Applications

Have you made any application(s) in this claim?   ☐ Yes   ☐ No

If Yes, what for?   _____   For hearing on _____
(e.g. summary judgment,
add another party)

Witnesses

So far as you know at this stage, what witnesses of fact do you intend to call at the trial or final hearing including, if appropriate, yourself?

Witness name	Witness to which facts

Experts

Do you wish to use expert evidence at the trial or final hearing?   ☐ Yes   ☐ No

Have you already copied any experts' report(s) to the   ☐ None yet   ☐ Yes   ☐ No
other party(ies)?   obtained

Do you consider the case suitable for a single joint expert in any field?   ☐ Yes   ☐ No

Please list any single joint experts you propose to use and any other experts you wish to rely on. Identify single joint experts with the initials 'SJ' after their name(s).

Expert's name	Field of expertise (e.g. orthopaedic surgeon, surveyor, engineer)

Do you want your expert(s) to give evidence orally at the trial or final hearing?   ☐ Yes   ☐ No

If Yes, give the reasons why you think oral evidence is necessary:

2   continue over ⅢⅢ➡

N150 Allocation (continued)

Track

Which track do you consider is most suitable for your claim? Tick one box
□ small claims track   □ fast track   □ multi-track

If you have indicated a track which would not be the normal track for the claim, please give brief reasons for your choice

E   Trial or final hearing

How long do you estimate the trial or final hearing will take?
_____ days _____ hours _____ minutes

Are there any days when you, an expert or an essential witness will not be able to attend court for the trial or final hearing?   □ Yes   □ No

If Yes, please give details

Name	Dates not available

F   Proposed directions *(Parties should agree directions wherever possible)*

Have you attached a list of the directions you think appropriate for the management of the claim?   □ Yes   □ No

If Yes, have they been agreed with the other party(ies)?   □ Yes   □ No

G   Costs

*Do **not** complete this section if you have suggested your case is suitable for the small claims track **or** you have suggested one of the other tracks and you do not have a solicitor acting for you.*

What is your estimate of your costs incurred to date?   £ _____

What do you estimate your overall costs are likely to be?   £ _____

In substantial cases these questions should be answered in compliance with CPR Part 43

3

N150 Allocation (continued)

H   Other information

Have you attached documents to this questionnaire? ☐ Yes ☐ No

Have you sent these documents to the other party(ies)? ☐ Yes ☐ No

If Yes, when did they receive them? [_____]

Do you intend to make any applications in the immediate future? ☐ Yes ☐ No

If Yes, what for? [_____]

In the space below, set out any other information you consider will help the judge to manage the claim.

[   ]

Signed [_____]   Date [_____]

[Counsel][Solicitor][for the][1ˢᵗ][2ⁿᵈ][3ʳᵈ][   ]
[Claimant][Defendant][Part 20 claimant]

Please enter your firm's name, reference number and full postal address including (if appropriate) details of DX, fax or e-mail

	if applicable
	fax no.
	DX no.
Tel. no. Postcode	e-mail
Your reference no.	

4

N150 Allocation (continued)

Notes for completing an allocation questionnaire

- If the claim is not settled, a judge must allocate it to an appropriate case management track. To help the judge choose the most just and cost-effective track, you must now complete the attached questionnaire.
- If you fail to return the allocation questionnaire by the date given, the judge may make an order which leads to your claim or defence being struck out, or hold an allocation hearing. If there is an allocation hearing the judge may order any party who has not filed their questionnaire to pay, immediately, the costs of that hearing.
- Use a separate sheet if you need more space for your answers marking clearly which section the information refers to. You should write the claim number on it, and on any other documents you send with your allocation questionnaire. Please ensure they are firmly attached to it.
- The letters below refer to the sections of the questionnaire and tell you what information is needed.

A Settlement

If you think that you and the other party may be able to negotiate a settlement you should tick the 'Yes' box. The court may order a stay, whether or not all the other parties to the claim agree. You should still complete the rest of the questionnaire, even if you are requesting a stay. Where a stay is granted it will be for an initial period of one month. You may settle the claim either by informal discussion with the other party or by alternative dispute resolution (ADR). ADR covers a range of different processes which can help settle disputes. More information is available in the Legal Services Commission leaflet 'Alternatives to Court' free from the LSC leaflet line Phone: 0845 3000 343

B Location of trial

High Court cases are usually heard at the Royal Courts of Justice or certain Civil Trial Centres. Fast or multi-track trials may be dealt with at a Civil Trial Centre or at the court where the claim is proceeding. Small claim cases are usually heard at the court in which they are proceeding.

C Pre-action protocols

Before any claim is started, the court expects you to have exchanged information and documents relevant to the claim, to assist in settling it. For some types of claim e.g. personal injury, there are approved protocols that should have been followed.

D Case management information

Applications

It is important for the court to know if you have already made any applications in the claim, what they are for and when they will be heard. The outcome of the applications may affect the case management directions the court gives.

Witnesses

Remember to include yourself as a witness of fact, if you will be giving evidence.

Experts

Oral or written expert evidence will only be allowed at the trial or final hearing with the court's permission. The judge will decide what permission it seems appropriate to give when the claim is allocated to track. Permission in small claims track cases will only be given exceptionally.

Track

The basic guide by which claims are normally allocated to a track is the amount in dispute, although other factors such as the complexity of the case will also be considered. A leaflet available from the court office explains the limits in greater detail.

Small Claims track	Disputes valued at not more than £5,000 except
	· those including a claim for personal injuries worth over £1,000 and
	· those for housing disrepair where either the cost of repairs or other work exceeds £1,000 or any other claim for damages exceeds £1,000
Fast track	Disputes valued at more than £5,000 but not more than £15,000
Multi-track	Disputes over £15,000

E Trial or final hearing

You should enter only those dates when you, your expert(s) or essential witness(es) will not be able to attend court because of holiday or other commitments.

F Proposed directions

Attach the list of directions, if any, you believe will be appropriate to be given for the management of the claim. Agreed directions on fast and multi-track cases should be based on the forms of standard directions set out in the practice direction to CPR Part 28 and form PF52.

G Costs

Only complete this section if you are a solicitor and have suggested the claim is suitable for allocation to the fast or multi-track.

H Other Information

Answer the questions in this section. Decide if there is any other information you consider will help the judge to manage the claim. Give details in the space provided referring to any documents you have attached to support what you are saying.

5

N170 Listing

Listing questionnaire
(Pre-trial checklist)

To be completed by, or on behalf of,

who is [1ˢᵗ][2ⁿᵈ][3ʳᵈ][   ][Claimant][Defendant]
[Part 20 claimant][Part 20 defendant] in this claim

In the

Claim No.

Last date for filing
with court office

Date(s) fixed for trial
or trial period

| This form must be **completed** and **returned** to the court no later than the date given above. If not, your statement of case may be struck out or some other sanction imposed. | If the claim has settled, or settles before the trial date, you must let the court know immediately. | **Legal representatives only:** You must **attach** estimates of costs incurred to date, and of your likely overall costs. In substantial cases, these should be provided in compliance with CPR Part 43. | For multi-track claims only, you must also **attach** a proposed timetable for the trial itself. |

A Confirmation of compliance with directions

1. I confirm that I have complied with those directions already given which require action by me.   ☐Yes ☐No

If you are unable to give confirmation, state which directions you have still to comply with and the date by which this will be done.

Directions	Date

2. I believe that additional directions are necessary before the trial takes place.   ☐Yes ☐No

If Yes, you should attach an application and a draft order.

*Include in your application all directions needed to enable the claim **to be tried on the date, or within the trial period, already fixed.** These should include any issues relating to experts and their evidence, and any orders needed in respect of directions still requiring action by any other party.*

3. Have you agreed the additional directions you are seeking with the other party(ies)?   ☐Yes ☐No

B Witnesses

1. How many witnesses (including yourself) will be giving evidence on your behalf at the trial? *(Do not include experts - see Section C)*   ☐

Continued over ➥

N170 Listing (continued)

Witnesses continued

2. If the trial date is not yet fixed, are there any days within the trial period you or your witnesses would wish to avoid if possible? *(Do not include experts - see Section C)*

Please give details

Name of witness	Dates to be avoided, if possible	Reason

Please specify any special facilities or arrangements needed at court for the party or any witness (e.g. witness with a disability).

3. Will you be providing an interpreter for any of your witnesses? ☐ Yes ☐ No

C Experts

You are reminded that you may not use an expert's report or have your expert give oral evidence unless the court has given permission. If you do not have permission, you must make an application (see section A2 above)

1. Please give the information requested for your expert(s)

Name	Field of expertise	Joint expert?	Is report agreed?	Has permission been given for oral evidence?
		☐ Yes ☐ No	☐ Yes ☐ No	☐ Yes ☐ No
		☐ Yes ☐ No	☐ Yes ☐ No	☐ Yes ☐ No
		☐ Yes ☐ No	☐ Yes ☐ No	☐ Yes ☐ No

2. Has there been discussion between experts? ☐ Yes ☐ No

3. Have the experts signed a joint statement? ☐ Yes ☐ No

4. If your expert is giving oral evidence and the trial date is not yet fixed, is there any day within the trial period which the expert would wish to avoid, if possible? ☐ Yes ☐ No

If Yes, please give details

Name	Dates to be avoided, if possible	Reason

2 of 3

N170 Listing (continued)

D Legal representation

1. Who will be presenting your case at the trial? ☐ You ☐ Solicitor ☐ Counsel

2. If the trial date is not yet fixed, is there any day within the trial period that the person presenting your case would wish to avoid, if possible? ☐ Yes ☐ No

If Yes, please give details

Name	Dates to be avoided, if possible	Reason

E The trial

1. Has the estimate of the time needed for trial changed? ☐ Yes ☐ No

If Yes, say how long you estimate the whole trial will take, including both parties' cross-examination and closing arguments ☐ days ☐ hours ☐ minutes

2. If different from original estimate have you agreed with the other party(ies) that this is now the **total** time needed? ☐ Yes ☐ No

3. Is the timetable for trial you have attached agreed with the other party(ies)? ☐ Yes ☐ No

Fast track cases only
The court will normally give you 3 weeks notice of the date fixed for a fast track trial unless, in exceptional circumstances, the court directs that shorter notice will be given.

Would you be prepared to accept shorter notice of the date fixed for trial? ☐ Yes ☐ No

F Document and fee checklist
Tick as appropriate

I attach to this questionnaire -

☐ An application and fee for additional directions   ☐ A proposed timetable for trial

☐ A draft order   ☐ An estimate of costs

☐ Listing fee

Signed [Counsel][Solicitor][for the][1st][2nd][3rd][ ] [Claimant][Defendant] [Part 20 claimant][Part 20 defendant] Date	Please enter your [firm's] name, reference number and full postal address including (if appropriate) details of DX, fax or e-mail Postcode

Tel. no.		DX no.		E-mail	
Fax no.		Ref. no.			

3 of 3

Appendix 10
FORMS (ENFORCEMENT)

N225 Request for Judgment and Reply to Admission

**Request for judgment
and reply to admission
(specified amount)**

In the	
Claim No.	
Claimant (including ref)	
Defendant (including ref)	

- Tick box A or B. If you tick box B you must complete the details in that part and in part C. Make sure that all the case details are given. Remember to sign and date the form. Your signature certifies that the information you have given is correct.
- If the defendant has given an address on the form of admission to which correspondence should be sent, which is different from the address shown on the claim form, you must tell the court.
- Return the completed form to the court.

A ☐ The defendant has not filed an admission or defence to my claim

Complete all the judgment details at C. Decide how and when you want the defendant to pay. You can ask for the judgment to be paid by instalments or in one payment.

B ☐ The defendant admits that all the money is owed

Tick only **one** box below and complete all the judgment details at C.

☐ **I accept the defendant's proposal for payment**

Say how the defendant intends to pay. The court will send the defendant an order to pay. You will also be sent a copy.

☐ **The defendant has not made any proposal for payment**

Say how you want the defendant to pay. You can ask for the judgment to be paid by instalments or in one payment. The court will send the defendant an order to pay. You will also be sent a copy.

☐ **I do NOT accept the defendant's proposal for payment**

Say how you want the defendant to pay. Give your reasons for objecting to the defendant's offer of payment in the space opposite. (Continue on the back of this form if necessary.) Send this form to the court **with defendant's admission N9A.** The court will fix a rate of payment and send the defendant an order to pay. You will also be sent a copy.

C Judgment details

I would like the judgment to be paid

☐ (immediately)

☐ (by instalments of £ [   ] per month)

☐ (in full by [   ])

Amount of claim as admitted
(including interest at date of issue) . . . .

Interest since date of claim (if any) . . . . . .

Period from . . . . to . . . .

Rate . . %

Court fees shown on claim

Solicitor's costs (if any) on issuing claim

Sub Total

Solicitor's costs (if any) on entering judgment

Sub Total

Deduct amount (if any) paid since issue

Amount payable by defendant

I certify that the information given is correct

Signed		Position or office held	
(Claimant) (Claimant's solicitor) (Litigation friend)		(if signing on behalf of firm or company)	
Date			

The court office at

is open between 10 am and 4 pm Monday to Friday. When corresponding with the court, please address forms and letters to the Court Manager and quote the Claim number.

N225 - w3   Request for judgment and reply to admission (specified amount) (4.99)   *Printed on behalf of The Court Service*

N316 Application for Order that the Debtor Attend Court for Questioning

Application for order that debtor attend court for questioning

In the

Claim No.

Appn. No.

Claimant

Defendant

The [claimant] [defendant] ('the judgment creditor') applies for an order that the [defendant] [claimant] ('the judgment debtor') attend court to provide information about the judgment debtor's means and any other information needed to enforce the judgment or order given on   20
[by the   in claim no.   ].

1. Judgment debtor

The judgment debtor is

whose address is

Postcode

2. Judgment debt or order

[The judgment or order required the judgment debtor to pay £   (including any costs and interest). The amount now owing is £   [which includes further interest payable on the judgment debt]].

[The judgment or order required the judgment debtor to

]

Note:

Questioning and documents

Questioning will be by a court officer unless a judge agrees there are compelling reasons for questioning to take place before a judge. Normally the court officer will ask the questions set out in Form EX140 and the judgment debtor will be told to produce all relevant documents including:

- pay slips
- bank statements
- building society books
- share certificates
- rent book

- mortgage statement
- hire purchase and similar agreements
- court orders
- any other outstanding bills
- electricity, gas, water and council tax bills for the past year.

and in the case of a business

- bills owed to it
- 2 years' accounts
- current management accounts.

Complete sections 3, 4 and 5 only if applicable.
The statement of truth overleaf must be completed.

N316 Application for order that debtor attend court for questioning (03.02)   *Printed on behalf of The Court Service*

N316 Application for Order that the Debtor Attend Court for Questioning (continued)

3. [Attached is a list of questions which the judgment creditor wishes the court officer to ask the judgment debtor in addition to those in Form EX140.]

4. [Attached is a list of documents which the judgment creditor wishes the judgment debtor to be ordered to produce in addition to those listed in the note above.]

5. [The judgment creditor requests that the judgment debtor be questioned by the judgment creditor before a judge. The reason for this request is

]

Statement of Truth

*(I believe)(The judgment creditor believes) that the facts stated in this application form are true.
* I am duly authorised by the judgment creditor to sign this statement.

signed _____ date _____
(Judgment creditor)(Litigation friend(where judgment creditor is a child or a patient)*)(Judgment creditor's solicitor)
delete as appropriate

Full name _____

Name of judgment creditor's solicitor's firm _____

position or office held _____
(if signing on behalf of firm or company)

Judgment creditor's or judgment creditor's solicitor's address to which documents should be sent.		if applicable	
		Ref. no.	
		fax no.	
		DX no.	
	Postcode		
Tel. no.		e-mail	

N323 Request for Warrant of Execution

Request for Warrant of Execution

to be completed and signed by the claimant or his solicitor and sent to the court with the appropriate fee

1 Claimant's name and address

In the

County Court

Claim Number

2 Name and address for service and payment (if different from above) Ref/Tel No.

for court use only

Warrant no.

Issue date:

Warrant applied for at   o'clock

Foreign court code/name:

3 Defendant's name and address

I certify that the whole or part of any instalments due under the judgment or order have not been paid and the balance now due is as shown

4 Warrant details

(A) Balance due at date of this request

◄

Signed

Claimant (Claimant's solicitor)

(B) Amount for which warrant to issue

Issue fee

Solicitor's costs

Land Registry fee

TOTAL

Dated

IMPORTANT
You must inform the court immediately of any payments you receive after you have sent this request to the court

If the amount of the warrant at (B) is less than the balance at (A), the sum due after the warrant is paid will be

You should provide a contact number so that the bailiff can speak to you if he/she needs to:

Daytime phone number: Evening phone number (if possible):

Contact name (where appropriate):

Defendant's phone number (if known):

If you have any other information which may help the bailiff or if you have reason to believe that the bailiff may encounter any difficulties you should write it below.

N323 -w3- Request for warrant of execution (4.99)   *Produced on behalf of The Court Service*

275

N324 Request for Warrant of Delivery of Goods

Request for Warrant of Delivery of Goods

to be completed and signed by the claimant or his solicitor and sent to the court with the appropriate fee

1 Claimant's name and address

In the

County Court

Claim Number

for court use only

Warrant No.

Issue date:

Warrant applied for at   o'clock

Foreign court code/name:

2 Name and address for service and payment *(if different from above)* Ref/Tel No.

3 Defendant's name and address

I apply for the issue of a warrant of delivery of goods (and execution) against the defendant(s) in respect of a judgment (an order) in this court for the delivery of the goods specified in the schedule below

4 Warrant details

*(Balance of) assessed value of specified goods due at date of this request/ unpaid balance of total price

(Debt/damages)

(Costs)

Issue fee

Solicitor's costs

AMOUNT TO BE LEVIED

*Delete where specific delivery is ordered

I certify that the whole or part of any instalments due under the judgment or order have not been paid (*and the balance now due is as shown)

Signed

Claimant (Claimant's solicitor)

Date

*delete if not applicable

IMPORTANT
You must inform the court immediately of any payments
you receive after you have sent this request to the court

Schedule of Goods *(Include here any other information that might assist the bailiff. You should also tell the court if you have reason to believe that the bailiff might encounter serious difficulties in attempting to execute the warrant.*

Warrant No.

N324 -w3 – Request for warrant of delivery (4.99)   *Printed on behalf of The Court Service*

N325 Request for Warrant of Possession of Land

Request for Warrant of Possession of Land

To be completed and signed by the claimant or his solicitor and sent to the court with the appropriate fee

1 Claimant's name and address

2 Name and address for service and payment (if different from above) Ref/Tel No.

3 Defendant's name and address

4 Warrant details

(A) Balance due at the date of this request

(B) Amount for which warrant to issue

Issue fee

Solicitor's costs

Land Registry fee

TOTAL

If the amount of the warrant at (B) is less than the balance at (A), the sum due after the warrant is paid will be

5 Property/land details

Date of judgment/order

Date of possession

Describe the land (as set out in the particulars of claim)

In the

County Court

Claim Number

For court use only

Warrant No.

Issue date:

Warrant applied for at   o'clock

Foreign court code/name (execution only):

I certify that the defendant has not vacated the land as ordered (* and that the whole or part of any instalments due under the judgment or order have not been paid) (†and the balance now due is as shown)

Signed

Claimant (Claimant's solicitor)

Dated

*   *delete unless defendant is in arrears with the suspended possession order or judgment*

†   *delete unless warrant is to issue for execution also*

IMPORTANT

You must inform the court immediately of any payments you receive after you have sent this request to the court

If there is more than one defendant and you are <u>not</u> proceeding against all of them, enter here the name(s) of the defendant(s) you wish to proceed against

You should provide a contact number so that the bailiff can speak to you if he/she needs to:

Daytime phone number: Evening phone number (if possible) :

Contact name (where appropriate):

Defendant's phone number (if known):

If you have any other information which may help the bailiff or if you have reason to believe that the bailiff may encounter any difficulties you should write it below.

N325 -w3- Request for warrant for possession of land (4.99)   *Produced on behalf of The Court Service*

N337 Request for Attachment of Earnings Order

Request for Attachment of Earnings Order

to be completed and signed by the claimant or his solicitor and sent to the court with the appropriate fee

1 Claimant's name and address

In the

County Court

Claim Number

2 Name and address for service and payment
(if different from above)
Ref/Tel No.

For court use only

A/E application no.

Issue date:

Hearing date:

on

3 Defendant's name and address

at   o'clock

at (address)

4 Judgment details

Court where judgment/order made if not court of issue

I apply for an attachment of earnings order

I certify that the whole or part of any instalments due under the judgment or order have not been paid and the balance now due is as shown

5 Outstanding debt

Balance due at date of request*
(excluding issue fee but including unsatisfied warrant costs)

Signed

Claimant(Claimants solicitor)

* you may also be entitled to interest to the date of request where judgment is for £5,000 or more, or is in respect of a debt which attracts contractual or statutory interest for late payment

Issue fee

AMOUNT NOW DUE

Date

6 Employment Details *(please give as much information as you can – it will help the court to make an order more quickly)*

Employer's name and address

7 Other details
(Give any other details about the defendant's circumstances which may be relevant to the application)

Defendant's place of work
(if different from employer's address)

The defendant is employed as

IMPORTANT
You must inform the court immediately of any payments you receive after you have sent this request to the court

Works No / Pay Ref

N337 - w3 Request for attachment of earnings order (4 99)   *Printed on behalf of The Court Service*

N342 Request for Judgment Summons

Request for Judgment Summons

to be completed and signed by the claimant and sent to the court with the appropriate fee

1 Claimant's
name and
address

In the

County Court

Claim Number

2 Name and
address for
service and
payment
(if different
from above)
Ref/Tel No.

For court use only

J/S no.

Issue date:

Hearing date:

3 Defendant's
name and
address[1]

[1] enter names
and addresses of
all defendants
against whom a
summons is
requested

On

at   o'clock

at (address)

4 Judgment details

Date of judgment/order

Court where judgment/order
made if not court of issue

I certify that the whole or part of any
instalments due under the judgment or
order have not been paid and the
balance now due is as shown

5 Judgment summons details

Balance due[2] at the date of this request

My evidence in support is attached

[2] and any interest
to date of request
where judgment
over £5,000 and
entered on or after
1 July 1991

Amount in arrears under
judgment or order
(including costs)

Signed

[3] Amount for which judgment
summons to issue

Claimant

[3] this figure
must not
include any
amounts on
previous
judgment
summons(es)
where debtor
imprisoned

Issue fee

Date

Travelling expenses to be
paid or offered to defendant

TOTAL

IMPORTANT

You must inform the court immediately of
any payments you receive after you have
sent this request to the court

Amount if any which will
remain outstanding when
the above sum has been paid

6 If service by post is required tick here

I request that the defendant(s) named here be served with the judgment summons in this action by post. I certify that I have reason to
believe that the summons, if sent to the defendant(s) at the address(es) given, will come to his/her (their) knowledge in time for him/her
(them) to comply with it.

I understand that no order of commitment will be made against the defendant(s) served by post unless he/she (they) appear(s) at the
hearing of the summons (or the judge is satisfied that the summons came to his/her (their) knowledge in sufficient time for him/her (them)
to appear) and I prove that the defendant has, or has had, the means to pay, but is refusing or neglecting, or has refused or has
neglected, to do so.

Signed   Dated

Claimant

N342 Request for judgment summons (03.02)

Printed on behalf of The Court Service

N349 Application for Third Party Debt Order

Application for third party debt order

In the

Claim No.

Appn. No.

Claimant

Defendant

Third Party

The [claimant] [defendant] ('the judgment creditor') applies for an order that the third party pay to the judgment creditor the debt which the third party owes to the [defendant] [claimant] ('the judgment debtor') (or so much of it as is necessary to discharge the amount owing under the judgment or order given on   20   [by the   in claim no.   ] and the costs of this application).

1. **Judgment debtor**
   The judgment debtor is
   whose address is

   Postcode

2. **Judgment debt**
   The judgment or order required the judgment debtor to pay £   (including any costs and interest). The amount now due is £   [which includes further interest].

   ☐ £   of the instalments due under the judgment or order has fallen due and remains
   unpaid.

   ☐ The judgment or order did not provide for payment by instalments.

3. **Third party**
   The third party is within England and Wales and owes money to (or holds money to the credit of) the judgment debtor.

   The third party is a bank or building society.
   Its name is
   Its head office address in England and Wales is:

   The branch at which the account is held is
   ☐ not known

   ☐ the
      whose address is

   The account number is   The sort code is
   ☐ not known   ☐ not known
   ☐   ☐

N349 Application for third party debt order (03.02)   *Printed on behalf of The Court Service*

N349 Application for Third Party Debt Order (continued)

[The third party is not a bank or building society.
☐ the third party is

whose address in England and Wales is

4. **Other persons' interests**
The persons (in addition to the judgment debtor) who have a claim to the money owed by the third party are
☐ None

☐ The following: *(names and address(es))*

Information known about each person's claim:

5. **Sources and grounds of information**
The judgment creditor knowns or believes that the information in section 3 and 4 is correct because:

6. **Other applications**
In respect of the judgment debt,
☐ the judgment creditor has made no other applications for third party debt orders.
☐ the judgment creditor has already made the following application(s) for third party debt order:
Details of application(s)

Third party's name
Address

Postcode

Statement of Truth
*I believe (the judgment creditor believes) that the facts stated in this application form are true.
*I am duly authorised by the judgment creditor to sign this statement

signed _____ date _____
*(Judgment creditor)(Litigation friend *(where judgment creditor is a child or a patient)*)(Judgment creditor's solicitor)
*delete as appropriate
Full name _____
Name of judgment creditor's solicitor's firm _____
position or office held _____ *(if signing on behalf of a firm or company)*

Judgment creditor's or
judgment creditor's
solicitor's address to
which documents
should be sent.

Postcode

if applicable

Ref. no.	
fax no.	
DX no.	
e-mail	
Tel. no.	

Appendix 11

Benefits recoverable from the defendant by the Department of Social Security

Under the Social Security (Recovery of Benefits) Act 1997

Benefits relating to earnings:

Disability working allowance
Disablement pension payable under section 103 Social Security Administration Act 1992
Incapacity Benefit
Income support
Invalidity pension allowance
Jobseeker's allowance
Reduced earnings allowance
Severe disablement allowance
Sickness benefit
Statutory sick pay (prior to 6th April 1994)
Unemployability supplement
Unemployment benefit

Benefits relating to the cost of care:

Attendance allowance
care component of disability allowance
Disablement pension increase payable under section 104 or 105 of the Social Security Act 1992

Benefits relating to loss of mobility:

Mobility allowance
Mobility component of disability allowance

Employment safety legislation

Mines and Quarries Act 1954
Agriculture (Safety Health and Welfare) Provisions Act 1956
Factories Act 1961
Offices Shops and Railway Premises Act 1963

GLOSSARY

Acknowledgement of Service – a form used by a defendant to tell the court that he has received the Claim Form and the Particulars of Claim.

acquittal – the formal order of a criminal court where the accused has been found 'not guilty' of the criminal offence for which he has been tried.

admission, Admission – the word has two meanings: a) the acceptance, in court or correspondence, of a fact by one party, which he then cannot later dispute without permission of the court, or b) a form used by the defendant to tell the court that he does not dispute or deny all or part of the claim.

affidavit, affirmation – a document containing the evidence of a witness who has 'sworn' (by a religious oath) or 'affirmed' (by a secular solemn promise) the truth of the contents.

aggravated damages – a sum unusually awarded by the court over and above the usual compensation to compensate the **claimant** for injury to his feelings of dignity and pride.

allocation – an order of the court assigning the case to one of the three trial tracks: small claims, fast and multi-track.

allocation questionnaire – a questionnaire filled out by claimants and defendants to tell the court about the case management aspects of their case (including number of witnesses, estimate length of **trial**, applications that will be made, number of expert witnesses, etc) so that the court can allocate the case to the appropriate trial track (small claims, fast and multi-track).

application, Notice of Application – where a party has a particular request to the court relating to the documents of the case (**disclosure**, witness statements, amendment, etc), management of the case (summary judgment, default judgment, etc) or to the conduct of the **trial** (adjournments, witness evidence, etc) or the grant of various permissions, he makes an 'application'. Applications are governed by **Civil Procedure Rules 1998**, Part 23. Pre-trial applications should be made on a form called a Notice of Application.

assault – where a person's deliberate action (not mere words) shows an immediate intention to commit a battery on the victim; an assault does not involve any physical contact with the victim (*see* **battery**).

association, *see* '**unincorporated association**'.

barrister – a lawyer who undertakes specialist advocacy and advisory work; the bulk of the work done by independent barristers is the representation of their clients in court. Barristers cannot take instructions direct from the public; they can generally only act on referral by a solicitor.

battery – the deliberate use of unlawful force on the body of another, ranging from mere touching to the use of physical violence.

breach of contract – failure to fulfil or comply with any term of an agreement.

breach of statutory duty – the failure of a person (or company) to comply with a duty imposed on him (or it) by Act of Parliament or Statutory Instrument.

case law – the body of reported cases, particularly judgments from the higher courts (High Court, **Court of Appeal** and the **House of Lords**), which create legal principles for application in other similar cases. Sometimes known as legal precedent.

case management conference (multi-track cases) – a hearing at court in front of a judge at which all parties attend, and at which the court will try to ascertain the matters which remain in dispute, take decisions as to how the case is to be managed, set timetables and give other appropriate directions.

cause of action – the legal basis of the claim for **damages** or other remedy. Over time the law has developed a series of situations (such as **negligence**, **breach of contract**, **breach of statutory duty**, **assault and battery**, **harassment**, etc) which give rise to a claim for damages; each cause of action has a very specific meaning and it is for the **claimant** to prove that the facts of his case amount to a claim in law.

charity – a type of trust or company which holds property and money for the purposes of doing specific charitable works.

child – any person who has not yet reached his 18th birthday. On the 18th birthday a child becomes an adult for the purposes of the law.

civil law, civil courts – the branch of the law dealing with people's rights and remedies against each other, the outcome of successful litigation being **damages** or some other court order putting right the wrong done to the **claimant** (*see by contrast* **criminal law**).

Civil Procedure Rules 1998 – the set of rules by which the **civil courts** (both **County courts** and the High Court) operate. They consist of 53 Parts each dealing with a specific area, various practice directions, a glossary, **pre-action protocols** and some of the old County Court Rules and Rules of the Supreme Court which continue to be in force; the rules can be found in publications by the main legal publishers and from The Stationery Office.

claimant – formerly known as 'the plaintiff'; someone who has brought a claim in the courts against the **defendant** for a remedy such as **damages**.

Claim Form – the form used by the **claimant** to initiate his claim (Form N1); it identifies the parties, gives a brief description of the claim and an indication of the value of **damages** expected.

common law – a general term for the legal system applying to England and Wales. It consists of judicially recognised customs and **case law**.

Community Legal Services Funding – CLSF has superseded Legal Aid; it is funding provided by the government for those who do not have the means to pay for legal advice and representation under the Access to Justice Act 1999; it is not available for most personal injury claims.

company, Ltd, plc – a business which by 'incorporating' (a legal process of registration) assumes its own identity, separate from the owners or shareholders; a company can, through its officers, therefore be negligent, breach contracts, breach statutory duties, etc. A company may also be vicariously liable for its employees' actions (*see* **vicarious liability**).

Compensation Recovery Unit clawback – the money that the **claimant** received in certain DSS benefits between the accident and the **trial** or **settlement**, which must be paid back to the DSS out of the **damages** agreed or awarded.

compromise – an out of court settlement of a claim (*see* **settlement**).

conditional fee agreement (CFA), no win, no fee – the agreement between a solicitor and his client that the solicitor will only be paid if the client 'wins' the case (whether he is the **claimant** or **defendant**).

consent – (defence to assault) permission.

contract – a legally binding agreement between two or more parties comprising various terms or separate promises, which may be explicit or may be implied (by the **common law** or statute); under the contract each party must fulfil the promises he has made, and breaches of those promises will only be lawful in certain circumstances. An unlawful breach of promise will entitle the other party to **damages**.

contribution – a type of **Part 20 claim** brought by the **defendant** (who becomes known as the **Part 20 claimant**) against a person (the Part 20 defendant); the Part 20 claimant must prove that the Part 20 defendant is liable either jointly or in his own right for the **claimant**'s loss and injury under the Civil Liability (Contribution) Act 1978.

contributory negligence – where the **defendant** proves that the **claimant**'s own negligence (failure to take reasonable care of his own safety in the circumstances) has contributed to the damage or injury suffered; if a court finds that the claimant is partly to blame for his own injury it will assess the percentage blame attributable to the defendant, and reduce the **damages** accordingly.

conviction – the formal finding of a criminal court (Magistrates or the Crown Court) that the defendant is guilty, either when he is found guilty at **trial**, or pleads guilty voluntarily.

costs – the legal cost of litigation, including the fees of solicitors, barristers, expert witnesses, court fees and other expenses.

counterclaim – an example of a **Part 20 claim** (after the **Civil Procedure Rule** governing such claims); a counterclaim is a claim for **damages** or other remedy brought by a **defendant** against the **claimant** or the claimant and another person. Where the claim and counterclaim arise out of the same incident or set of facts, the court will usually order that both are heard together in one **trial**.

County court – The lowest tier of civil courts – where cases are heard at 'first instance' (i.e where the **trial** is held, evidence heard and judgment given on the merits of a case).

Court of Appeal – A senior court where appeals from decisions in cases tried in the lower courts (**County court** and High Court – and other courts of 'first instance') are held.

criminal law, criminal courts – that part of the law which deals with the State's (The Crown's) condemnation and punishment of people who commit criminal offences; criminal law is generally dealt with in the criminal courts (magistrates courts or the Crown Court).

cross-examination – the series of questions put to a witness by the other party at **trial** designed to test the evidence of that witness for inconsistencies or inaccuracies, etc. Any witness whose oral or written evidence is put before the court may be cross-examined by the other side, although the judge has the power to limit cross-examination (**Civil Procedure Rules 1998**, Part 32).

damages – monetary compensation awarded by the court to people who have suffered loss or injury; the person found to be negligent or in breach of duty (or his insurer) pays.

default judgment, judgment in default of defence – an order of the court deeming the **claimant** to have 'won' and usually awarding him the **damages** sought, or fixing a date for the assessment of the amount to be paid; it can only be obtained in circumstances set out in **Civil Procedure Rules 1998**, Part 12. The **defendant** can apply to set aside such a default judgment in circumstances set out in **Civil Procedure Rules 1998**, Part 13.

defence, Defence – a defence is a legal excuse or justification to all or part of the claim; a **defendant's** defence is set out in a document called a Defence, which is designed to assist the court and the **claimant** to know exactly what parts of the claim are disputed.

defendant – the person against whom the **claimant** has a claim, i.e. the claimant must prove that the defendant is legally liable for his loss and injury.

directions – actions required of a party or parties imposed by the court and set out in an order.

directions hearing – a hearing in front of the judge at a preliminary stage during the preparations for **trial** at which the parties discuss the management of the case, and the court makes an order directing the parties to take certain actions, such as **exchange of witness statements**, etc; usually will be given a strict timetable for compliance with directions.

disclosure/discovery – the revealing by one party to another of documents in his possession. Disclosure is a formal stage in the steps taken towards **trial** involving a party stating to the other side that a particular document exists or has existed. All documents, except **privileged documents** or where inspection would be disproportionate, may then be inspected by the other side.

disposal hearing – a type of hearing or **trial** at which the court hears evidence relating only to the amount of **damages** to be paid (the defendant's liability to pay damages having been decided at an earlier hearing, or having been conceded by the defendant himself).

domicile – the country or legal jurisdiction where a person lives (unless his stay is only temporary or transitory), or where a company has its 'seat of business'.

evidence – material (oral testimony, written testimony, artefacts, measurements or documentation) put before the judge which proves a fact alleged by the **claimant** or **defendant**.

exchange of witness statements – the formal process whereby, instead of a party merely sending the witness statements he wishes to rely upon to the other party, both parties agree to exchange their witness statements simultaneously. This is a requirement frequently placed on parties by the judge at the directions stage of preparation for **trial**.

exemplary damages – a sum of money that is over and above the compensation awarded to a **claimant** which marks the court's disapproval of the **defendant's** conduct; they are only awarded in certain types of case (including where the government is a defendant and has acted oppressively, or where the defendant has calculated that he will gain a profit from his wrongdoing even if he has to pay damages).

expert evidence – the evidence (usually oral or written testimony, plus measurements or other observations) of a professional who can assist the court with his opinion from the viewpoint of a particular discipline.

false imprisonment – where the **defendant** unlawfully deprives the **claimant** of his liberty.

fast track – a trial track to which medium-size claims may be allocated (**allocation**).

firm, *see* **partnership**.

group litigation order – an order of the court made under **Civil Procedure Rules 1998**, Part 19 which provides for the joint case management of claims which raise similar or common issues of fact or law.

harassment – a course of conduct by the **defendant** which amounts to harassment of the **claimant**.

hearsay, hearsay evidence – testimony that is not eyewitness but rather is the report of someone else's eyewitness; as in 'Ruth told me that Gary was driving the car' – where 'Ruth told me' is the speaker's direct evidence, and '...Gary was driving the car' is the speaker's hearsay evidence.

Highway Code – a publication issued by the Department of Transport, Local Government and the Regions, and published by The Stationery Office; it contains written guidance for use of the roads (for all road users) and material related to criminal offences.

House of Lords – the highest **Court of Appeal** within the British court system (although it may be possible to go to an international court).

indemnity – a type of **Part 20 claim** in which the **defendant** (known as a **Part 20 claimant**) invokes a contractual right to recoup certain sums – an indemnity – from the Part 20 defendant.

intentional causation of harm – a **tort** created by the case of *Wilkinson v Downton* where the defendant has deliberately done or said something in order to harm the **claimant**, and the claimant duly suffers physical (including psychiatric) harm.

issue of claim – the formal beginning of litigation, when the court stamps the **Claim Form** and notes the date (the date of issue).

judgment – the formal process by which the judge communicates his decision to the parties; it may be automatic in some circumstances (*see* **default judgment**) but generally is delivered orally (or in writing) at the end of the **trial**. The judge will tell the parties in his judgments of the findings of fact he has made, and of any rulings of law.

Judicial Studies Board Guidelines – a set of guidelines used by the courts and by lawyers to determine the amount of **damages** for the 'pain, suffering and loss of amenity' part of a claim.

Legal Aid – now defunct, *see* **Community Legal Services Funding**.

limitation, limitation period – the period after the accident or onset of loss and injury in which the **claimant** may bring a claim; once the period has expired the **defendant** will be able to raise a defence that the claim is 'statute barred' under the Limitation Act 1980.

listing questionnaire – a questionnaire sent to the parties by the court during the preparations for **trial** stage; the information sought will assist the court in allocating the appropriate court time for the trial, and dealing with any other trial issues such as witnesses' needs, etc.

litigant-in-person – a party in litigation who is conducting his own case and representing himself, rather than hiring a lawyer to do so.

litigation friend – a person who acts as a representative for a **child** (or **patient**), **claimant** or **defendant** in order to conduct the litigation – including instructing lawyers, complying with court orders, etc.

Mckenzie friend – a layman (non-lawyer) who may, with the permission of the judge, act as an advisor and moral support to a **litigant-in-person** whilst in court; the Mckenzie friend may generally not, however, speak on behalf of the litigant-in-person.

minor, *see* **child**.

mitigation of loss – the duty of the **claimant** to take reasonable steps to lessen his loss or injury where he can.

Motor Insurers' Bureau – industry-wide group of motor insurers who has made various agreements with the government to provide insurance in certain situations.

multi-track – a trial track to which large or complex claims may be allocated (**allocation**).

negligence – a breach of the duty imposed by the **common law** to take care for the safety of a person; in other words, situations where the law holds the **defendant** liable for the costs and injury caused to the **claimant** by his carelessness.

no win, no-fee, *see* **conditional fee agreement**.

nuisance (private) – a **tort** based on the unreasonable and substantial interference with a person's use and enjoyment of land (including buildings). The torts of private and public nuisance are separate and distinct.

Ogden Tables – actuarial tables used by lawyers to calculate **damages** representing future financial loss.

order – the formal decision of the court, consisting of pronouncements and requirements; delivered (usually verbally) by the judge and typed up or 'drawn up' by the court who then sends it to the parties.

pain, suffering and loss of amenity – elements which are taken into consideration when calculating the amount of **damages** for injury; 'loss of amenity' is the effect that the injury has on one's ability to carry out the everyday activities and enjoyments of life (housework, personal care, mobility, social interaction, confidence, hobbies, aspirations and expectations, etc).

Part 20 claim – a claim for **damages** or other remedy made under Part 20 of **Civil Procedure Rules 1998**; examples include **counterclaims** and claims for a **contribution** and/or **indemnity**.

Part 20 claimant – a defendant bringing a **counterclaim** (against the **claimant**) or a person claiming against a third party for a **contribution** or **indemnity** towards any **damages** that are awarded against him. The procedure is governed by **Civil Procedure Rules 1998**, Part 20 – hence the name.

Part 36 offer (fast and multi-track claims only) – an offer made by the **claimant** or other party in litigation to settle a claim under the provisions of Part 36 of **Civil Procedure Rules 1998** (*see* **settlement**).

Particulars of Claim – a formal document submitted to the court usually with the **Claim Form** in which the **claimant** gives details of the facts on which his claim is based (including financial losses and costs).

partnership – a relationship between two or more people carrying on a business in common with a view to profit, where the business is not 'incorporated' (or 'mining' in certain areas). The partners are collectively known as a firm and is not the same thing in law as a **company**; however, a firm can employ personnel, and the partners will be legally liable for the acts of their employees (**vicarious liability**) and also for the acts of other partners acting in the course of the business.

patient – a person suffering from a mental disorder (as defined in the Mental Health Act 1983) which renders him incapable of managing and administering his own affairs; a patient must conduct litigation through a **litigation friend**.

payment into court – the payment of a sum of money to the court by the **defendant** or a **Part 20** defendant by way of an offer to settle proceedings under Part 36 of **Civil Procedure Rules 1998** (*see* **settlement**).

personal representatives – a general term used to describe the people who formally wind up the estate of someone who has died (call in the moneys owing, and pay the appropriate sums to the tax man and beneficiaries, etc); personal representatives either operate under the deceased's Will, in which case they are granted 'probate' and are called 'executors', or they operate under the statutory provisions for intestacy in which case they take out 'letters of administration' and are called 'administrators'.

plaintiff, *see* **claimant.**

pre-action protocol – a code of conduct setting out the steps that potential parties to personal injury litigation must observe before litigation starts; the protocol aims to promote early **settlement.**

privileged documents – documents which are exempt from having to be shown to the other side, or the judge. All letters and communications between a client and his legal advisors made for the purpose of seeking and giving legal advice are 'privileged', as are communications between a solicitor and third parties or agents made for the purpose of the litigation, and also **without prejudice** communications between parties which show a genuine intention to negotiate the terms of a settlement.

pro bono – work that is undertaken by a lawyer for no fee.

representative order – an order of the court made under **Civil Procedure Rules**, Part 19 (Part II) where one person is deemed to represent others for the purposes of a case – such an order may be suitable where many potential litigants have the same interests as each other.

Response Pack – the pack of documents sent to the defendant by the court with the **Claim Form.**

Retail Price Index (RPI) – an official indicator of indication, produced monthly; the RPI is used by lawyers to calculate what general **damages** awarded are worth in today's money.

settlement – an agreement between the parties to litigation which ends the claim, either before the claim begins or at any time (including during the **trial**) before the judge gives his **judgment.**

small claims track – one of the three trial tracks; normally personal injury claims where the **damages** for **pain, suffering and loss of amenity** are expected to be £1,000 or less and the total value of the claim is £5,000 or less.

solicitor – a lawyer who undertakes a range of legal services.

solicitor-advocate – a solicitor who has rights of audience in the higher courts, and who therefore may represent a party before the judge at **trial.**

special damage – the quantifiable costs, losses and expenses (although not the legal costs) suffered by the **claimant** between the accident and the **trial** or those that he knows he will incur in the future.

standard of proof – where there is a dispute about what happened (i.e. a factual rather than a legal dispute about liability), to find a claim proved, the judge must believe that the **claimant**'s version is probably the correct one. Similarly, to prove a defence, the judge must find the **defendant**'s version to be probably correct. These legal tests applied by the judge to the evidence before him at **trial** are known as the 'standard of proof'. In civil matters the standard of proof is 'on the balance of probabilities' (as opposed to 'beyond reasonable doubt', which is the criminal standard).

statement of case – a general description for a class of documents used by parties in litigation to set down the precise facts of their respective cases; **Claim Forms, Particulars of Claim** and **Defences** are all examples of statements of case.

statement of truth – a phrase which must be included on certain documents put before the court in which the person whose document it is verifies the contents as true. Statements of truth must be included in **Particulars of Claim, Defences,** Application Notices and **witness statements**.

statutory duty – a duty imposed on a person (such as an employer) or a body (such as a Highway Authority) for the benefit of specific persons (such as employees or road users) by an Act of Parliament or statute. In certain cases, a breach of such a duty gives rise to a civil claim for **damages**; in others, a criminal penalty arises.

stay, to stay a case – an order made by a judge suspending any further action on a case. The stay may later be lifted, and the litigation recommence.

striking out a statement of case – an order made by a judge removing a portion or portions of a **statement of case**. The party will no longer be able to rely on matters which have been thus deleted. Where the whole statement of case has been struck out the party will have lost (although it may be possible to begin a fresh claim or **defence**, etc).

subpoena – the old term for a **witness summons**.

summary judgment – a **judgment** obtained by a party under **Civil Procedure Rules 1998,** Part 24 at a private hearing (rather than a **trial**), where he can satisfy the court that his opponent has no real prospect of success and that there is no other compelling reason for there to be a trial.

tort – a Norman French word still used to describe a class of **common law** civil wrongs; from time to time the law extends the list which includes **negligence, assault, battery, false imprisonment,** etc.

trespass (to land) – a **tort** where the **defendant** directly causes his person or another object to encroach on to the land possessed by the **claimant**.

trial – the formal hearing at which the court considers the evidence (oral, written, documentary and physical) relating to the claim and **defence**, hears the legal argument and gives a **judgment**.

unincorporated association – a group of people who have collected together for a particular reason (such as a club) but who have not formed a **partnership** (firm),

company, friendly society or industrial society. Often the members are bound by a contractual relationship, or have agreed to abide by a set of rules or constitution. Unincorporated associations may own property, enter contracts and employ people; however, they do so through one or more individuals (such as a club chairman) and since the association takes on no 'legal personality' of its own, it cannot be sued as such. Thus members can only sue or be sued individually or through a **representative order**.

vicarious liability – a legal rule which makes someone legally liable for the (civil) wrongs committed by someone else; thus employers are responsible for the **torts** committed by employees in the course of their employment; the rule enables the **claimant** to claim against the employee for his 'primary' liability, and the employer for his 'vicarious' liability.

without prejudice – a phrase used in many situations (including negotiation letters) meaning that the writer retains the right to assert his full legal rights or position at a future date, but for the purpose of the current situation puts them to one side.

witness statement – a written statement ordered by the court containing the evidence of a witness and verified by a **statement of truth** by the maker of the statement. Usually a witness statement, after being formally 'adduced' (in other words, identified and confirmed by a witness who has just taken an oath or affirmation) is allowed to be read by the court as the witness' 'evidence in chief'. The statement then becomes the basis for **cross-examination**.

witness summons – a court order compelling a witness or other person to attend court.

BIBLIOGRAPHY

Legislation sources

Halsbury's Current Statutes Service

Halsbury's Laws (4th edition)

Halsbury's Statute Citator 2003

Halsbury's Statutes (4th edition)

Is it in force? – Butterworths

Textbooks and other reference works

Bingham's Negligence Cases (5th edition), 2002 – His Honour Judge David Maddison, et al – Sweet & Maxwell

Bingham's & Berryman's Motor Claims Cases (11th edition), 2000 – Paul Taylor, et al – Butterworths

Butterworths Health Services Law and Practice, 2001 - Butterworths

Butterworths Personal Injury Litigation Service, 1995 – Iain S. Goldrein, et al – Butterworths

Current Law, 2000 – Sweet & Maxwell

Defending Posession Proceedings (5th edition), 2002 – Jan Luba, et al – Legal Action Group

Encyclopaedia of Health and Safety at Work, 1996 – Neil Brailsford QC et al – Sweet & Maxwell

Cheshire Fifoot and Furmstone's Law of Contract (14th edition), 2001 – Furmston, et al – Butterworths

The White Book Service (*Civil Procedure*), 2003 – The Right Hon. Lord Justice May – Sweet & Maxwell

Clerk and Linsdell on Torts (18th edition), 2001 – Anthony Dugdale – Sweet & Maxwell

Kemp and Kemp: the Quantum of Damages, 1975 – David a. Mci Kemp – Sweet & Maxwell

McGregor on Damages (17th edition), 2003 – Harvey McGregor QC – Sweet & Maxwell

Megarry & Wade: The Law of Real Property (6th edition), 2000 – Charles Harpum, et al – Sweet & Maxwell

Powers and Harris on Medical Negligence (3rd edition), 2000 – Michael J. Powers, et al – Butterworths

Street on Torts (11th edition), 2003 – John Murphy – Butterworths

Websites

Action for Victims of Medical Accidents (AVMA) – www.avma.org.uk

The Association of British Travel Agents (ABTA) – www.abtanet.com

Butterworths Lexis Nexis – www.butterworths.co.uk

Criminal Injuries Compensation Authority – www.cica.gov.uk

Court Service – www.courtservice.gov.uk

Department for Transport – www.dft.gov.uk

INDEX